AT THE HEART OF POWER

'Through this meticulously researched book, Shyamlal Yadav tells the story of Uttar Pradesh through personalities that dominated and defined its politics. Yadav's deep understanding of politics—at the grassroots level and in the corridors of power—is evident in this work, which is an essential guide for anyone who needs to know why and how India's most politically significant state has changed over the last seven decades. That is also, in more ways than one, the story of how politics changed in India.'

—**Unni Rajen Shanker**, editor, *The Indian Express*

'Shyamlal Yadav's new book is a sterling account of the democracy, parliamentary politics and style of functioning of all 21 chief ministers of the country's most populous state. It explains in a distinct manner their interests and specialities. This is a must-read for anyone who wants to understand the political culture of Uttar Pradesh.'

—**Ram Bahadur Rai**, chairman,
Indira Gandhi National Centre for the Arts, New Delhi

'Shyamlal Yadav's book fills the critical gap in the knowledge about the dramatis personae of Uttar Pradesh's political theatre, from G.B. Pant to Yogi Adityanath.'

—**Shekhar Gupta**, editor-in-chief, *The Print*

'The road to Delhi has often led through Lucknow. By exploring the lives and times of Uttar Pradesh's storied list of chief ministers, Shyamlal Yadav has enhanced our understanding of India's most politically crucial state. Richly anecdotal and sharply analytical, this is a fine read.'

—**Rajdeep Sardesai**, consulting editor, India Today TV

'Shyamlal Yadav's new book, well researched, shows the pros and cons, highs and lows of the post-Independence politics of Uttar

Pradesh. He has been successful in rising to the challenge to encapsulate everything in such a concise and comprehensive book. It is a must-read for anyone who is interested in Uttar Pradesh, its people, its politics, its society.'

—**Ashok Mehta,** additional advocate general of Uttar Pradesh and former additional solicitor general to the Government of India

'Shyamlal Yadav has combined his vast range of skills and experience in reportage and research to put together a very readable and informative book on the largest and the most complex state in India. It is a must-read compendium for those interested in the political history of India.'

—**Shankkar Aiyar,** journalist and author

'It is my firm conviction that without proper understanding of the social and political processes in Uttar Pradesh, one cannot fully comprehend the political dynamics of India. This is precisely where Shyamlal Yadav's latest book comes as a great help. I wholeheartedly recommend this as a must-read book for students of political science, political analysts, public administrators, public policymakers and, of course, political activists, not only in Uttar Pradesh but in the entire country and abroad.'

—**Narendra Jadhav**, author and former Rajya Sabha MP

'This is an outstanding, detailed and stunning book of depth and width. The book chronicles the lives and careers of chief ministers of Uttar Pradesh like V.P. Singh, Mayawati, Kalyan Singh, Mulayam Singh Yadav and Yogi Adityanath through their actions. It is a valuable book for politicians, historians, bureaucrats, social scientists, academics and media persons.'

—**Late K.S. Sachidananda Murthy,** former resident editor, *Malayala Manorama* and *The Week*

AT THE HEART OF POWER

THE CHIEF MINISTERS OF UTTAR PRADESH

SHYAMLAL YADAV

RUPA

Published by
Rupa Publications India Pvt. Ltd 2024
7/16, Ansari Road, Daryaganj
New Delhi 110002

Sales centres:
Bengaluru Chennai
Hyderabad Jaipur Kathmandu
Kolkata Mumbai Prayagraj

Image courtesy: Directorate of Information, Government of Uttar Pradesh

P-ISBN: 978-93-6156-969-2
E-ISBN: 978-93-6156-181-8

First impression 2024

10 9 8 7 6 5 4 3 2 1

Dear Shreeti, my daughter,

You were a rare gift from god; you brought joy and happiness in my life from the day you were conceived. I am writing this for you, the one who loved to write and receive long letters, never satisfied with one-line messages. Your laughter, even your satiric shouts, were my favourite things to listen to at home. You were a part of my heart that beat outside my body. Losing you has been the saddest event of my life. You were fully fit, you had dreams for the future and, still, for over six months, you kept reminding me about the uncertainty of life, kept asking me to live every moment in a better way. Most days, I was busy with things like work and this book, and you frequently asked me to try to live in the present. If I had any inkling that you were making your own case of final leave, I would have spent much more time with you, would have made many more memories with you. I am full of regrets about this. However, the concern and care you showed for us until the moment you were able to speak will be a source of strength and inspiration for me forever. You had read three chapters of this manuscript and suggested modifications. But before you could read it in full, I lost you. This book, now complete, is proudly dedicated to you, betu.

CONTENTS

PREFACE

Work on this project began when I realized that a comprehensive and consolidated account of the pedigree, personality, politics, policies, promises, programmes and patrimony of all the chief ministers (CMs) of Uttar Pradesh (UP)—the country's most populous state—did not exist.

From people known for their simplicity to those known for their luxurious lifestyles, from the truthfulness of some to the corruption of others, from certain commendable actions to a host of misdeeds, the 21 CMs of UP till date, in all their complexity, are the subjects of this book.

Since the first post-Independence government was formed in the state on 20 May 1952, it has been, up to 29 February 2024, governed by single-party majority governments for nearly 49 years and coalition governments for over 18 years, and was under President's Rule 10 times for over four years and seven months.

I was born in 1970 and grew up in a village in UP. My peers and I have witnessed the transformation of politics in UP: the change from one party to the other—the Congress, Janata Party, Janata Dal, Bharatiya Janata Party (BJP), Samajwadi Party (SP), Bahujan Samaj Party (BSP)—and from single-party majority governments to governments of alliances and also governments under President's Rule. Fighting corruption and casteism along with the all-round development of the state were part of the *electoral rhetoric* for almost all of them, but for some, it was more about a *hissedari* (share) in power.

These CMs have taken UP from where it was in 1952 to what it is today. In the early years, deaths due to hunger were a matter of routine in parts of the state; water scarcity was a big problem; there were cases of police atrocities, a sad reminder of the British Raj; there were no proper roads and no access to electricity in a majority of areas; large parts of the land were rain-fed, that is, there weren't sufficient irrigation facilities, or the land was not being cultivated; and dacoity was a big challenge for the police administration until the 1980s.

Towns like Kanpur, where industries had been flourishing, were reduced to ruins. Because of its proximity to Delhi, Noida, a new industrial township in UP established in 1976, attracted investments, but industries hardly looked towards other underdeveloped regions in the state. In the state's 596 institutions imparting engineering and technologies degrees and diplomas, there was an intake of 2.07 lakh students, as per data for the year 2022–23 posted by the AICTE.[1] However, a pertinent question arises here: does UP have employment opportunities for even 10 per cent of the students that graduate every year? Governments of different ideologies kept coming with rosy promises, and the state remained known for migration of unskilled labourers. Moreover, in a state where lakhs of aspirants apply for a few dozen government jobs, holding a fair examination without paper leaks has become a big challenge.

Uttar Pradesh is a state where, as Chaudhary Charan Singh once said, '[People] believe in caste by birth, and caste by birth means one person is not equal to another; some are inferior and some are superior. The inferior one is superior to another and the superior one is inferior to someone else. It means, everyone is either inferior or superior to someone. How can

---

[1]Approved intake for engineering and technology courses, https://tinyurl.com/3nj2n22f. Accessed on 1 March 2024. Figures include data for undergraduate, postgraduate, diploma, post diploma and postgraduate diploma levels.

democracy survive [in this]?'[2] Things have not changed much in the state, and those who claim to be against casteism are often the most casteist. More than politicians, the government machinery itself is often divided along, and functions on, caste lines.

There is progress and there are failures; there are hits and there are misses. Some of these CMs made great contributions, some tried to contribute but could not, and some were not allowed to work by their own parties. Problems have been plenty and politics has been everywhere. If you talk to politicians and bureaucrats, you will realize that the elected representatives in UP are flooded with requests to settle land disputes, to help with registering a case with the police of a crime that one is a victim of, and to help acquire arms licenses. People also visit them to request for development schemes, water, electricity, education and employment, and to get benefits of different government schemes. You will find government officials criticizing 'political interference', but if you go to them as a complainant or as an applicant, they will not act unless you are a 'somebody' or know one. This is UP and these are its people.

While reading this book, many questions may come to your mind. Would UP have been more developed if the Congress had not destabilized its own state government by changing CMs frequently? Would mass industrialization of the state have been possible, as former CM Chandra Bhanu Gupta had dreamt, if he had got a full term post 1962? What would have been the outcome if Sucheta Kripalani had stayed in the state politics in 1967? Would Charan Singh's dream of village empowerment have been fulfilled had he got a full tenure in 1967? Would things have changed had Mulayam Singh Yadav been able to

---

[2] *Vidhan Sabha ki Karyawahi,* 2 August 1972, UP Assembly Secretariat, Lucknow, p. 830; author's translation.

rule for five years from 1989, or even from 1993? Would Kalyan Singh have been able to change UP had he managed to continue for five years from 1991? Would there have been more empowerment of the downtrodden had the BJP allowed Mayawati to be the CM for rest of the assembly term in 1995?

Voters of the state have expected of the people they vote for to create a UP where there is no difference in the living standards of people, be it in Noida, Lalitpur, Shrawasti or Maharajganj; a UP where there is no bias based on caste, creed or religion; a UP from where people are not forced to migrate for livelihood as unskilled labourers.

It was a challenge for me to encapsulate everything in a concise and comprehensive manner. Much more needs to be researched, written and discussed about these CMs. Paul R. Brass, an American political scientist, had spent most of his career studying and writing on Indian politics, particularly on Chaudhary Charan Singh. In a similar manner, academics and researchers from Indian universities and journalists with a thorough understanding of the state must take up this mantle.

The purpose of writing this book is to make people aware of the electoral and political history of UP through the lives of its CMs. I start from 1952 and stop at 2024 to paint as comprehensive a picture as possible of one of India's most economically significant and politically important states. As you delve into the chapters that follow, I hope that you'll discover new perspectives, and I look forward to the conversations they may inspire.

INTRODUCTION

The Political Significance of Uttar Pradesh

When Narendra Modi was the chief minister (CM) of Gujarat, he was appointed as the chairman of the Bharatiya Janata Party's (BJP's) election campaign committee on 9 June 2013, for the 2014 Lok Sabha elections. Three weeks prior to that, on 19 May, his close confidant Amit Shah was put in charge of the party in Uttar Pradesh (UP), and then, heading the government at the Centre, the Congress had appointed Madhusudan Mistry, the general secretary of the All India Congress Committee (AICC) (like Modi and Shah, he is also from Gujarat), as incharge of UP on 16 June 2013. India's largest state in terms of population and Lok Sabha seats was in national focus. By that time, Modi was popular in several states, but everyone—the BJP workers, Modi's supporters, his opponents—was wondering where Modi was going to contest the Lok Sabha elections from. On 13 September 2013, he was declared as the prime ministerial candidate of the BJP. He launched his election campaign in UP from Kanpur on 19 October. Clearing all doubts, the BJP announced that Modi would contest from two seats—Varanasi in UP and Vadodara in Gujarat. When he won from both, he retained the former and resigned from the latter. The BJP won 71 (+2 by its ally Apna Dal [S]) of the 80 seats in UP, and Modi became the prime minister (PM) of India.

The journey from UP to the prime ministerial chair began with Jawaharlal Nehru, the first PM of India, who was a Member of Parliament (MP) from Allahabad Dist (East)-cum-Jaunpur Dist (West) (now Phulpur). He was followed by Lal Bahadur Shastri, an MP from Allahabad (now Prayagraj), and Indira Gandhi, Lok Sabha MP from Raebareli (prior to that a Rajya Sabha MP from UP). The list doesn't end here—Charan Singh from Baghpat, Rajiv Gandhi from Amethi, V.P. Singh from Fatehpur, Chandra Shekhar from Ballia and Atal Bihari Vajpayee from Lucknow, all went on to become PMs. In all probability, if Narayan Dutt Tiwari had won the 1991 polls from Nainital (which was in UP at the time), he, and not P.V. Narasimha Rao, might have become the PM in 1991. It is a widespread perception that *kendra ki sarkar ka raasta UP se hokar gujarata hai*—the way to the central government goes through UP. Except Gulzarilal Nanda, Morarji Desai, P.V. Narasimha Rao, H.D. Deve Gowda, Inder Kumar Gujral and Dr Manmohan Singh, all other nine PMs of India have been either residents of UP or were elected from UP.

A land-locked state, UP touches Nepal as well as the states of Himachal Pradesh, Uttarakhand, Bihar, Jharkhand, Chhattisgarh, Madhya Pradesh, Rajasthan, Haryana and the union territory of Delhi. Much of its area is covered by a deep layer of extremely fertile alluvial soil along the Ganga, the Yamuna and their tributaries. During an election trip in 2012, when Nitin Gadkari, then president of the BJP, travelled across UP for the first time, he said in the course of a conversation with me, 'If we find such fertile land in Maharashtra, we can get yields many times more than what UP farmers might be getting presently.'[1] That is only one of the capabilities of the state.

Uttar Pradesh's political importance is certainly because of its size, a fact that was discussed in the 1955 report by the States Reorganisation Commission (SRC) headed by Justice Fazl Ali. In those days, the Congress dominated the nation's politics, and UP was its strength. There were suggestions to divide the state, but in its report submitted in 1955, the commission rejected such demands, stating, 'We feel that the case for the division of Uttar Pradesh on the ground of its position in all-India affairs is somewhat overstated.'[2]

G.B. Pant, who was appointed Union home minister after serving as the CM of UP, said in the Lok Sabha on 23 December 1955:

> I have lived and laboured in Uttar Pradesh, and I have enjoyed the advantages that accrue from being in charge of the administration of a big State. I know what it means, and I know what benefits flow from it, benefits which harm nobody, but which advance all who live within that State. So, I would like still bigger States to be carved out, because then the economy is stabilized, the weaknesses of one are made up by the strong points of the other, and there is the need, the imperative need, of developing and cultivating a spirit of accommodation and understanding.[3]

---

[1] I had accompanied him for two days in the first week of March 2012 during the assembly elections to cover his rallies in central UP and Rohilkhand region. Another party leader, Narendra Singh Tomar, had also accompanied us.

[2] *Report of the States Reorganisation Commission 1955,* Government of India Press, New Delhi, p. 164, https://tinyurl.com/5n6trsnw. Accessed on 5 March 2024.

[3] *Lok Sabha Debates,* 23 December 1955, Lok Sabha Secretariat, Delhi, p. 326.

Those who were ruling it or dreamt of ruling it hardly appreciated the idea of a divided UP. Narayan Dutt Tiwari, who later became the CM of the newly carved Uttarakhand, supported the move when he was out of power from UP. Hemwati Nandan Bahuguna was also against the division of UP, a position he reinforced repeatedly. Once, alleging that Chaudhary Charan Singh wanted to divide the state, Bahuguna had said, '*Is pradesh ka vibhajan nahin hoga, nahi hoga, nahi hoga*' (This state will never, never, never be divided).[4] But those who had lost hope to rule the undivided state advocated for division. The Rashtriya Lok Dal (RLD) chief back then, late Ajit Singh, launched a movement prior to the 2002 assembly polls for the creation of what he called Harit Pradesh, consisting of 22 districts of the western part of the state, but gradually fell silent, as it did not garner much on-ground support.

After that, on 21 November 2011, the last day of the assembly session of Mayawati's last government, she tabled a resolution to recommend to the Union government to divide the state into four parts, namely Bundelkhand, Purvanchal, Awadh Pradesh and Paschim Pradesh. This resolution was adopted.[5] Had UP been divided as per her government's plan, she might have imagined the possibility of power for her party in some of the proposed new states. But the proposal was returned by the United Progressive Alliance (UPA) government at the Centre, which was headed by Dr Manmohan Singh, seeking clarifications on issues like proposed capitals, boundaries and the spiralling debt burden.[6] However, the assembly polls

---

[4] *Vidhan Sabha ki Karyawahi,* 28 June 1974, UP Assembly Secretariat, Lucknow, p. 425; author's translation.

[5] *Vidhan Sabha ki Karyawahi,* 21 November 2011, UP Assembly Secretariat, Lucknow, p. 73; author's translation.

[6] 'Centre Returns UP Split Resolution with Queries', *India Today,* 19 December

happened within three months, and Mayawati lost the mandate. In the present setup of the BJP, there are certain people in favour of division of the state, and they keep raising the issue during informal discussions.

The political importance of UP becomes clear when we look at the performance of various parties in UP in Lok Sabha polls and the role of those parties in national politics. The Congress has formed single-party majority governments at the Centre seven times, and this can be attributed to the substantial number of seats it won in UP. Similarly, when the Janata Party had come to power in 1977, it had bagged all 85 seats of the state. On the other hand, in the Congress's three coalition regimes, it had won only five of 85 seats in 1991; nine of 80 in 2004; and 21 of 80 in 2009. The coalition government of the United Front (UF) at the Centre in 1996 had the Samajwadi Party (SP) as its crucial ally, but it managed to win only 16 of the 85 seats in the state. In the BJP's coalition governments at the Centre, the party had won 57 of 85 seats in UP in 1998, and though the tally was reduced in 1999, it still won 29 of 85 seats. The BJP's majority governments at the Centre in 2014 and 2019 bagged 71 and 62 seats (excluding ally Apna Dal [S]), respectively, out of 80 from the state.

Such has been the state's importance. Many of the leaders of British India and independent India as well as an array of luminaries from other fields were students of the University of Allahabad, Banaras Hindu University (BHU) and Aligarh Muslim University (AMU), among others. It is not surprising that a large state like UP has produced a number of stalwarts who have left their mark on the country's politics and also on society. Dr Ram Manohar Lohia, one of the most fearless Opposition leaders, was born in UP and was active in politics;

2011, https://tinyurl.com/mr3swj5k. Accessed on 2 March 2024.

he reached Lok Sabha from here. Dr Lohia had delivered his historic *sapta kranti* (seven revolutions)[7] for the first time in a training camp of Samajwadi Yuvajan Sabha (SYS) in Nainital on 26 June 1962. His party's slogan of '*Pichhde paaven sau me saath*' (Other Backward Classes [OBCs] should get 60 per cent [of all opportunities]) got momentum in UP and Bihar. Jayaprakash Narayan gave his historic speech on *sampoorn kranti* (total revolution)[8] in Patna, Bihar, on 5 June 1974, but UP was the ground for his experiments, and the Janata Party won all 85 seats in the state in 1977, including the formerly unshakeable Raebareli seat of PM Indira Gandhi. Jayaprakash Narayan founded Gandhi Vidya Sansthan in Varanasi.

Additionally, it was the Allahabad High Court—the country's largest high court—that brought a sitting PM into the witness box and, in its historic judgement in 1975, set aside PM Indira Gandhi's election of 1971 from Raebareli. Kashmiri Pandit families also migrated to Allahabad for education and settled there for legal practice; the Nehru (Motilal Nehru and Jawaharlal Nehru), Sapru (Tej Bahadur Sapru) and Katju (Kailashnatha Katju) families played key roles in the freedom struggle as well as in independent India.

Besides Atal Bihari Vajpayee, the Bharatiya Jan Sangh (BJS) founder Deen Dayal Upadhyay was from UP. Nanaji Deshmukh and Bhaurao Deoras, Rashtriya Swayamsevak Sangh (RSS) ideologues, had come from Maharashtra, but their field

[7]Equality among men and women; equality against differences on the basis of the colour of one's skin; equality against ritualistic caste system plus special opportunities for the backward; freedom from foreign slavery; freedom from disparities of private capital and economic inequality, and increasing production by planning; freedom from unjust interference in private life and ensuring a democratic system; and struggle against weapons and for satyagraha.

[8]This translated into political, economic, social, cultural, intellectual, educational and spiritual revolution.

of activities was UP. The second *sarsanghchalak* (chief) of RSS, Madhavrao Sadashiv Golwalkar 'Guruji', had studied and taught at the BHU. The BJS was formed in UP on 2 September 1951 before it was formed at the central level on 21 October the same year. With merely two Lok Sabha seats in the 1984 Lok Sabha elections, the BJP started to revamp its strategy by becoming part of the Sangh Parivar's movement for a Ram temple at Lord Ram's birthplace in Ayodhya. The Bahujan Samaj Party (BSP) founder, Kanshi Ram, made this land his experimental ground and not his own state of Punjab (despite Punjab having the largest percentage of Scheduled Caste [SC] population), as UP has the largest number of SC individuals, creating an opportunity for parties to work towards uplifting the SCs in particular. Kanshi Ram changed the dynamics of UP politics and was actively involved in its political affairs for several years.

Three CMs of UP—G.B. Pant, Sucheta Kripalani, and Kamalapati Tripathi—were members of the Constituent Assembly. Two former CMs, G.B. Pant and Charan Singh, have been awarded the Bharat Ratna, while Mulayam Singh Yadav and Kalyan Singh were honoured with the Padma Vibhushan, highlighting their significant contributions to Indian society and politics.

Uttar Pradesh was the battleground of the First War of Independence in 1857, from Meerut and Jhansi to Bithoor and Kanpur. Cities like Ballia, Banaras (now Varanasi) and Allahabad, among others, became hot centres for revolutionaries during the Quit India Movement. Prior to that, cases including the Banaras Conspiracy Case (1915), Chauri Chaura incident (4 February 1922), Kanpur Conspiracy (1924), Kakori Conspiracy (1925) and Meerut Conspiracy (1929) had played their key roles in the fight for Independence.

The state is not only politically relevant because of its size but is also equally important from a historical and cultural point of view, both of which ultimately loop back to its political significance. From Mathura to Ayodhya to Kashi, from Gorakhpur to Sitapur to the Sangam (the confluence of the three holy rivers Ganga, Yamuna and the mythical Saraswati) at Prayagraj, UP has a host of significant Hindu sites. The state houses several Buddhist holy places—Sarnath, Kushinagar, Shravasti, and so on—as well as birthplaces of many Jain *tirthankara*s (ford makers, saviours), and also places of Islamic interest like Darul Uloom in Deoband. From Kannauj, the capital of Harshvardhan's kingdom, to Agra, the capital of the Mughal Empire before it was moved to Delhi, UP has had a place on the country's map through the ages.

While this book discusses the people who have governed the state since 1952, it is only prudent to have an overview of its governance prior to that. Under the British rule, its political map and system of government were in constant flux. Between 1775 and 1834, it was under the Bengal Presidency. In November 1834, it was separated from the Bengal Presidency and a new presidency was established in Agra. Initially, Allahabad was established as the capital of the Agra Presidency, but it was shifted to Agra in 1836, and the presidency was renamed as North-Western Provinces. In February 1856, Oudh (Awadh) was annexed to the British, and in 1858, its capital was again shifted to Allahabad. In 1902, the region was renamed as the United Provinces of Agra and Oudh, and, in 1921, its capital was shifted to Lucknow. There was a further change in its name in 1937, when it was renamed as the United Provinces. Finally, on 24 January 1950, it got its present name. Its other name was suggested as Aryavart, but it was not approved by Congress leaders in the meeting of the State Congress Committee on 9 December 1949 in Farrukhabad, and, thus, the present name was chosen. Many decades later, its boundary was changed, with the creation of a new state named Uttaranchal in 2000 (later renamed as Uttarakhand).

However, its size was always a bone of contention, and because of protest from the southern states, the number of Lok Sabha seats in states has remained frozen since 1976, even though it can be argued that high population growth should have resulted in more seats in the state. As per the 2011 census, the population of UP was 19.98 crore, accounting for 16.51 per cent of the total population of the country; with 240,928 sq. km (7.33 per cent of the total area of the country), UP is fourth largest in terms of area.[9] With 75 districts divided into 18 divisions, 351 tehsils, 826 development blocks and 58,189 gram panchayats with 1.07 lakh villages, UP is quite enormous. Its society, economic status, dialects, farming, village life, city life and eating habits as well as its rituals and local festivals vary from region to region.

But more than all of the above, what adds to the importance of UP is that the state has 80 Lok Sabha seats (14.7 per cent of the total seats), 31 seats (12.4 per cent of total seats) in the Rajya Sabha, 403 assembly segments (9.77 per cent of the total seats of all state assemblies) and 100 seats in the Legislative Council. It is one of only six states (others being Maharashtra, Andhra Pradesh, Karnataka, Telangana and Bihar) having an Upper House in the state legislature. As a result, UP has acquired political importance that is arguably incomparable to any other state in India.

[9]'A-01: Number of Villages, Towns, Households, Population and Area (India, States/UTs, Districts and Sub-districts) – 2011', *Census Tables,* https://tinyurl.com/ymhxwtvr. Accessed on 2 March 2024.

1

GOVIND BALLABH PANT

The First 'Ratna' of UP

First CM: Govind Ballabh Pant

Party: Indian National Congress

Tenure: 20 May 1952–27 December 1954

Constituency: Bareilly Municipality

Days in Office: 2 years and 222 days (since the first assembly election in independent India)

Govind Ballabh Pant was one of the key figures in India's freedom movement who fought alongside Mahatma Gandhi, Sardar Vallabhbhai Patel and Jawaharlal Nehru. Pant was also a member of the Constituent Assembly from the United Provinces. Among its 55 members were luminaries such as Feroze Gandhi, Jawaharlal Nehru, Abdul Kalam Azad, Rafi Ahmad Kidwai and B.V. Keskar, among others.[1]

---

[1]'Constituent Assembly', *Parliament of India*, https://tinyurl.com/3p7dwyu8. Accessed on 5 March 2024.

The first assembly elections were held in 1936–37, and the Indian National Congress got clear majority in five provinces. There were negotiations about the functioning of governments that would soon be formed between the Congress and the governors of the states it had majority in. The Congress wanted certain assurances before forming governments in the provinces. In the meantime, Muhammad Ahmad Said Khan Chhatari (known as Nawab Chhatari), who was elected from Bulandshahr West as the candidate of the National Agriculturist Party of Agra, was administered the oath as CM (the designation back then was 'premier') of the United Provinces on 3 April 1937 by Governor Harry Graham Haig as an interim arrangement. When the viceroy Lord Linlithgow assured on 22 June that a governor was not free or entitled to interfere with the day-to-day administration of a province, Govind Ballabh Pant replaced Nawab Chhatari on 17 July. The Congress was able to form governments in eight out of 11 provinces, including the United Provinces. Jawaharlal Nehru wanted Purushottam Das Tandon for the post as he had struggled a lot for farmers' rights in the United Provinces. But the decision was left to the Congress Working Committee (CWC), which finalized Pant's name—no other name was considered.[2] Tandon was elected as the Speaker of the assembly on 31 July 1937.

That is how Pant became a premier for the first time. However, during the Second World War, the Congress asked its premiers to resign in protest against the decision of Lord Linlithgow to engage India in the War without consulting the elected representatives of the country. Therefore, Pant resigned on 2 November 1939. The assembly was dissolved and, in 1945, the new British Labour government ordered new elections for

---

[2]Gupta, Chandra Bhanu, *Oral History*, Nehru Memorial Museum and Library, New Delhi, 1973, p. 10.

the provincial legislatures. These were held in March 1946, and the Congress was victorious again. Governor Francis Verner Wylie administered oath of office to Pant on 1 April 1946.

After Independence, the first assembly election in UP was completed in March 1952. Only 38.01 per cent of the 3.17 crore electors had voted.[3] The UP Assembly then had 347 constituencies, which involved 263 single-member and 83 double-member constituencies, besides one nominated seat.[4] Fourteen were reserved for SCs. The Congress won 388 seats, the Socialist Party 20 and the BJS two, with 15 going to independent candidates and a few to other parties.[5] Pant won from the Bareilly Municipality constituency, defeating the BJS candidate Manmohan Lal Mathur.[6] The Congress leadership decided that Pant should continue as the UP CM as the party had swept the polls under his leadership. Thus, he was sworn in as the first elected CM of UP in independent India on 20 May 1952.[7]

Even before Independence, the Congress was transforming from a nationalist movement into an electioneering machine. A caucus within the Congress established the Congress Socialist Party (CSP) in 1934, and its leaders began creating conflicts and personality clashes with Congress leaders everywhere. In the Kanpur conclave of the CSP on 26–28 February 1947, they decided to remove 'Congress' from 'Congress Socialist Party' and it was reduced to 'Socialist Party'.[8] In a meeting in

[3]*Statistical Report on General Election 1951 to the Legislative Assembly of UP*, Election Commission of India, New Delhi, p. 3.

[4]Ibid.

[5]Ibid. 14.

[6]Ibid. 35.

[7]'Former CMs of UP', *State Portal, Government of Uttar Pradesh*, https://tinyurl.com/4y55r72f. Accessed on 5 March 2024.

[8]Sharad, Onkar, *Lohia: Ek Pramanik Jivani,* Lok Bharti Prakashan, Allahabad, 1993, p. 151.

Nasik in March 1948, Socialist Party leaders decided to have the party separate from the Congress.[9] After this, several prominent Congressmen, notably Acharya Narendra Dev, Jayaprakash Narayan, Dr Ram Manohar Lohia, Damodar Swarup Seth, Aruna Asaf Ali and Achyut Patwardhan, left the Congress. These dissident Congressmen then started the Socialist Party as a new party.

In the United Provinces, a dozen of them, considering it an ethical move, resigned from the assembly and the Legislative Council because they were elected on Congress tickets. In June 1948, by-elections were held for 13 seats, and all candidates of the Socialist Party were defeated. Notable among them was Pant's old friend Acharya Narendra Dev (from Ayodhya). The government under Pant had made every effort to outmatch Dev, including dividing the elections on religious lines. A candidate named Baba Raghav Das (born in Maharashtra, settled in Deoria) was fielded against Dev in the Ayodhya Assembly by-poll, and many tactics were applied in favour of Baba, including the distribution of *tulsi* leaves during the campaign. Thereafter, the Congress, under Pant, managed to take effective control of the political affairs of the region, as many of his competitors—his potential successors—got out of the race one after the other because they had either left the party or moved to central politics.

Pant was born in Khoont village in Almora district (now in Uttarakhand) on 10 September 1887. He graduated from the University of Allahabad in 1907, from where he also acquired a law degree in 1909. While studying in Allahabad, he stayed at the MacDonnell Hindu Boarding House (later renamed as

[9] Ibid. 181.

Hindu Hostel). He started participating in political activities during his student days. In 1905, as a first-year student of BA, he went to Banaras to participate in the Congress session as a volunteer. This session was chaired by Gopal Krishna Gokhale. In 1908, during a camp organized by the Congress at Kumbh in Allahabad, Pant made a strong speech, which prompted the university authorities to issue an order prohibiting him from appearing in the examination. However, the order was revoked with the intervention of one of his teachers and of Madan Mohan Malviya.

After the completion of his law degree, he returned home and started practising as a lawyer in 1910 (first in Almora, then in Ranikhet and finally in Kashipur) before he ventured into politics. In Kashipur, he founded a social organization called Prem Sabha in 1914 to help the needy. He was also behind the founding of Kumaon Parishad in 1916, which advocated for the abolishment of *coolie-begar* (a tradition forcing villagers to work for government officials without any payment). In the same year, he attended the Lucknow session of the AICC and remained its member until his demise.

In the meantime, Mahatma Gandhi had returned to India from South Africa in 1915 and his influence on the freedom movement was increasing. In 1919, the Jallianwala Bagh massacre in Amritsar marked the beginning of immense political turmoil in the country. In 1923, general elections were held for the central Legislative Assembly and provincial legislatures.[10] Pant was elected to the Legislative Council from the Swaraj Party in 1923 and 1926, and in 1924, he was elected as leader of the Swaraj Party in the House. In the meantime, there was a truce in the Congress in November 1924 to end the infighting, and

[10] *Uttar Pradesh Vidhanmandal: Ek Aitihasik Ruprekha,* UP Assembly Secretariat, Lucknow, 1977, p. 22.

Gandhi, and Motilal Nehru and C.R. Das signed an agreement, whereby the Congress conceded that the Swarajists were in the Legislative Councils on the Congress's behalf. On the other hand, the Swarajists agreed that only those people who spun khadi could be members of the Congress.[11]

Pant was one of the lawyers who defended the revolutionaries in the Kakori Conspiracy Case of 9 August 1925. He was elected as president of the Congress committee of the United Provinces of Agra and Oudh in 1927. He became a member of the CWC in 1931 and remained so till his last days.

In October 1928, the Indian Statutory Commission (Simon Commission) arrived in India. Widespread opposition to it was seen everywhere in the country. When the Simon Commission reached Lucknow on 30 November 1928, a huge protest was held under the leadership of Jawaharlal Nehru and Pant. Protestors were lathi-charged. Nehru writes in his autobiography *Toward Freedom*:

> Almost every part of me seemed to ache, and I was covered with contused wounds, and marks of blows. But fortunately I was not injured in any vital spot. Many of our companions were less fortunate and were badly injured. Govind Ballabh Pant, who stood by me, offered a much bigger target being six feet off in height, and the injuries, received then, have resulted in a painful and persistent malady which prevented him for a long time from straightening his back or leading an active life.[12]

Nehru escaped serious injury in the lathi-charge due to Pant's presence there, and he showed his gratitude and respect for Pant

---

[11] '1915–1925: Brief History of Congress', *Indian National Congress*, http://tinyurl.com/4trm6pj4. Accessed on 3 April 2022.

[12] Nehru, Jawaharlal, *Toward Freedom: An Autobiography of Jawaharlal Nehru*, The John Day Company, New York, 1941, p. 137.

his whole life. Since Pant was actively engaged in provincial politics in the United Provinces of Agra and Oudh, he gradually came in close contact with top leaders of the Congress amidst the freedom movement. It was Pant who prevented a potential split of the factions of Mahatma Gandhi and Netaji Subhas Chandra Bose in the Congress at the Tripuri session on 10–12 March 1939.[13]

However, his legislative career saw a brief halt in 1929–30 when, following a resolution at the Lahore session of the AICC, all its members had to resign from the legislative bodies. However, in 1934, he was elected to the central Legislative Assembly, and on 18 February 1937, he was elected to the Legislative Assembly of the United Provinces. Soon after, on 7 March 1937, he was elected as the leader of the Congress Legislative Party (CLP). However, when he formed his government in 1937, Pant's cabinet had 13 parliamentary secretaries and six members—himself, Rafi Ahmed Kidwai, Kailash Nath Katju, Vijaya Lakshmi Pandit, Pyarelal Sharma and Hafiz Mohammad Ibrahim (Dr Sampurnanand was appointed in March 1938 after the death of Pyarelal Sharma).[14]

When statues of Ram Lalla and Sita appeared at the disputed site in Ayodhya on the night of 22–23 December 1949, Pant was the premier. Three days later, on 26 December 1949, PM Jawaharlal Nehru wrote to him, 'I am disturbed at developments at Ayodhya. Earnestly hope you will personally interest yourself in this matter. Dangerous example being set there which will have bad consequences.'[15] After that, Sardar Patel wrote a letter to Pant on 9 January 1950, suggesting ways to resolve the dispute. Among other things, Patel said:

---

[13]Kashyap, Subhash C., and Mahesh C. Joshi, *Govind Ballabh Pant: Parliamentarian, Statesman and Administrator,* National Publishing House, Delhi, 1988, p. 13.

[14]*Mantrimandalon ka Gathan 1921–1988*, UP Assembly Secretariat, Lucknow.

[15]Advani, L.K., *My Country My Life,* Rupa & Co., New Delhi, 2008, pp. 360–1.

> I think it has been one of the outstanding achievements of your administration that despite many upsetting factors, communal relations have generally improved very considerably since 1946… It would be most unfortunate if we allowed any group advantage to be made on this issue. On all these grounds, therefore, I feel that the issue is one which should be resolved amicably in a spirit of mutual toleration and goodwill between two communities.[16]

Later, L.K. Advani, lamenting the fact that the Pant government did not adopt the suggestions of Sardar Patel, wrote: 'The letter [by Patel] outlined an approach to the resolution of the Ayodhya dispute which was flawless. Had it been adopted, the problem could have been solved long ago—and that too, amicably and expeditiously.'[17] This turned into the Ram Janmabhoomi–Babri Masjid dispute that has influenced India's politics for several decades since then, and was finally settled by the Supreme Court on 9 November 2019.

During his tenure as the premier of the United Provinces, Pant took some historic decisions and implemented them effectively. One of the decisions of his government, which was admittedly revolutionary, was the abolition of the zamindari system. He is also credited with passing the Hindu Code Bill in the state, which made monogamy compulsory for Hindu men while giving Hindu women the rights to divorce as well as inheritance of ancestral property.

The Congress, which was well-acquainted with the agrarian movements in the United Provinces of Agra and Oudh during the 1920s and 1930s, felt that only someone like Pant would be able to effectively deal with the situation this province was facing, as he was very much connected to and aware of

[16]Ibid.

[17]Ibid.

the problems of the farmers. Activist and political leader B. Pattabhi Sitaramayya stated:

> The agrarian condition of the tenants in the U.P. mostly of those under Talukdars and Zamindars, was anything but enviable. Their distress was appalling. There was no relaxation shown in the methods of collecting rents. The intermediaries had neither the sense of responsibility that animates a Government, nor did they understand the pinch of depression which was oppressing the poor cultivators. They were middlemen, happily situated, secure in the protection afforded by a benevolent Government, free from the cares and worries of labour, and always invoking the interference of the authorities on grounds of sedition, non-cooperation, lawlessness and anarchy, of any friends of the ryot and public men, who chose to plead his cause… Pandit Govind Ballabh Pant was specially appointed by the Provincial Congress Committee to bring to the notice of Government the various grievances of the people and to put before them the view-point of the Congress.[18]

So, Pant was the choice of the party legislators.

On 14 March 1952, a little over two months before he was formally appointed the CM of UP, Pant announced while presenting the interim budget for 1952–53 in the assembly, 'This budget is prepared keeping in mind that we will be able to implement the Zamindari Abolition Act from the next financial year.'[19] Subsequently, he had to face some challenges as it was not an easy task to implement this legislation, which was considered revolutionary for UP farmers. Surprisingly,

---

[18]B. Pattabhi Sitaramayya, *History of The Indian National Congress,* Volume I, S Chand & Co., Delhi, 1969, pp. 499–500.

[19]*Vidhan Sabha ki Karyawahi,* 14 March 1952, UP Assembly Secretariat, Lucknow, p. 113.

there was no significant backlash from the zamindars, and it was carried out without any notable social turmoil. The Uttar Pradesh Zamindari Abolition and Land Reforms Act, 1950, was applied to the entire state with the exception of certain areas of the Kumaon and Garhwal regions, urban areas and some other specific areas.

After the first assembly elections, when the then governor, Homi Modi, addressed the first sitting of the newly constituted assembly on 21 May 1952, most of his speech was devoted to reforms like the zamindari abolition. He said:

> Everything that can be done to bring a new robust life, and good cheer, to our rural population has naturally the first call on our attention. We have long looked forward to the promulgation of the Zamindari Abolition and Land Reforms Act, which, more than any other single measure, is designed to secure that end. With this pronouncement, the final stage has been reached for putting an end to an age-long, but outmoded, feudal system and to place the hitherto suppressed peasantry of our State on its feet, so that it may lead a manly and full life free from all impediments and hindrances.[20]

Zamindari abolition was followed by more reforms. Direct collection of land revenue was introduced in the state in 1952 after the abolition of intermediaries. As a result, about 15 lakh tenants and sub-tenants came into direct relationship with the state. Later, the UP Consolidation of Holdings Act, 1953, was passed and was implemented from 1954.

The UP Legislative Assembly debates show that for more than three decades after Independence, the state faced

[20] *Vidhan Sabha ki Karyawahi,* 21 May 1952, UP Assembly Secretariat, Lucknow. p. 33.

grievous problems, including dacoity and absence of roads, electricity and connectivity in many parts. Under Pant's chief ministership, the construction of the Rihand Dam was started in 1954; it was operationalized in 1962. It was later renamed as Govind Ballabh Pant Sagar. Located in Sonbhadra district of the state, this is India's largest man-made lake.

As the CM, Pant enjoyed an enormous following among the masses in the state and was admired by leaders from both the Congress and Opposition parties. His government had several ambitious leaders, such as Dr Sampurnanand (minister of home affairs, prisons, labour, statistics and religious affairs), Chandra Bhanu Gupta (minister of food and civil supplies), Chaudhary Charan Singh (minister of revenue, agriculture, food production, sugarcane development and animal husbandry) and Kamalapati Tripathi (minister of information and irrigation), all of whom subsequently went on to become CMs. Pant was able to keep them all together while also ensuring that they performed their duties well. Paul R. Brass wrote:

> Pandit Pant was one of the most astute political managers Indian politics has produced. Although he rarely participated directly in political controversies, he knew how to make men work for him and he knew how to make enemies work together under him. Indeed, it was part of his political strategy to permit those under him to fight amongst themselves, a certain way of assuring that they would not fight him.[21]

As UP's first CM, Pant is credited with providing a stable government and ensuring communal harmony in the state when neighbouring states like Punjab and Bihar were in the

---

[21]Brass, Paul R., *Factional Politics in an Indian State: The Congress Party in Uttar Pradesh*, University of California Press, Berkley and Los Angeles, 1965, p. 45.

throes of communal conflagrations in the post-Independence years. In his farewell speech for Pant, Dr Sampurnanand, who replaced him as CM, said:

> After Independence, the government came into our hands and communal violence was spread and flames were coming towards us from two sides, if not all. If things had not been controlled at that time, the situation of our state could have been like that in parts of Punjab and Bihar. As far as communal riots are concerned, there is no such incident in our state so far. Much credit for this goes to Pant ji.[22]

Chandra Bhanu Gupta, who later became the CM, named Pant as one of the five most influential people of UP. He said, 'Pandit Jawaharlal Nehru brought enthusiasm among our youth; Rajarshi [Purushottam Das] Tandon taught us ideals of abandonment in life; Acharya Narendra Dev and Dr Sampurnanand brought us towards idealism; and respected Pant ji applied those ideals in his life. All these are going to be part of the political history of the state.'[23] In his farewell speech for Pant, Raja Virendra Shah of Kalpi, who was then Uttar Pradesh Praja Party's Member of Legislative Assembly (MLA), said, 'I was also one of the affected zamindars. We suffered economic losses. But we were silent because of the good behaviour, gentleness and politeness of Pant ji.'[24]

Pant said in his last speech in the UP Assembly on 27 December 1954, 'I am thankful to the zamindars; I am obliged. We tightened up on them, and they suffered a lot, but for this country they did not care about that. Bearing public interest

[22]*Vidhan Sabha ki Karyawahi,* 27 December 1954, UP Assembly Secretariat, Lucknow, p. 414; author's translation.

[23]Ibid. 431.

[24]Ibid. 430.

in mind, they faced all these difficulties.'[25]

On 3 January 1955, Pant was called to Delhi by PM Nehru to take oath as a minister without portfolio, and a week later, he was appointed as the minister of home affairs. He was elected to the Rajya Sabha on 2 March 1955 and again on 3 April 1958.[26] In the Rajya Sabha, he was the leader of the House between March 1955 and February 1961.[27] Pant is one of the only two CMs of UP who have been conferred with the highest civilian award, the Bharat Ratna. This was on 26 January 1957. He was the Union home minister at that time. Next was Chaudhary Charan Singh, who was conferred posthumously in 2024 by the Narendra Modi government.

When the home minister in Pant's government, Dr Sampurnanand, replaced him as the CM, UP's political stability also started waning. Congress leaders and workers, who were ready to give everything for the country during the freedom movement, had changed in a few years after Independence. Conflicts cropped up among the ambitious leaders of the party who suddenly seemed hungry for power. These were the same people with whom Pant had successfully managed to work jointly with in his government. Beginning from Pant, the CMs of UP were frequently changed by the Congress leadership sitting in Delhi. No Congress CM was allowed to serve the state for a full term till 1989, when the party was wiped out and, post that, it never returned to power. Leaders in UP started to ditch one another, some even defecting from the Congress. By then, political aspirations of several social groups were also rising, and it would only be a matter of time before

---

[25]Ibid. 434.

[26]*Rajya Sabha Members: Biographical Sketches, 1952–2019*, Rajya Sabha Secretariat, New Delhi, 2019, p. 343.

[27]Rajya Sabha Secretariat, *Rajya Sabha: The Journey since 1952*, The Secretary-General, Rajya Sabha, New Delhi, 2019, p. 13.

the era of single-party majority regime would disappear for several years. All this continued till 2007, when BSP President Mayawati took over as the CM with a single-party majority and became the first CM to complete a single five-year tenure on the post. This had happened for the first time since 1952.

Despite his political life being exemplary, Pant's personal life was quite disturbed—he married thrice because of the untimely death of two of his wives. He was first married at the age of 12 in 1899, but his wife Gangadevi died along with their newborn in 1909. He married again in 1912, but merely two years later, his second wife died too. He got married for a third time in 1916.

G.B. Pant passed away on 7 March 1961. After his demise, his son K.C. Pant was elected to the Lok Sabha in 1962. He was the Union minister of state (MoS) for home affairs, minister of education and then minister of defence. Later, he joined the BJP and was deputy chairman of the erstwhile Planning Commission. K.C. Pant's wife Ila Pant was also a Lok Sabha MP from Nainital in 1998.

On Pant's demise, J.B. Kripalani said, 'Words are not adequate to do justice to the great qualities of head and heart that he had. In him we have lost a great patriot, a great guide and a great parliamentarian, a man who was never ruffled and who always had a sweet word for everybody.'[28]

---

[28]*Lok Sabha Debates,* 7 March 1961, Lok Sabha Secretariat, New Delhi.

2

DR SAMPURNANAND

The Ambitious Scholar

Second CM: Dr Sampurnanand

Party: Indian National Congress

Tenure: 28 December 1954–9 April 1957

10 April 1957–6 December 1960

Constituency: Banaras City South

Days in Office: 5 years and 344 days

On 3 January 1955, Govind Ballabh Pant was sworn in as a Union Cabinet minister after summons from PM Jawaharlal Nehru, and on 10 January 1955, he was appointed as the minister of home affairs. But before Pant was shifted, the Congress had already decided to replace him with Varanasi-based Sanskrit scholar and former journalist Dr Sampurnanand as the CM of UP. He was sworn in on 28 December 1954 by Governor K.M. Munshi, who later became the president of India.

Prior to Independence, Varanasi was among the prominent centres of the Non-Cooperation and Civil Disobedience movements and also a prime centre for the Hindu Mahasabha activities. Dr Sampurnanand had become one of the key figures in the Varanasi unit of the Congress by the early 1930s. Along with Purushottam Das Tandon, he was at the forefront of the campaign for Hindi being associated with the Hindi Sahitya Sammelan. He was among the leaders who were mentored by Mahatma Gandhi. It was Dr Sampurnanand's government that officially changed the name of the historic city from Banaras to Varanasi, effective from 24 May 1956.[1]

When Govind Ballabh Pant formed his government for the second time on 1 April 1946, Dr Sampurnanand was appointed as the minister of education and finance in the 17-member cabinet. (The first time he was appointed as the minister of education was on 2 March 1938, after the demise of the then minister, Pyarelal Sharma.) He also handled the portfolios of home and labour at various points in his career. During the national movement, and later as part of the government, Dr Sampurnanand and Chandra Bhanu Gupta (the third CM of UP) became close to Govind Ballabh Pant and their relations remained cordial for decades. However, they worsened after Dr Sampurnanand became the CM.

In both the first and second assembly polls in independent India (1952 and 1957, respectively), Dr Sampurnanand was elected from Banaras City South Assembly constituency, defeating Rustam Satin of the Communist Party of India (CPI). Considering that the CPI candidate's victory would have been a setback for them, Hindu nationalist groups helped Dr Sampurnanand win by strategically voting for him in large

[1]Uttar Pradesh District Gazetteers, *Varanasi*, Government of UP, Lucknow, 1965, p. vi, http://tinyurl.com/2vw72ar4. Accessed on 3 April 2022.

numbers to stop Rustam. They did not vote for their candidate but for Dr Sampurnanand. Like C.B. Gupta, Dr Sampurnanand was also among the socialists within the Congress, and both were members of the CSP since its beginning in 1934. But they did not leave the Congress in 1948 with other colleagues led by Acharya Narendra Dev. However, Dr Sampurnanand continued to maintain his friendship with them.

Born on 1 January 1890 in Banaras, Dr Sampurnanand did his BSc and LLB from the University of Allahabad. Before joining active politics, he taught at London Mission High School (Varanasi), Prem Mahavidyalaya (Vrindavan, Mathura), Princess College (Indore, Madhya Pradesh), Dungar College (Bikaner, Rajasthan) and Kashi Vidyapeeth (Varanasi). He quit as the principal of Dungar College in 1921 to take part in the Non-Cooperation Movement.

Dr Sampurnanand authored a number of books, including the first biography of Mahatma Gandhi. He edited *Maryada,* a monthly newspaper started by Madan Mohan Malviya, and other newspapers like *Aaj* and *Today* published from Varanasi. For some time, he had served as the secretary to Motilal Nehru as well.[2] Despite being a member of the Congress, Dr Sampurnanand kept writing articles in *Panchjanya*, a weekly newspaper close to the RSS family.[3] Paul R. Brass says, 'Sampurnanand was one of the many Congressmen in Uttar Pradesh who managed to combine "socialism" with Hindu revivalism and cultural nationalism. A well-known socialist thinker, he was esteemed even more for

[2] *Who's Who in UP Legislative Assembly,* UP Assembly Secretariat, Lucknow, 1959, p. 420.

[3] Sampurnanand, *Adhuri Kranti,* Bhanu Pratap Shukla (ed.), Lokhit Prakashan, Lucknow, 2013, p. 5.

his traditional learning in Sanskrit.'[4]

During G.B. Pant's chief ministership, Congress stalwarts like Rafi Ahmed Kidwai and Lal Bahadur Shastri were called to the Centre by PM Nehru, leaving state politics in Pant's hands. But once Pant moved to Delhi too, Dr Sampurnanand got his hold on the UP Congress and on the state's politics. At this time, the Congress was rapidly converting itself into an electioneering and election-winning machine, and the socialists or other groups like the BJS were unable to create any obstacles to its widening popularity. Results of the second assembly polls under Dr Sampurnanand's chief ministership confirmed this fact. In the 1957 assembly elections, there were 252 single-member constituencies and 89 double-member constituencies (one seat in each reserved for SCs) for a 431-member House (including one nominated member). The Congress won 286 seats and retained power. Dr Sampurnanand was unanimously elected as the leader of the CLP again on 7 April 1957, and took oath to continue as CM on 10 April.

Dr Sampurnanand's government established educational institutions in the state that would go on to become famous. His government elevated the Government Sanskrit College of Varanasi to Varanaseya Sanskrit University in March 1958, which, after his demise, was renamed as Sampurnanand Sanskrit University in December 1974.[5] Uttar Pradesh Agricultural University (renamed as G.B. Pant University of Agriculture in 1972, now in Uttarakhand) was also inaugurated during his tenure on 17 November 1960, a few days before he relinquished the CM post.[6] This was the first university of its kind in India

[4]Brass, Paul R., *Factional Politics in an Indian State: The Congress Party in Uttar Pradesh*, University of California Press, Berkeley and Los Angeles, 1965, p. 45.
[5]*Vidhan Sabha ki Karyawahi*, 27 September 1977, UP Assembly Secretariat, Lucknow.
[6]'About the University', *Indian Council of Agricultural Research*, https://tinyurl.com/36cfrtk3. Accessed on 2 March 2024.

at the time. He was associated with Mahatma Gandhi Kashi Vidyapeeth till the last days of his life. Gorakhpur University (now named after Deen Dayal Upadhyay), Kanpur Medical College (renamed as Ganesh Shankar Vidyarthi Memorial Medical College) and the country's first Sainik School in Lucknow (now named after a Kargil war hero, the Param Vir Chakra awardee Captain Manoj Kumar Pandey) were established during his tenure.

As the home minister of UP in the Pant government, Dr Sampurnanand had initiated key reforms, including starting open prison camps and modernizing the jails. In 1960, towards the end of his tenure as the CM, he constituted the Jail Reforms Evaluation Committee. His open prison camp idea was later implemented in Rajasthan when he was the governor of the state (1962–67). Dr Sampurnanand's government also prepared a plan for the beautification of the ghats of the Ganga in Varanasi.[7]

His government tried to reform the management of social and religious organizations. It decided 'to appoint a committee for a state-wide survey of social organisations'.[8] His government also intended to implement a state-wide ban on cow slaughter. Those were the years when the RSS and the BJS were trying to strengthen their relevance through a movement in support of a nationwide ban on cow slaughter. A legislation was passed, but it was challenged in the Supreme Court, which ruled that:

> As regards the U. P. Act we uphold and declare, for reasons already stated, that it is constitutionally valid in so far as it prohibits the slaughter of cows of all ages and calves of cows, male and female, but we hold that in

[7] *Vidhan Sabha ki Karyawahi*, 10 February 1955, UP Assembly Secretariat, Lucknow, p. 6.
[8] Ibid. 8. Author's translation.

> so far as it purports to totally prohibit the slaughter of breeding bulls and working bullocks without prescribing any test or requirement as to their age or usefulness, it offends against Art. 19 (1) (g) and is to that extent void.[9]

Dr Sampurnanand, being an academic, often articulated his concern that the MLAs participating in debates in the assembly did not read the subject properly. One incident can be cited here. During a discussion on a motion of thanks on the governor's address before the assembly in 1958, he said:

> It seems that no one bothered to listen to or read the Governor's address, otherwise they would have given me some suggestions, some lights. For example, there are some members here who love so much the Hindu dharma. They must love, but some love it so much. The Governor's address has mention of the fact that we are going to introduce a Bill on cow protection. At least some [MLAs] should have thought about it, about what we are going to do. This also has mention of control on properties of temples. Some [MLAs] should have asked our views on the control of temples, because this is going to impact crores of lives. But, no one asked. No one has seen. Someone should have seen that something is going to be done.[10]

This must, in all probability, have been a comment on the 17 MLAs of the BJS in that assembly. Though they were part of the discussion on the governor's address, these MLAs appeared to be disinterested in talking about the issues mentioned in that

---

[9]*Mohd. Hanif Quareshi & Others vs The State Of Bihar (And Connected Petitions)*, 1958 AIR 731.

[10]*Vidhan Sabha ki Karyawahi*, 24 July 1958, UP Assembly Secretariat, Lucknow p. 297; author's translation.

address, apparently because they had not bothered to read it.

Less than a decade after Independence, governments were making every effort to implement schemes for the development of the states. Industry was, of course, a focus area. In this regard, in 1956, Dr Sampurnanand's government constituted a fact-finding committee, headed by B.M. Birla and comprising prominent industrialists and some MPs and MLAs, to suggest ways for the industrial development of the state.[11] Dacoity was also a big law-and-order problem in those days, and efforts to deal with dacoits were ongoing. His government also constituted a committee to inquire the reasons for the poor representation of SCs in government employment and suggest measures to raise that level.[12]

In the government machinery during those days, the level of representation of various social groups, particularly SCs and backward classes (BCs), was quite poor. Among the 96 superintendents of police in UP, only one came from an SC and two from BCs; among the 422 inspectors of police, none belonged to SCs and 15 were from BCs. Among the 285 deputy superintendents of police, 12 were from SCs and only four from BCs.[13] The ratio started improving over the years, but the process went very slowly for OBCs (BCs are now known as OBCs). It only started improving after the Janata Party government implemented 15 per cent reservation in government services for them.

Dr Sampurnanand had to cope with various other problems immediately after he resumed his second stint as the CM

---

[11] *Vidhan Sabha ki Karyawahi*, 17 February 1956, UP Assembly Secretariat, Lucknow, p. 6.

[12] *Vidhan Sabha ki Karyawahi*, 25 July 1960, UP Assembly Secretariat, Lucknow, p. 14.

[13] Response of Ram Swarup Yadav, Deputy Minister of Home, on Questions of Garib Das, *Vidhan Sabha ki Karyawahi*, 31 July 1959, UP Assembly Secretariat, Lucknow, p. 448.

in 1957. Reeling under infighting and factionalism within the Congress, he was drawing fire not only from Opposition leaders like Raj Narain and Triloki Singh, but also from his own ambitious party colleagues like Chandra Bhanu Gupta, Kamalapati Tripathi and Chaudhary Charan Singh. Gupta, who had lost the assembly election in 1957 from the Lucknow City East seat to the Praja Socialist Party (PSP) candidate Triloki Singh, started opposing Dr Sampurnanand. Triloki Singh was elected as the leader of Opposition (LoP) in the second assembly. In 1958, Gupta made another unsuccessful attempt to enter the assembly through a by-election in Maudaha in Bundelkhand region, but he again lost to another PSP nominee, Maharani Rajendra Kumari. Interestingly, despite these two consecutive losses, Gupta's hold on the Uttar Pradesh Congress Committee (UPCC) was intact. Confrontations between the Congress party and Dr Sampurnanand's government were aggravating. While these pressures from various quarters were growing against his government, there was also a chorus of allegations of corruption, casteism and ineffectiveness.

In 1958, when Dr Sampurnanand's government decided to increase the retirement age of government employees from 55 to 58, it was criticized by the employees and many leaders of the Congress party. He was not ready to take back his decision, and so the government issued an order prohibiting cabinet ministers from expressing their opinion against government decisions in party meetings.[14] Dr Sampurnanand was also criticized for caste biases and for appointing officials from his own caste to top posts, including Govind Narain, who was appointed as the chief secretary. The CM had shifted Aditya Nath Jha, who had been the chief secretary since 16 August 1954, to the post of

[14]Gupta, Chandra Bhanu, *Safar Kahin Ruka Nahin, Jhuka Nahin*, Naman Prakashan, Lucknow, 2021, pp. 145–6.

the vice-chancellor of Varanaseya Sanskrit University in March 1958 in order to replace him with Govind Narain as the chief secretary. Allegations of nepotism were also made regarding university appointments during his government. A debate in the UP Assembly provides a glimpse of these allegations. On 31 July 1959, within a few years of the establishment of Gorakhpur University, Ugra Sen, an MLA from the Socialist Party elected from Salempur (West), alleged in the assembly: 'One thing I want to mention about Gorakhpur University is that there is so much corruption and nepotism there that 118 teachers belonging to a particular caste only have been appointed. Third-class teachers are appointed there.'[15]

However, neither the Govind Ballabh Pant government nor Dr Sampurnanand's government had faced a single vote of confidence or no-confidence motion in their respective tenures in the first Legislative Assembly.[16] In the second assembly, though, Dr Sampurnanand's government faced three no-confidence motions consecutively in 1957, 1958 and 1959, out of the total five tabled during his tenure.

The first no-confidence motion against his government was moved by the socialist leader Raj Narain on 10 December 1957 and discussed in the assembly on 23–24 December. However, only 106 MLAs voted in its favour and 265 against it, so his government survived. The second no-confidence motion was moved by another socialist leader, Triloki Singh, on 22 August 1958 and discussed in the assembly on 3–4 September. Only 95 members voted in its favour, while 269 voted against it. The third no-confidence motion against his government was also moved by Triloki Singh on 31 July 1959 and discussed

---

[15] *Vidhan Sabha ki Karyawahi*, 31 July 1959, UP Assembly Secretariat, Lucknow, p. 431; author's translation.

[16] Malhotra, G.C., *Cabinet Responsibility to Legislature*, Lok Sabha Secretariat, New Delhi, 1998.

on 6–7 August. This time, 112 MLAs voted in its favour and 285 against it, so the government survived again.

However, for Dr Sampurnanand, problems were worsening. A no-confidence motion is not an unusual thing, but what happened during the discussion on the third no-confidence motion was something that had not been witnessed in the UP Assembly till then. Just before the discussion was to start that day, Acharya Jugal Kishore of the Congress party (MLA from Govardhan) stood up and claimed that 96 Congress MLAs had given him a letter stating:

> We wanted to participate in the discussion in the House in favour of the no-confidence motion but we can't do that. In our opinion, the way Dr Sampurnanand is running the government is not up to the expectations of the ordinary people and Congressmen. Administration has been very weak and its strength is deteriorating. It does not have the reputation it had nearly five year ago ... there is wastage of money ... government employees are behaving arbitrarily ... corruption is growing... Ministers don't seem to be concerned to improve financial condition of the state ... due to factionalism ministers have no time to see the files of their departments... Congress party has now become a party of groups.[17]

Including Kishore and another member, the number of those dissident Congress MLAs increased to 98. The names of signatories on that letter, as claimed by Kishore, also included Charan Singh, who was elected from the Kotana seat in 1957. Charan Singh had resigned from the Sampurnanand Cabinet on 22 April 1959 due to differences, including on some policy issues. Allegations of nepotism were being raised time and again.

---

[17] *Vidhan Sabha ki Karyawahi,* 7 August 1959, UP Assembly Secretariat, Lucknow, pp. 849–50; author's translation.

Finally, a time came when Dr Sampurnanand, an educationist and academic, made a grave political blunder, something that no seasoned politician could have done. It was widely believed that all the problems, including those of ministers resigning from Dr Sampurnanand's government as well as dissident MLAs being led by Jugal Kishore, were instigated by C.B. Gupta. So, when Gupta was contesting elections for the UPCC presidentship, Dr Sampurnanand opposed him and made it a prestige issue, reinforcing his differences with Gupta. Dr Sampurnanand announced that if Gupta won, he would resign from the CM's post.[18] The UPCC elections held on 4 October 1960 had very high stakes. The CM put in his own nominee, Munishwar Dutt Upadhyay of Pratapgarh, as the candidate against Gupta. Now all his opponents needed to do to unseat Dr Sampurnanand was to defeat Upadhyay. That was done effectively as Gupta won the election by a majority of 630 votes and took charge as the UPCC president in October 1960.

Stung by Gupta's victory, Dr Sampurnanand was contemplating on how best to deal with the issue when PM Nehru intervened, and on his advice,[19] Dr Sampurnanand resigned as the CM on 26 November 1960. Although a majority of the Congress MLAs were still with him, the Congress leadership had finally decided to replace Dr Sampurnanand with C.B. Gupta as the CM on 7 December 1960. Dr Sampurnanand bid goodbye to electoral politics at that point and did not contest the 1962 assembly elections. In an article in August 1963, he wrote, 'The Indian citizen has no outline for him. All their dreams are focused on themselves. The emotional power which had mobilized them,

---

[18]Gupta, Chandra Bhanu, *Safar Kahin Ruka Nahin, Jhuka Nahin*, Naman Prakashan, Lucknow, 2021, pp. 145–6.

[19]Ibid.

is gone... Perhaps our leaders think that the era of idealism ended with Mahatma Gandhi.'[20]

To say that Dr Sampurnanand's tenure as the CM started the regime of political instability in UP would be fair. His ministers, like Kamalapati Tripathi, faced allegations of corruption, and his government faced allegations of working in the interests of corporates.

During his tenure, Dr Sampurnanand's relations with Governor V.V. Giri were also not cordial. Giri was transferred to Kerala in June 1960 before he could complete his tenure in UP, though he had later clarified that his transfer was due to his 'domestic circumstances'.

On 15 May 1961, the then Union government under PM Nehru constituted a National Emotional Integration Committee headed by Dr Sampurnanand. Initially, it had 10 members, including Indira Gandhi (by then, she had already served as the Congress president).The committee made 214 recommendations with regard to several aspects of education policy planning and its implementation. One of the recommendations was to impart education in regional languages. But along with this, the committee also recommended that 'for purely intellectual purposes, students in universities should have a good knowledge of the English language so that they can express themselves with facility. It is necessary, therefore, that they should frequently listen to lectures and write tutorials in English.'[21]

Dr Sampurnanand was appointed as the governor of Rajasthan in April 1962, and he remained in the post until 15 April 1967. During this time, his experiment with open prison camps in UP was applied in Rajasthan by the Mohanlal

---

[20]Sampurnanand, *Adhuri Kranti*, Bhanu Pratap Shukla (ed.), Lokhit Prakashan, Lucknow, 2013, p. 15; author's translation.

[21]*Report of the Committee on Emotional Integration*, Ministry of Education, Government of India, 1962, paras 13.87 and 13.91.

Sukhadia government. However, his tenure as the governor was also rife with controversy. The appointment of leaders like him as governors was criticized by many, who alleged that the Congress leadership had started appointing those leaders who had become 'spent forces' as governors of states.

Dr Sampurnanand passed away in Varanasi on 10 January 1969. Chandra Bhanu Gupta, on the demise of his predecessor, said:

> He was a progressive person. He wanted to abolish pernicious customs and wanted to see emerging new ideas in society. As a leading member of the Congress Socialist Party he tried from the beginning to bring new thoughts in the Congress and he remained with those thoughts till his last. He was a believer in Indian culture and wanted to change education systems in accordance with that.[22]

On 27 August 2021, President Ramnath Kovind attended the diamond jubilee function of Captain Manoj Kumar Pandey Sainik School, Lucknow, which was founded by Dr Sampurnanand during his tenure as the CM. More than 15 members from Dr Sampurnanand's family also attended the function.

---

[22] *Vidhan Sabha ki Karyawahi*, 17 March 1969, UP Assembly Secretariat, Lucknow, p. 16; author's translation.

3

CHANDRA BHANU GUPTA

A Behemoth of UP Politics

Third CM: Chandra Bhanu Gupta

Party: Indian National Congress

Tenure: 7 December 1960–14 March 1962

14 March 1962–1 October 1963

14 March 1967–2 April 1967

26 February 1969–17 February 1970

Constituency: Member of Legislative Council, Ranikhet South (later renamed as Ranikhet)

Days in Office: 3 years and 308 days

On 26 November 1960, Dr Sampurnanand resigned from the post of CM and Congress President Neelam Sanjiva Reddy called Chandra Bhanu Gupta to Delhi. Gupta writes in his memoir, 'Reddy took me to [Jawaharlal] Nehru to discuss the successor of Dr Sampurnanand. I suggested the names of Sri Prakash, Vijaya Lakshmi Pandit and Charan

Singh. Pandit Nehru did not like Charan Singh. He and Reddy advised me to take on the responsibility. Indira Gandhi was also present there and she endorsed their plan.'[1]

After his return to Lucknow from Delhi, Gupta was elected as the CLP leader on 1 December 1960. Governor B. Ramakrishna Rao was then in Hyderabad, so on 2 December, Dr Sampurnanand sent him a telegram requesting him to accept his resignation and advised him to 'invite Gupta to form the government'.[2] On the governor's return to Lucknow, Gupta was administered oath of CM of UP on 7 December 1960. He ended up being sworn in as the CM not once but four times, though his chief ministership lasted for less than four years.

Born in Atrauli (Aligarh) on 14 July 1902, Gupta was a key figure in the freedom movement. He studied law at the University of Lucknow and was a part of the team of advocates that defended revolutionaries in the Kakori Conspiracy Case.

Gupta was elected as an MLA for the first time in 1937 and was the treasurer of the UPCC during 1946–58. When the second Govind Ballabh Pant government was formed before Independence in July 1946, Gupta was appointed as the parliamentary secretary attached to Premier Pant. On 9 September 1947, he was elevated to the rank of minister of health and food in Pant's government.[3] Lal Bahadur Shastri (who later became the PM) and Charan Singh (who later became the CM of UP and then the PM) were also parliamentary

[1]Gupta, Chandra Bhanu, *Safar Kahin Ruka Nahin, Jhuka Nahin,* Naman Prakashan, Lucknow, 2021, p. 147.

[2]*Vidhan Sabha ki Karyawahi,* 7 February 1961, UP Assembly Secretariat, Lucknow, p. 86; author's translation.

[3]*Mantrimandalon ka Gathan 1921–1988,* UP Assembly Secretariat, Lucknow.

secretaries of the Pant government during that assembly.[4]

Post Independence, Gupta was elected to the first assembly in 1952 from the Lucknow City East constituency by defeating BJS candidate Krishna Gopal Kalantri.[5] In Dr Sampurnanand's first government, Gupta was the minister of planning, health, public health, industry, food and civil supplies.[6] But when Dr Sampurnanand was sworn in to continue as CM after the 1957 elections, Gupta was dropped as he had lost his assembly seat.

In fact, Gupta, who was among the probable chief ministerial candidates during the 1957 assembly polls, faced a major electoral setback when he lost his assembly seat Lucknow City East to the PSP's Triloki Singh. It became a double setback for him when he tried his luck for the Maudaha seat in Bundelkhand region in 1958 in a by-poll and lost there as well.[7] There were allegations that Gupta had distributed valuable gifts among hundreds of voters in the area, but even if he had done so, it did not work in his favour. His opponents in the Congress had also applied all tricks to defeat him.[8]

Despite the two electoral losses of 1957 and 1958, Gupta's hold on the state unit of the Congress was intact; so was his capability to shake Dr Sampurnanand's government and influence state politics through his friends and supporters in the party and the government. Being among the heavyweights of the Congress, Gupta's influence on the UPCC and state politics remained unhindered at least until the early 1970s. But

---

[4]Ibid.

[5]Ibid.

[6]Ibid.

[7]'Details of Assembly Bye Elections since 1952', *Election Commission of India*, https://tinyurl.com/484cmv3d. Accessed on 2 March 2024.

[8]Gupta, Chandra Bhanu, *Safar Kahin Ruka Nahin, Jhuka Nahin*, Naman Prakashan, Lucknow, 2021, p. 119.

PM Nehru and Indira Gandhi never liked him, a fact he has narrated in his memoirs as well.[9]

When he was sworn in for the first time, his administration was struggling to check the soaring expenses of the government. To reduce unnecessary expenditure, his government, on the very first day of his tenure—7 December 1960—issued an ordinance to curtail the salaries and allowances of ministers and deputy ministers and to appoint unpaid parliamentary secretaries in place of paid ones.[10] His government applied other austerity measures as well.[11] Since he was not a member of either House of the state legislature when he took oath as the CM, he was nominated to the Legislative Council on 23 January 1961 on a seat vacated by B.B. Bhatia. But Gupta's entry into the Upper House was controversial as Bhatia's resignation was submitted on 20 January 1961 and accepted on 28 January, but Gupta was nominated in his place on 23 January. Amid several accusations and allegations, Lakshman Singh Adhikari, an MLA from Ranikhet South, vacated his seat, offering it to Gupta to contest. Gupta did so and won.

Opposition leaders were also observing the growing factionalism in the Congress. Within three months of Gupta taking the oath, on 20 February 1961, two no-confidence motions were moved against his government, one by Raj Narain and another by Gupta's bête noire, Triloki Singh, and members of three other parties (Swatantra Party, the CPI and the BJS). Speaker Atmaram Govind Kher accepted the one moved by Raj Narain, which contained 21 reasons, including 'not implementing the report of the Backward Commission by the government is a loss to BCs... Government ignored the

---

[9]Ibid. 166–73.

[10]*Vidhan Sabha ki Karyawahi,* 6 February 1961, UP Assembly Secretariat, Lucknow, p. 3.

[11]Ibid.

demand for constituting a committee to inquire into allegations made in this House against ministers and senior officials'.[12] A discussion was held in the assembly on 23–24 February 1961, during which Narain demanded that Gupta should first resign from the Legislative Council, contest an assembly by-poll and then declare that if he lost the by-poll, he would quit. But Gupta replied that the motion was 'unreal, impractical and misleading'.[13] His government survived.

The Opposition was utilizing every opportunity to destabilize the Gupta government. In August 1961, Swatantra Party MLA K.D. Paliwal brought in a no-confidence motion, which was discussed on 22–24 August in the assembly. Paliwal alleged that the ruling party was facing factionalism, and due to that, it had little time to attend to the affairs of the state, thereby resulting in inefficiency and slackness in the administration.[14] On his part, Gupta replied forcefully, and among other accusations, he responded to the allegation of non-payment of sugarcane dues to farmers by saying that his government was doing what it could.[15] The Gupta government survived as the no-confidence motion fell through once again.

Dirty politics started in the UP Congress soon after Gupta took oath. On 3 February 1961, Gupta's predecessor Dr Sampurnanand wrote to the governor, 'You are going to address a joint sitting of both Houses of the assembly... Since this government was formed, it has done nothing which can

---

[12] *Vidhan Sabha ki Karyawahi,* 20 February 1961, UP Assembly Secretariat, Lucknow, p. 851; author's translation.

[13] *Vidhan Sabha ki Karyawahi,* 23 and 24 February 1961, UP Assembly Secretariat, Lucknow, p. 208; author's translation.

[14] *Vidhan Sabha ki Karyawahi,* 22 August 1961, UP Assembly Secretariat, Lucknow, p. 39.

[15] *Vidhan Sabha ki Karyawahi,* 23 August 1961, UP Assembly Secretariat, Lucknow pp. 166–74.

create enthusiasm. I don't want to listen to what the government is going to do and, therefore, I would not like to attend the joint sitting.'[16] A similar letter was written on 6 February 1961 by Kamalapati Tripathi, another prominent Congress leader, on behalf of a small group of Congress MLAs. Clashes of ego were seen among titans of the UP Congress.

Amid such problems playing out within the UP Congress, the tenure of the second assembly came to an end—it was adjourned sine die on 6 March 1962. Back then, the assembly was a 430-member House (excluding one nominated member). In the assembly polls held in March 1962, the Congress retained its majority. Gupta won again from the same Ranikhet South seat by defeating the PSP's Balwant Singh. Though Ajit Prasad Jain, UPCC president, had been hoping to replace Gupta, and Charan Singh and Kamalapati Tripathi had not felt at ease with him,[17] Gupta took oath on 14 March 1962 to continue as the CM.

In August 1962, a few months after the assembly polls, a no-confidence motion was moved against Gupta by the BJS's Yadavendra Dutt Dubey (from Jaunpur), and it was supported by members of the Socialist Party, the PSP, Swatantra Party and the CPI as well as an independent MLA. After being discussed in the assembly on 10 August and 13 August 1962, the no-confidence motion was negated, and his government, once again, survived.

In the following months, due to the Indo-China War and the declining health of PM Nehru, there was a sense of disquiet and uncertainty on the political front in the country. In late 1963, at an informal meeting at the Tirupati temple in Andhra Pradesh, a caucus called the Syndicate was formed by

---

[16]Gupta, Chandra Bhanu, *Safar Kahin Ruka Nahin, Jhuka Nahin,* Naman Prakashan, Lucknow, 2021, p. 150; author's translation.

[17]Ibid

the then Madras CM Kumaraswami Kamaraj, Andhra Pradesh CM Neelam Sanjiva Reddy, Karnataka CM Siddavanahalli Nijlingappa, Congress stalwart from West Bengal Atulya Ghosh and Union minister from Maharashtra Sadashiv Kanoji Patil. Under what came to be known as the Kamaraj Plan, PM Nehru was advised to reorganize the party and the central and state governments. He accepted the advice, and all Union ministers and CMs started to put in their papers from 29 September 1963; Gupta did not resign easily.

The UP CM considered the Kamaraj Plan to be humbug. 'I wanted to make them aware that I understood the game behind their plan, so I resigned only when he [Nehru] wrote me to do so.'[18] On 1 October 1963, Gupta also resigned as the CM. On 9 October, Kamaraj was elected as the president of the Congress. Except Kamaraj, Jagjivan Ram and Lal Bahadur Shastri, none of the others got back their old portfolios. Sucheta Kripalani had said in an interview that PM Nehru, due to his declining health, was contemplating his possible successor. Though Nehru wanted to transfer power to his daughter Indira Gandhi, he was reluctant to mention it. But, as Kripalani explained, 'The Kamaraj Plan of resigning from the chief ministership to strengthen the organization came in as a very handy cue for him.'[19] She proved to be the biggest beneficiary of the Kamaraj Plan in UP (she replaced Gupta as the CM).

After resigning under the Kamaraj Plan, Gupta contested for the post of the UPCC president in 1965 and won against Kampalati Tripathi, but the Congress leadership was not happy with the result, and a recounting was ordered with

---

[18]Gupta, Chandra Bhanu, *Safar Kahin Ruka Nahin, Jhuka Nahin,* Naman Prakashan, Lucknow, 2021, p. 168.

[19]'Interview: Mrs S. Kripalani – Part 5', *Centre of South Asian Studies,* University of Cambridge, http://tinyurl.com/297n4bvu. Accessed on 9 April 2022.

the stipulation that the votes of delegates who had taken any government quota/permit be declared as invalid. Gulzarilal Nanda scrutinized the votes; after recounting, Gupta's votes reduced and Tripathi was declared the winner.[20]

However, another opportunity was in the offing for Gupta. A few years later, in the 1967 elections, for the first time since Independence, the Congress fell short of the majority in UP as it won just 199 seats—14 short of a simple majority in a 425-seat House. Gupta won from Ranikhet again, though with a very narrow margin of just 70 votes.[21]

Since Sucheta Kripalani had already left for Delhi and was out of the race for chief ministership for multiple reasons, and Opposition parties had found themselves unable to form the government despite efforts, Gupta, being the leader of the single largest party, was sworn in as CM for the third time along with 12 ministers on 14 March 1967. An independent MLA, Ram Chandra Vikal, was elected as the LoP. Gupta said in the new assembly, 'I am among those who support the idea of a two-party system, as soon as it is possible. Then people will elect as per their wishes. I am happy that people from six-seven parties are trying.'[22] The day he took over as the CM for the third time, government employees withdrew their *kalamband hadtaal* (pen-down strike).[23] The Gupta government also decided to withdraw the levy imposed on *lagaan* (land tax) during the 1965 Indo-Pak War.[24] At the same time, he

---

[20]Gupta, Chandra Bhanu, *Safar Kahin Ruka Nahin, Jhuka Nahin,* Naman Prakashan, Lucknow, 2021, p. 172.

[21]*Statistical Report on General Election 1967 to Legislative Assembly of UP,* Election Commission of India, New Delhi.

[22]*Vidhan Sabha ki Karyawahi,* 1 April 1967, UP Assembly Secretariat, Lucknow, p; 485; author's translation.

[23]*Vidhan Sabha ki Karyawahi,* 17 March 1967, UP Assembly Secretariat, Lucknow, p. 36.

[24]Ibid. 40.

appealed to his ministers to practise austerity: 'The need of the hour is that we should curtail unnecessary expenses of the government. These can be curtailed. Ministers and officials should set an example by curtailing their own expenses so that others can get inspiration from them.'[25]

But Gupta could continue as CM only for 19 days in his third stint, as the UP Congress faced the first major defection engineered by Chaudhary Charan Singh, who was not part of Gupta's new 13-member ministry. Stunned by the move orchestrated by his old friend, on 1 April 1967, Gupta said in the assembly, '[S]ince the Opposition has got majority, I request adjourning the proceedings of the House. I will go to the Honourable Governor to submit my resignation.'[26] This was considered a big ethical move on his part. Gupta wrote in his memoirs that he had information that Charan Singh had contacted dissident Congress leaders as well as some Opposition leaders, but ministers H.N. Bahuguna and Govind Sahay had assured him that Charan Singh was an old Congressman and would never do that.[27] However, after Gupta's resignation, Charan Singh, as leader of a coalition called Samyukta Vidhayak Dal (SVD), took the reins from Gupta and became the CM.

An interesting example illustrates how difficult it was to deal with Gupta even for PM Indira. On his sixty-fifth birthday just before the 1967 assembly polls, Gupta was presented with ₹36 lakh, and Indira Gandhi was said to have been annoyed with him for accepting the money. This was a considerable amount in those days. Gupta has written that one day, the managing director of *National Herald*, Umashankar Dikshit, came to him

---

[25]Ibid. 36. Author's translation.

[26]*Vidhan Sabha ki Karyawahi,* 1 April 1967, UP Assembly Secretariat, Lucknow, p. 498.

[27]Gupta, Chandra Bhanu, *Safar Kahin Ruka Nahin, Jhuka Nahin,* Naman Prakashan, Lucknow, 2021, p. 209.

and told him that Indira Gandhi wanted a part of the amount from the collection for *National Herald*. He refused: 'I was not ready to fulfil the wishes of Indira Gandhi because she always helped my political opponents silently. I categorically said that no fund is left to me.'[28]

Gupta continued to remain active and relevant to UP politics even after resigning from the post of CM. Due to the failure of the SVD government, a fourth chance to be CM presented itself to Gupta after the mid-term polls in 1969. On 25 February 1968, after the fall of the Charan Singh government, President's Rule was imposed in the state for the first time since Independence. It ended with the swearing in of a new government after the 1969 mid-term polls.

In the 1969 mid-term polls, there were several allegations by several members, including Charan Singh, that the Congress misused the government machinery and that voters from the downtrodden were not allowed to vote. However, the Congress won 211 seats, and the biggest chunk from among the Opposition parties went to Charan Singh's newly formed Bharatiya Kranti Dal (BKD), which won 98 seats.[29] Gupta was elected from two seats—Ranikhet and Sarojini Nagar.[30] He retained Ranikhet and resigned from Sarojini Nagar.

Though the Congress was short of just two seats from a simple majority, Gupta was invited to form the government and took oath as CM for the fourth time on 26 February 1969. The year 1969 was among the most politically volatile in India. President Zakir Husain had passed away, and the Congress was virtually divided into two groups. What was known as the Syndicate within the Congress favoured Neelam

[28]Ibid. 204. Author's translation.

[29]*Statistical Report on General Election 1969 to Legislative Assembly of UP,* Election Commission of India, New Delhi.

[30]Ibid.

Sanjiva Reddy as the candidate for the president of India. The Indira Gandhi faction fielded its own candidate, V.V. Giri, who ultimately won, proving that it held the reins. But on 12 November 1969, Congress leaders Kamaraj, Sanjiva Reddy and Morarji Desai expelled PM Indira Gandhi from the Congress, which resulted in a split with one faction known as Congress (Organisation) (Congress [O]) and the other, headed by Indira Gandhi, as Congress (Requisitionists) (Congress [R]). Gupta went with Congress (O).

The impact of a split in the Congress on Gupta's chair was obvious. He started facing problems not only from his colleagues in the state but also from the Centre, since he was close to the leaders who were rivals of PM Indira. He alleged that PM Indira had made 49 trips to the state before the 1969 mid-term polls and 17 trips after the polls between 12 September 1969 and 23 December 1969.[31] He suggested that expenses on those trips should have been borne by the central government because of the poor fiscal condition of the state.[32] Prime Minister Indira responded that the state's leadership was responsible for UP's backwardness. Gupta countered these allegations and blamed the central leadership instead.

A week after the historic split of the Congress on 20 November 1969, UP's deputy CM Kamalapati Tripathi and ministers N.D. Tiwari (Kashipur), Chaturbhuj Sharma (Jalaun), Lakshmi Shankar Yadav (Khuthan), Ateek-ur-Rahman (Nagina) and Ajit Pratap Singh (Pratapgarh) resigned from the Gupta Cabinet. Later, ministers Vidyawati Rathore (Mohammadabad) and Swami Prasad Singh (Rath) also resigned. On 23 November 1969, Gupta expanded his cabinet, but the situation seemed to have gone out of his control. In those stressful days, while

---

[31]Gupta, Chandra Bhanu, *Safar Kahin Ruka Nahin, Jhuka Nahin,* Naman Prakashan, Lucknow, 2021, p 243

[32]Ibid.

returning from Gorakhpur after delivering a Republic Day speech on 26 January 1970, he fell unconscious. His poor health was one of the reasons for his resignation on 10 February 1970.[33]

The downfall of a titan had truly begun. For decades, Gupta had not only dominated UP politics but was also on the forefront of fund collection for the Congress. But in the 1974 assembly polls, he had to face a big setback. Though booth-capturing at the social level was complained about at several places since Independence, it was H.N. Bahuguna as the CM in the 1974 assembly polls who faced severe criticism for the misuse of government machinery. Bahuguna, whom Gupta used to call Natwarlal, ensured Gupta's defeat from his Lucknow Cantt seat, and Gupta not only stood fourth but also lost his deposit. That was the last poll Gupta contested. When both Gupta and Bahuguna were in the Janata Party in 1977, the former asked the latter how he had defeated him; Bahuguna told him that the ballot boxes (in Gupta's assembly seat) had been swapped.

The Congress (O) was first headed by K. Kamaraj and later by Morarji Desai, before it was merged with the Janata Party prior to the 1977 polls. By then, Gupta was with the Janata Party and was appointed its treasurer, but he could not play a major role in the Janata Party government in 1977 due to his poor health. Known for his simple living, helpful nature, straightforwardness and outspokenness, Gupta remained a bachelor and did not promote his family members in politics. As the CM, he never stayed at his official residence; after finishing the day's work, he used to return at night to his room at Pandariba in Lucknow. Gupta was known for working 15–18 hours a day, sitting in his vest.[34] He was actively involved

---

[33]Ibid. 247.

[34]*Vidhan Sabha ki Karyawahi,* 3 July 1980, UP Assembly Secretariat, Lucknow.

in various educational, social welfare and cultural activities in Lucknow, especially those undertaken by Motilal Memorial Society and Bharat Sewa Sansthan, which were founded by him.

Gupta had a dream to spread industry in the entire state. As the industry minister in Dr Sampurnanand's government, he announced several concessions for industrialists who wanted to invest in the state, but that gave the opportunity to his opponents to publicize that he was a friend of the corporates.

Chandra Bhanu Gupta passed away on 11 March 1980, after a few years of steadily deteriorating health. On Gupta's demise, V.P. Singh, who went on to become the CM of UP, said:

> He [Gupta] gave a new definition to politics in our state. While working with him, I realized that he wore iron gloves but his heart had no doors. It was always open. He lived like a poor man, and in spite of being in contact with the richest people, his personal life was unaffected by that. I believe that whenever any youth tries to enter politics in this state or think of doing so, they will always keep Shree Chandra Bhanu Gupta in their mind, in their beliefs, in their future.[35]

[35]Ibid. 17.

4

SUCHETA KRIPALANI

The First Female CM of India

Fourth CM: Sucheta Kripalani

Party: Indian National Congress

Tenure: 2 October 1963–13 March 1967

Constituency: Mehndawal

Days in office: 3 years and 162 days

In the last week of September 1963, when the Congress leadership was considering probable successors of Chandra Bhanu Gupta, who had been asked to resign as the CM of UP under the Kamaraj Plan, Gupta was in Delhi to pay a courtesy call to the ailing Acharya J.B. Kripalani, a former Congress president and a Gandhian stalwart. His wife Sucheta Kripalani, who was a cabinet colleague of Gupta, was also in Delhi at that time, taking care of her husband. During a conversation, J.B. Kripalani, in a lighter vein, asked Gupta, 'Why don't you give the CM's post to her [Sucheta]?' The idea appealed to him, and he, at an opportune moment, suggested to PM Nehru to consider replacing him with Sucheta as the new leader of the CLP, ignoring the likes of Kamalapati Tripathi.[1]

Sucheta Kripalani, while recounting the story, said that when J.B. Kripalani had had a heart attack and was being treated at the Willingdon Hospital (now Dr. Ram Manohar Lohia Hospital) in New Delhi where she had been taking care of him, K.C. Pant (the son of G.B. Pant) had come to see J.B. Kripalani, and he had told Sucheta that her name was being considered as Gupta's successor.[2] However, a final decision was taken after a meeting of the CLP was held in Lucknow, where party MLAs were given blank papers to write the name of the person they favoured as leader of the CLP. There were only two contenders—Sucheta Kripalani and Kamalapati Tripathi. When the counting was completed, it turned out that Sucheta won by a margin of 99 votes.[3] That is how she was elected as the CLP leader. She was sworn in as the fourth CM of UP on 2 October 1963 and, thus, became the first female CM of not only UP, but of any Indian state.

The politics of Sucheta Kripalani cannot be understood in isolation; her contributions were multidimensional. She was associated with several relief activities, be it for the 1934 earthquake in Bihar; the pre-Partition riots in Noakhali in 1946; the rehabilitation of Tibetan refugees, including the Dalai

---

[1]Gupta, Chandra Bhanu, *Safar Kahin Ruka Nahin, Jhuka Nahin*, Naman Prakashan, Lucknow, 2021, p. 169.

[2]'Interview: Mrs S. Kripalani – Part 5', *Centre of South Asian Studies*, University of Cambridge, http://tinyurl.com/297n4bvu. Accessed on 9 April 2022.

[3] Gupta, Chandra Bhanu, *Safar Kahin Ruka Nahin, Jhuka Nahin*, Naman Prakashan, Lucknow, 2021, p. 170.

Lama, in 1959; or providing help to the East Pakistan refugees during the Indo-Pak War of 1971.

Daughter of S.N. Majumdar, a government surgeon posted in Punjab, Sucheta was born in Ambala (now in Haryana) on 25 June 1908. She studied at the University of Delhi (Indraprastha College for Women and St. Stephen's College) and, in April 1936, married the former Congress president J.B. Kripalani, a Gandhian who later quit Congress to work with socialist leaders but left them after almost five years. He had taught at the BHU during 1919–20 after working as secretary to the Congress president Madan Mohan Malviya in 1918. A decade later, in 1929, Sucheta had also joined BHU to teach Constitutional History, and J.B. used to visit the campus in search of volunteers for the freedom movement. Their marriage was against the wishes of their families, as well as Mahatma Gandhi's, as J.B. was 20 years older than Sucheta.[4] Both husband and wife were social workers and freedom fighters, and were with the Congress, but in later years, they became members of different parties.

Sucheta resigned from BHU in 1939, and the couple lived in Allahabad for some time. During this period, Sucheta, along with her cousin 'Dhiren' Majumdar, stayed for a while in Faizabad (now Ayodhya) to work among disadvantaged women. She participated in a satyagraha while living in Faizabad and was imprisoned for nearly a year in 1940. When she joined the Congress, she was put in charge of organizing the foreign affairs wing of the AICC, but when Dr Ram Manohar Lohia joined this wing, she was assigned to organize the party's newly created women's wing. Thus, she was the founder of the All India Mahila Congress. During the Quit India Movement, she

[4]Rai, Ram Bahadur, *Shashwat Vidrohi Rajneta Acharya JB Kripalani,* National Book Trust, New Delhi, 2013, pp. 98–9.

worked underground to evade arrest but was finally taken into custody in Patna and spent several months in a jail in Lucknow. When the Kripalanis were elected to the Constituent Assembly in 1946, they moved to Delhi.

In the Meerut session of the AICC on 23–24 November 1946, J.B. Kripalani was elected the Congress's forty-seventh president. Those were crucial years as freedom was achieved nine months later, on 15 August 1947. The country was in the throes of historic changes after Partition, having faced the after-effects of widespread communal riots. Sucheta, a member of the Constituent Assembly, sang 'Vande Mataram' at the Independence session of the Constituent Assembly on 14 August 1947 midnight, before Nehru delivered his speech titled 'Tryst with Destiny'.

Sucheta was elected to the United Provinces Assembly from Kanpur District North East (comprising parts of Kanpur and Bilhaur tehsils) unopposed in a by-poll in 1948. The seat had been vacated by Vijaya Lakshmi Pandit as she was appointed as India's ambassador to the Soviet Union in 1947. But Sucheta resigned from this assembly seat in 1950; she decided to quit the Congress, following J.B.'s plan to leave the party. When J.B. quit the Congress in 1951 to form the Kisan Mazdoor Praja Party (KMPP), Sucheta joined him and in the Lok Sabha poll she won from the New Delhi seat on a KMPP ticket. J.B. merged his KMPP with the Socialist Party in 1952 to form the PSP and was appointed its president. But in 1954, he resigned as the PSP president, and from 1960, he separated from the PSP to be in non-partisan politics. Within two years of J.B. resigning as president of the PSP, Sucheta returned to the Congress, and, in 1957, she won from the same New Delhi Lok Sabha seat as a Congress candidate. She was among the most eloquent and outspoken members of the Lok Sabha. When Indira Gandhi was elected as the Congress president in

May 1959, on the advice of PM Nehru and Indira Gandhi, Sucheta joined the latter as a general secretary of the party; being senior to Indira, she did so unwillingly.[5]

It was sometime in 1960 that the Kripalanis visited Lucknow after returning from a trip to the United States (US). C.B. Gupta called on them and said to Sucheta, 'You have been out of your state for a long time. Why don't you come and serve your state?'[6] J.B. Kripalani responded, 'Alright, you become the chief minister; then she will come and help you.'[7] Sucheta has mentioned that J.B. had meant it as a joke, but Gupta had taken it seriously, and later, after he had become the CM, he invited her to join his government, which she did, and was allotted a portfolio of her own choice.[8] Elaborating on the background to this story, Sucheta explained that 'at that time, C.B. Gupta was working against Sampurnanand and it looked as if he might be able to supersede Sampurnanand as chief minister. He had serious differences with Sampurnanand and his supporters and told us all about it.'[9]

That is how Sucheta Kripalani was sent to Lucknow and entered state politics. On 12 December 1960, she took oath as a cabinet minister in the five-day-old Gupta government. She was allotted the portfolios of community development and small industries and labour.[10] She resigned from the Lok Sabha and was elected to the Legislative Council on 4 May 1961. Later, in the third assembly elections in March 1962, she

---

[5]'Interview: Mrs S. Kripalani – Part 4', *Centre of South Asian Studies*, University of Cambridge, http://tinyurl.com/297n4bvu. Accessed on 9 April 2022.

[6]'Interview: Mrs S. Kripalani – Part 5', *Centre of South Asian Studies*, University of Cambridge, http://tinyurl.com/297n4bvu. Accessed on 9 April 2022.

[7]Ibid.

[8]Ibid.

[9]Ibid.

[10]*Mantrimandalon ka Gathan, 1921–1988,* UP Assembly Secretariat, Lucknow.

contested from the Mehndawal Assembly seat and won. She was again sworn in as a minister in the Gupta government that was formed in March 1962, having the same portfolios as before.

Later events show that the CM's chair was inching towards her. From the memoirs of Gupta and Sucheta, it appears that before Gupta resigned as the CM on 1 October 1963, he wanted someone other than his old colleagues in the cabinet to replace him. As per his wishes, Sucheta was sworn in as the fourth CM of UP on 2 October 1963. However, she has narrated another reason as well behind her selection:

> Gupta ji ultimately decided on my name because the various caste clashes were such that if he had taken a man from any caste, the other caste-members would have opposed him, because none of the leaders had the stature like that of Gupta ji and different caste blocks were there. Secondly, he wanted a person against whom there could be no charge of corruption.[11]

Sucheta was known for her many qualities, including her strictness, straightforwardness and simplicity. In his well-researched book *Shashwat Vidrohi Rajneta Acharya JB Kripalani,* Ram Bahadur Rai, senior journalist and chairman of the Indira Gandhi National Centre for the Arts (IGNCA), wrote, 'She used to reach [CM's] office at 10 a.m. and leave only after 6.00 p.m. She had directed that no one should bring any gift for her. The same was the instruction for her staff.'[12] J.B. Kripalani wrote:

---

[11]'Interview: Mrs S. Kripalani – Part 5', *Centre of South Asian Studies*, University of Cambridge, http://tinyurl.com/297n4bvu. Accessed on 9 April 2022.

[12]Rai, Ram Bahadur, *Shashwat Vidrohi Rajneta Acharya JB Kripalani,* National Book Trust, New Delhi, 2013, p. 105; author's translation.

> [S]he did not occupy the usual palatial house, where lived her predecessors [except Gupta] in office. She contented herself with the annexe of that big bungalow, occupied by the personal staff of her predecessors in office. When Lal Bahadur [Shastri], after he became prime minister, went to Lucknow and visited her house, he remarked in surprise, 'Is this the house where the chief minister of the biggest State of India lives?' All her cabinet colleagues and departmental secretaries occupied biggest houses.[13]

As the CM, Sucheta waived school fees for all girls up to Class 10 from January 1965.[14] Meerut University (now named after Chaudhary Charan Singh) and Kanpur University (now named after Chhatrapati Shahu Ji Maharaj) were established.[15] Concerned with the fact that 18 per cent reserved posts in government jobs for the SCs (called harijans at that time) were not filled, her government decided to increase reservation of posts in Group C to 24 per cent and in Group D to 45 per cent until the 18 per cent target was achieved.[16] A Sainik School was established in Ghorakhal and a new medical college was started in Meerut.[17] Many dacoits were neutralized in the Chambal Valley with the help of the Police Radio Unit.[18] During her regime, the UP Awas Vikas Parishad was established,

---

[13]Kripalani, J.B., 'In Memoriam', in Kripalani, Sucheta, *Sucheta: An Unfinished Autobiography,* K.N.Vaswani (ed.), Navajivan Publishing House, Ahmedabad, 1978, p. xxi.

[14]Governor's address before UP Assembly on 8 February 1965, *Vidhan Sabha ki Karyawahi,* 8 February 1965, UP Assembly Secretariat, Lucknow, p. 27.

[15]Ibid.

[16]Ibid. 28.

[17]Governor's address before UP Assembly on 3 February 1964, *Vidhan Sabha ki Karyawahi,* 3 February 1964, UP Assembly Secretariat, Lucknow, pp. 10, 13.

[18]Ibid. 10.

and the post of the agriculture production commissioner as a coordinator for all departments related to agriculture production was created.[19]

However, Opposition parties, and sometimes even members of her own party, often criticized her for the corruption in the government machinery and accused her government of being run by bureaucrats. Sucheta realized the curse of corruption; her government once underlined in the assembly, while welcoming the Union government's initiative to appoint a vigilance commission, 'Growing corruption in public services is an obstacle in the progress and growth of our people, and it needs to be dealt with strictly.'[20] Records suggest that corruption and casteism, which have become rampant today, are not new; even Sucheta Kripalani was dealing with these in the 1960s.

With regard to caste equations, she said, 'Caste did play an important part, in the sense that ministers readily trusted men belonging to their own caste. In some way or the other, the caste link has a lot of weight.'[21] Regarding the pressure from MLAs, she mentioned:

> In every district, powerful MLAs would try to twist the administration to their liking, to their way of thinking, and each minister was under heavy pressure by MLAs from different districts and the pressure was on small matters like transfers of officers (even petty officers), or condoning the wrong done by particular persons or on

[19]Sucheta Kripalani informed the assembly during her reply on the governor's address on 5 February 1964.

[20]Governor's address at UP Assembly on 3 February 1964, *Vidhan Sabha ki Karyawahi,* 3 February 1964, UP Assembly Secretariat, Lucknow, p. 10; author's translation.

[21]'Interview: Mrs S. Kripalani – Part 5', *Centre of South Asian Studies*, University of Cambridge, http://tinyurl.com/297n4bvu. Accessed on 9 April 2022.

> shielding people who had done some wrong so that they might not be taken to task and things like that.[22]

Though Sucheta was among those leaders who were staunch supporters of Hindi, she faced criticism for being influenced by the English mindset of government officials. When a Socialist Party MLA, Kashi Nath Mishra (Bansdih East), alleged this, she responded, 'I am ready to speak in Hindi despite being Bangla-speaking, but you are not… Only the CM cannot do this. You have to create an atmosphere [for Hindi].'[23]

It was during her tenure that the foundation of the Green Revolution in UP was laid—notably, the state had been facing drought conditions during the entirety of her tenure as CM. She once said, 'Recently, the Union Finance Minister [T.T. Krishnamachari] came here and he had meetings with each department. He met 80–90 officials. He returned satisfied that in UP now there is good work being done and there is progress. The Central Government had a negative image about the state earlier but now that is not the case.'[24]

When UP was heading for polls for the fourth assembly along with polls for the fourth Lok Sabha in 1967, many political events taking place in the state and some other parts of North India had been troubling Sucheta. The campaign of Socialist Party stalwart Dr Ram Manohar Lohia for non-Congress governments in states and at the Centre was at its peak. In 1963, he was elected from Farrukhabad in a by-poll as a Socialist Party candidate, and in 1964, he formed the Samyukta Socialist Party (SSP). Away from UP, in Madhya Pradesh, a tribal king, Pravir Chandra Bhanj Deo, was killed

---

[22]Ibid.

[23]*Vidhan Sabha ki Karyawahi*, 2 February 1966, UP Assembly Secretariat, Lucknow, p. 423; author's translation.

[24]Ibid. 419. Author's translation.

in a police encounter in Bastar (now in Chhattisgarh) on 25 March 1966. J.B. Kripalani was part of a delegation of Opposition parties that inquired into the incident and held the then Madhya Pradesh CM, Dwarka Prasad Mishra, responsible for the killing. The repercussions were felt in UP.

But these were not the only reasons for Sucheta's disquiet. Her unfinished autobiography gives some glimpse of the political turmoil UP was facing in those days, and how it was becoming difficult day by day for her. Problems, it appears, had started from the very beginning. Annoyed with some news items published in newspapers against her, she wrote to PM Nehru on 6 November 1963, a little over a month of her taking oath as the CM:

> I sincerely feel that UP has not had a fair chance to develop in recent years mainly because the leaders of the State have been too preoccupied with politics and the administration was given secondary consideration if at all… Unfortunately, at such a time, the release of the news in the manner it has appeared in the papers has created an atmosphere of uncertainty regarding the tenure of this ministry… But if I have to carry on a continuous struggle on three or four fronts, the task will be too overwhelming even for somebody more able and clever than myself.[25]

On 28 August 1966, she wrote to the Congress president K. Kamaraj, 'I may be allowed to tender my resignation from my office, which has been far from comfortable and which as days go by is becoming increasingly uncomfortable.'[26] On this, Kamaraj had consulted PM Indira and announced that there

---

[25]Kripalani, Sucheta, *Sucheta: An Unfinished Autobiography,* K.N. Vaswani (ed.), Navajivan Publishing House, Ahmedabad, 1978, pp. 204–5.

[26]Ibid. 208.

would be no change of the CM till the end of the existing assembly in February 1967.[27] Then, on 8 September 1966, she wrote to the governor of UP, Bishwanath Das:

> I have approached the High Command to give me leave to resign from my office that as you know has not been quite a bed of roses. This is as you are aware due to ambition of two friends [C.B. Gupta and Kamalapati Tripathi] who both want the same place, namely the Chief Ministership… Under these circumstances, when no control is exercised by the Central Party or Government authority, it becomes my painful duty to submit my resignation.[28]

Her resignation was not accepted.

However, just a month later, when PM Indira called her to Delhi and asked if she would like to resign as the CM and accept a governorship (PM Indira thought that her resignation would facilitate the Congress election campaign in UP), Sucheta said that she was not prepared to resign.[29] But she wrote to Governor Bishwanath Das again in January 1967 that 'I am, therefore, constrained to place before you my resignation. It is quite possible that some of my critics in the party may do better than me… If, however, you may think that this is not possible with the general election so near, you may advise the Rashtrapati to suspend the Constitution and order President's Rule.'[30] On receiving the letter, the governor called her personally and told her that as she had somehow pulled along so far, she might as well do it for a month more.[31] The troubles were mostly associated with her party colleagues. She said:

---

[27]Ibid. 224.

[28]Ibid. 208.

[29]Ibid. 225.

[30]Ibid. 212.

[31]Ibid. 212.

> At one time I had as Chief Secretary a Christian, the next officer, the Development Commissioner, a Mussalman, and another head of the department, a Harijan. Instead of appreciating this, my detractors from Kamalapati's group wrote an article saying that 'Mrs Kripalani is carrying on the Government with the help of the minority' and that I was ignoring the interests of the majority community.[32]

When the last session of the UP Assembly with her as the CM was going on, the non-gazetted government employees were on strike with the demand for a hike in salary. Opposition parties were raising the issue and criticizing the Kripalani government. The strike started over two months back, and she had refused to accept their demands. While responding to an adjournment motion on the issue on 8 December 1966, she had categorically stated, 'We have a limit. We can give only a part of what we [government] are earning. It is true that inflation has increased. But Congress alone is not responsible for it… We will not talk to them [striking employees] until they change their attitude [of indiscipline].'[33] The next day, on 9 December, the assembly was adjourned sine die. Her government had to face three consecutive no-confidence motions in 1964, 1965 and 1966; all three were negated and her government survived.[34]

For these reasons, Sucheta Kripalani did not contest the assembly polls in 1967. Evidently, the party leadership did not want her to be repeated as the CM; she did not want to continue on the chair after the 1967 polls either. On why she left UP and returned to central politics, she had mentioned

---

[32]'Interview: Mrs S. Kripalani – Part 6', *Centre of South Asian Studies*, University of Cambridge, http://tinyurl.com/297n4bvu. Accessed on 9 April 2022.

[33]*Vidhan Sabha ki Karyawahi,* 8 December 1966, UP Assembly Secretariat, Lucknow, p. 926.

[34]Malhotra, G.C., *Cabinet Responsibility to Legislature,* Lok Sabha Secretariat, New Delhi, 2004.

earlier, 'The responsibility [as CM] I am given is too much and my shoulders don't have that much strength, but I have tried to do everything in the last two years, whatever was possible for me to do.'[35] The feeling of the central leaders back then about UP can be best understood from one of her speeches before the UP assembly: 'I must say that for our state, here and outside of it, there is much *tiraskar* [disdain] and *laanchhan* [stigma].'[36]

The fourth assembly polls were held in March 1967, simultaneously with the Lok Sabha polls, and for the first time since 1952, the Congress was reduced to a minority. Sucheta contested the Lok Sabha polls from Gonda on a Congress ticket. She won and returned to Delhi. She lost the 1971 Lok Sabha poll from Faizabad as the Congress (O) candidate. After that, the Kripalanis decided to leave politics, and they settled in Delhi.

A true Gandhian, Sucheta wore khadi right from her student days. She was known for helping even her opponents. During the 1974 elections in UP, she visited the state and tried to help even those candidates who had made her chief ministership difficult. She went to the constituency of C.B. Gupta and took charge of his campaign, despite J.B. Kripalani's objection due to her ailing health. When the JP Movement started in early 1974 against the Indira Gandhi government, J.B. Kripalani was made chairman of the Delhi Committee.[37] She was also active

[35]Sucheta Kripalani in the UP Assembly on 2 February 1966, *Vidhan Sabha ki Karyawahi*, 2 February 1966, UP Assembly Secretariat, Lucknow, p. 426; author's translation.

[36]Ibid.

[37]Rai, Ram Bahadur, *Shashwat Vidrohi Rajneta Acharya JB Kripalani,* National

in the JP Movement, but her health had been deteriorating.

The Kripalanis had no children and donated their assets to a Delhi-based trust, Lok Kalyan Samiti, which Sucheta had formed with some others in the early 1950s. She passed away on 1 December 1974 in Delhi. On her demise, then PM Indira said, 'The news came as a blow. Suchetaji was a person of rare courage and character. She brought credit to Indian womanhood. Her death is a loss to the country.'[38]

Book Trust, New Delhi, 2013, p. 105.

[38]Kripalani, Sucheta, *Sucheta: An Unfinished Autobiography,* K.N. Vaswani (ed.), Navajivan Publishing House, Ahmedabad, 1978, p. 228.

5

CHAUDHARY CHARAN SINGH

The First Non-Congress CM of UP

Fifth CM: Chaudhary Charan Singh

Party: Jan Congress, Bharatiya Kranti Dal

Tenure: 3 April 1967–25 February 1968

18 February 1970–1 October 1970

Constituency: Chhaprauli

Days in Office: 1 year and 188 days

The fourth UP Assembly polls held in 1967 were different from previous assembly elections for the ruling Congress party. For one, the sitting CM, Sucheta Kripalani, did not contest them. Around that time, Dr Ram Manohar Lohia of the SSP had emerged as a major force in Opposition politics and launched a campaign for non-Congress governments after having won the Lok Sabha by-poll from Farrukhabad in 1963. In order to give voice to the neglected BCs, he had coined a new slogan: '*Sansopa ne baandhi gaanth, pichhde paaven sau mein saath*' (SSP has resolved that the OBCs should get 60 per cent [of all opportunities]). The electorate was in distress due to continued drought and price rise, and an additional contributor was a campaign for the ban on cow slaughter. All these factors helped the Opposition parties broaden and strengthen their presence in UP. The BJS won 99 seats (including one that was won by one of its leaders as an independent candidate), and several young faces from the BCs like Mulayam Singh Yadav and Kalyan Singh (both became CMs later) had won for the first time from different parties.

The Congress's hold on the state was reduced to 14 seats short of a majority as it won only 199 out of 425 assembly seats. This provided an opportunity for the Opposition leaders to try to unseat the Congress. Opposition members, comprising a group of small parties and independents, who had formed the SVD under the leadership of Ram Chandra Vikal,[1] attempted to form a government but failed.

By this time, non-Congress governments were being sworn in one after the other in other states like West Bengal, Bihar, Kerala, Madras, Orissa (now Odisha), Punjab and Haryana. In Rajasthan, the Congress was short of a majority by four seats, but Governor Hukum Singh administered oath to Mohanlal Sukhadia of the Congress as the CM amid accusations of 'mockery of democracy'.

In UP, equations had been changing for the past several years. Relations between Charan Singh and C.B. Gupta had been deteriorating day by day. Charan Singh had a significant following among the farmers and rural populace. Gupta wrote in his memoir that while he was finalizing the names of his cabinet colleagues in March 1967, Charan

[1]Vikal had been a Congress MLA from Sikandarabad in 1957 and from Dadri in 1962, but in 1967, he was denied a Congress ticket and was elected as an independent MLA from Sikandarabad.

Singh had come to him and advised not to take certain MLAs into his government. Those MLAs were Chaudhary Girdharilal (Afzalgarh, Bijnor), Jaganprasad Rawat (Kheragarh, Agra), Chaturbhuj Sharma (Orai) and Dr Sitaram (Rudrapur, Deoria). However, Gupta took Dr Sitaram in his 13-member cabinet. Gupta further mentioned that Charan Singh had wanted Jairam Verma (Akbarpur) and Udit Naraian Sharma (Jhansi) to be inducted into the Gupta government.[2] But they did not find place in the Gupta Cabinet, and this was one reason why Charan Singh was annoyed.

Gupta had an inkling that Charan Singh was in touch with Vikal and other Opposition leaders, but party colleagues H.N. Bahuguna and Govind Sahai allayed his fears and assured him that being an old Congressman, Charan Singh would not leave the party.[3] Besides Charan Singh, parties like the BJS were also actively trying to unseat the Congress by dividing it since the day Gupta assumed office. Defections in other states gave them, as well as Charan Singh, added confidence. Finally, with the backing of socialist leaders like Dr Lohia, Raj Narain and the BJS's Nanaji Deshmukh, Charan Singh managed to manufacture a historic defection in the Congress.

On 1 April 1967, a total of 418 members and two ministers who were not members of either House were present in the assembly during a discussion on the motion of thanks on Governor Bishwanath Das's address. Gupta had given his reply, and Krishnanand Rai, a Congress MLA from Dildarnagar (Ghazipur), was speaking. Suddenly, Charan Singh, the Congress MLA from Chhaprauli, stood up. The Speaker, Jagdish Saran Agrawal, asked him, 'What do you want to speak on?'[4] Charan

---

[2]Gupta, Chandra Bhanu, *Safar Kahin Ruka Nahin, Jhuka Nahin,* Naman Prakashan, Lucknow, 2021, p. 208.

[3]Ibid. 209.

[4]*Vidhan Sabha ki Karyawahi*, 1 April 1967, UP Assembly Secretariat, Lucknow,

Singh replied, 'I want to make a small statement and that is that some members of the Congress have left the party and they have formed a new party named Jan Congress.'[5] Slogans of 'Charan Singh zindabad' rang out from the Opposition benches and continued in spite of the Speaker ordering them to maintain silence. Charan Singh continued, 'Political parties are just an instrument of public service, and if a party does not remain so, the duty of its true members is that they must depart from that party. With the beliefs with which we have lived our lives, if we want to protect them, it is not possible in the Congress, but only outside of it.'[6]

The assembly session continued. There was voting on the 19-point ammendments proposed by Jharkhande Rai, the CPI MLA from Ghosi, on the motion of thanks on the governor's address. Out of all the members present, 215 voted in favour and 198 voted against the amendments, which were then adopted. This meant that the ruling government lost its majority. Immediately, Gupta stood up and said, 'Hon'ble Speaker Sir, I wanted to say that since the Opposition is now in a majority, I request adjournment of the proceedings of the House. I will go to the Governor to submit resignations of myself and of my colleagues.'[7]

After Gupta's resignation was accepted, Charan Singh took oath as the fifth CM of UP on 3 April 1967. Nearly 20 years after Independence, Charan Singh became the first non-Congress CM of the state.

Prior to Charan Singh's switch in parties, Agrawal had already been elected as the Speaker on 17 March. In the changed scenario, he wrote to Charan Singh, conveying that

---

p. 490.

[5]Ibid.

[6]Ibid. 490–1.

[7]Ibid. 498.

he was willing to step down from his post, but Charan Singh said that he should continue.

Charan Singh was born in Noorpur village of Meerut (now in Hapur district) on 23 December 1902 in a Jat family. After completing his MA and law degrees from Agra University (now named after Dr B.R. Ambedkar), he started practising as a lawyer in Meerut's Ghaziabad tehsil (a district since 1976). He joined the Congress in 1931 and was jailed for several months during the freedom struggle. In 1937, standing for election for the first time, he was elected to the United Provinces Assembly from Chhaprauli on a Congress ticket. After Independence, he was part of the interim government of UP headed by G.B. Pant. As the minister of revenue in the Pant government, he gained popularity as he was at the forefront of the implementation of the zamindari abolition. The United Provinces Assembly passed a resolution on 8 August 1946 for the abolition of zamindari system in the province and appointed a committee headed by G.B. Pant, which included Charan Singh, who was then the parliamentary secretary to Pant. Charan Singh helped write the report of the Zamindari Abolition and Land Reforms Committee in 1948. As the revenue minister, he continued its implementation very effectively after Independence. Because of this, several lakh farmers and landless people became owners of land, even if small in size. In February 1953, the patwaris—revenue employees at the grassroots—started a strike and submitted their resignations. After serving two warnings, Charan Singh accepted the resignations of nearly 27,000 patwaris. To replace them, he created a new cadre, which he called lekhpal, to maintain the village revenue and land records. Later, as the home minister in the Gupta government, he was behind several police reforms. In 1964, he directed the police to register every complaint as even in those days first information reports (FIRs) were not registered easily by the police, to give the impression that crime rate was not increasing.

He took oath as the CM at a time when the farming communities were asserting their power; a large number of MLAs in the 1967 assembly were from these communities. There was no reservation for OBCs, but there was a demand for it as it was recommended by the First OBC Commission formed in 1953. There was 18 per cent reservation for the SCs, but even their representation was very low.

Soon after his oath-taking as the CM, the Charan Singh government was able to convince government employees to end a protest that had been going on for months and reached an amicable agreement with them. From 13 June 1967, non-gazetted employees of the UP government had been on a strike, setting forth various demands, a tactic that Sucheta Kripalani had said was one of the two key methods to destabilize any UP government during those years (the other one, according to her, was creating trouble in university campuses). However, in a few days, the strike was withdrawn by the employees at the intervention of Charan Singh. In early July 1967, there were protests for promotion of Urdu. In a matter of days, on 26 July 1967, Charan Singh announced that in the districts where more than 15 per cent population spoke Urdu, important government orders, rules, regulations and laws were to be provided in Urdu as well, up to the tehsil-level government offices. Before this announcement, this facility was available only up to the district level.[8]

When Charan Singh quit the Congress, a number of other Congress MLAs left the party one after the other in

---

[8] *Vidhan Sabha ki Karyawahi*, 26 July 1967, UP Assembly Secretariat, Lucknow.

the following months, though there were some who returned to the party later. During the assembly sessions, the Speaker would often read out notices of some MLA joining one party after leaving another.

On 26 July 1967, a no-confidence motion was moved by Gupta against the Charan Singh government. The next day, after a debate, the motion was put to vote. The government survived: 200 members voted in favour of the motion and 220 members against it. During the assembly session in June 1967, there was a huge uproar in the House when Charan Singh said Gupta was eyeing the post of the CM again. Gupta responded that it was Charan Singh who had coveted the CM's post since the 1950s.

In reference to Charan Singh's ambitions, Nanaji Deshmukh, one of the BJS founders, had written that when Charan Singh resigned from the Sampurnanand government in 1958 along with C.B. Gupta and others, Sampurnanand called Deshmukh and said, 'Your Chaudhary [Charan Singh] Sahib also wants to leave. Is he also with [C.B.] Gupta ji?'[9] After that, Deshmukh went to Charan Singh to request him to take his resignation back, and Charan Singh told him, 'I will withdraw my resignation. This perception that I am with Gupta ji is not good. But tell me, when will you make me the CM?'[10] At that time, the BJS had 18 MLAs in UP. Deshmukh wrote that he had replied to Charan Singh that the latter will become CM when the BJS has 100 MLAs.[11] In 1967, the BJS's tally reached 99, and Charan Singh became the CM.

To run the coalition, the Charan Singh government had a 19-point programme, agreed to by all coalition partners.

---

[9]Nanaji Deshmukh in his letter dated 1 February 1985 to Rajendra Singh of RSS, *Virat Purush Rashtrarishi Nanaji,* Volume 6, Prabhat Prakashan and Deendayal Research Institute, New Delhi, 2014, p. 105; author's translation.

[10]Ibid.

[11]Ibid.

However, the coalition encountered many problems. Among its partners, the socialists had been active in promoting Hindi for many years. The issue of language was hot, as the Official Language (Amendment) Bill was tabled by the Union government in Parliament on 27 November 1967. Some of Charan Singh's ministers courted arrest against it.

Charan Singh took several initiatives over the course of his chief ministership. On 6 April 1967, three days after taking oath and a day before portfolios of ministers were allotted, his government decided that castes must be removed from names of schools and colleges by 30 June, else their aid would be stopped. During his first regime, a motion stating that young men marrying inter-caste be given preference for government employments was tabled. But when it was brought before the cabinet, the BJS members in his government voted against it.[12]

Always known as a tough administrator, he was in favour of recovery of damage to public property from protestors. Once, as the home minister of UP, he visited Vinoba Bhave along with then CM Gupta. Bhave was talking about pardon to former dacoits and asked Charan Singh's opinion. He told Bhave that if dacoity was at Charan Singh's own home, he would not hesitate to pardon them, but as a home minister, he represented the sentiments of an ordinary person. He added that saints like Bhave are needed in society to run it peacefully, but where preaching of saints and religious books fail, the government comes in. Society cannot run if there are no governments.[13]

Nine months after Charan Singh became CM, the Jan Congress was renamed as the Bharatiya Kranti Dal.[14] After

---

[12]*Vidhan Sabha ki Karyawahi*, 21 March 1970, UP Assembly Secretariat, Lucknow, p. 474.

[13]Ibid. 499.

[14]*Vidhan Sabha ki Karyawahi*, 18 December 1967, UP Assembly Secretariat, Lucknow, p. 179.

the new party was formed, he shared his vision with his party workers—beliefs like 'god decides fate' are 'hurdles in economic development' and will have to be changed. He said that the 'caste system is against democracy' and that 'communism does not prompt a large section of people to make progress through hard work'. He promised that 'there will be no place for so-called armies of NGOs formed for narrow self-interest'.[15]

The winter session of the assembly was declared sine die on 22 December 1967, and the budget session was planned for 15 January 1968, which was rescheduled to 19 February 1968. However, the SSP, which was annoyed by the government not fulfilling its demand to waive lagaan on agriculture land up to 6.25 acres, withdrew support on 5 January 1968; a few other parties, too, withdrew from the coalition. Charan Singh finally resigned and recommended dissolution of the assembly on 17 February 1968, two days before the assembly session was to start. Heading a coalition government of conflicting ideologies, from right to left, he faced many problems and termed himself on more than one occasion as an 'unhappy man'.

After resignation, Charan Singh said:

> While the constituent units of the SVD are making preparations for seizure of public lands, or have already launched upon a mass agitation, in utter violation of law, others are engaged in publicly condemning the administration… A coalition of so many disparate elements necessarily involves an adjustment with principles… In my case, this limit has been reached, that is, a stage has arrived when I can no further compromise with the future and interests of the people as I see it.[16]

[15]'1968 Pictorial Manifesto of BKD', *Charan Singh Archives*, http://tinyurl.com/42b88hv4. Accessed on 22 May 2022.

[16]'HT This Day: Feb 18, 1968—Charan Singh Quits as CM', *Hindustan Times*,

His conflicts with BJS and the socialists were out in the open, and while he had recommended to Governor B. Gopala Reddy to dissolve the assembly, President's Rule was imposed on 25 February 1968. A month-and-a-half later, on 15 April 1968, the assembly was dissolved, making way for mid-term polls.

The mid-term polls of 1969 strengthened the position of BKD as it won 98 seats out of the 402 seats it had contested.[17] Charan Singh won from Chhaprauli. The Congress was short of just two seats from a simple majority; C.B. Gupta was again invited to form the government and took oath on 26 February 1969.

Charan Singh's efforts to make new social alliances were objected to by established players like Gupta who were constantly criticizing him. However, within a year of Gupta's oath, the Congress encountered a country-wide split and it was divided into Congress (O) and Congress (R). Gupta's supporters started deserting him. He was with Congress (O) and was able to retain 90 MLAs with him; the Congress (R) had 120 members with Kamalapati Tripathi as its leader in the House. Gupta was also ailing, and he finally resigned on 10 February 1970.

Now, Charan Singh again saw a chance to lay claim to the CM's chair. Though he was offered support from the Congress (O) and some other parties, after talking to both sides, he decided to go with the support of a new ally, the Congress (R). He took oath on 18 February 1970 for the second time.

The first thing Charan Singh did after taking the oath was to review all the decisions the previous government had taken in the preceding months. Coincidently, Charan Singh claimed the chair of the CM for both his tenures from Gupta.

---

16 February 2022, http://tinyurl.com/t8wxaakp. Accessed on 25 June 2022.

[17] *Statistical Report on General Elections 1969 to the Legislative Assembly of UP*, Election Commission of India, New Delhi.

In his second tenure, he announced in the assembly that no new liquor shops would be opened in the state.[18] Charan Singh was an Arya Samaji and a teetotaller.

But problems soon emerged in his new coalition. Some MLAs protested against Charan Singh wanting to establish a bench of the Allahabad High Court in Meerut. Udit Narain Sharma, who was once among Charan Singh's favourite MLAs and had quit the Congress with him in April 1967, started a campaign against him, making several allegations against him in public. The end of the coalition appeared imminent.

In the meantime, a resolution was brought on 28 April 1970 by a BJS MLA from Dehradun, Nityanand Swami, before the assembly: 'This House resolves that Uttar Pradesh Legislative Council should be abolished.' Later, this resolution was negated by another. Problems continued as Genda Singh (MLA from Seorahi), the minister of information, economic census, culture and scientific research, resigned soon after, on 11 July 1970, and after some time, there were rumours of resignation of N.D. Tiwari, the minister of finance.

There was another development. On 5 September 1970, a bill was tabled in the Lok Sabha and Rajya Sabha to abolish Privy Purses given to erstwhile rulers. Disregarding the wishes of Indira Gandhi, the BKD voted against the bill. The BKD's relations with the Congress (R) started deteriorating fast. The political environment was heating up. On 24 September 1970, Charan Singh met the governor to ask for the dismissal of 13 of his ministers (belonging to his party's ally, the Congress [R]), but Governor B. Gopala Reddy did not accept his recommendation; instead, he asked Charan Singh to resign. The same day, some leaders of the Congress (O), the BJS and Swatantra Party also met the governor to express their support for the Charan

---

[18]Ibid.

Singh government. On 27 September 1970, Charan Singh took away the portfolios of those 13 ministers of Congress (R). However, finally he resigned as the CM on 1 October 1970 and President's Rule was imposed on the same day.

Charan Singh's second government had brought an ordinance, which was later tabled as the Uttar Pradesh Control of Goondas Bill, 1970, in the assembly and sent to Select Committee of both Houses. In the meantime, the new government headed by T.N. Singh had taken over and taken forward the bill. On 15 December 1970, it was passed by the Legislative Council and, on 24 December 1970, by the assembly. President of India V.V. Giri gave his assent to this historic legislation on 13 January 1971, which is famous in the state as Goonda Act and has been used by all governments since then.[19] His government banned compulsory membership of university unions and student union elections to check student political activities. He was against agitations and strikes and was in favour of recovery of damage to public property from protestors. However, his opinion on some issues changed after Emergency.

Charan Singh looked towards the Centre and contested the 1971 Lok Sabha polls on a BKD ticket from Muzaffarnagar but lost to the CPI's Vijaypal Singh. The Congress had not put up a candidate and supported Vijaypal Singh. The BKD's performance in the 1971 Lok Sabha polls was dismal as it had contested 97 seats in nine states, including 67 in UP and 14

---

[19]The most useful provision of this Act is Section 3, which states that if 'any person is a Goonda; and (b)(i) that his movements or acts in the district or any part hereof are causing, or are calculated to cause alarm, danger or harm to persons or property', the District Magistrate can 'direct him to remove himself outside the area within the limits of his local jurisdiction or such area and any district or districts or any part thereof, contiguous thereto, by such route, if any, and within such time as may be specified in the order and to desist from entering the said area or the area and such contiguous district or districts or part thereof, as the case may be from which he was directed to remove himself'.

in Bihar, but won just one in UP (Shive Kumar Shastri from Aligarh).[20] Later, some of his MLAs in UP also deserted him.

However, Charan Singh played a crucial role in the fight against the imposition of Emergency and formation of the Janata Party. Congress leaders made many attempts to reach out to Charan Singh, who was the LoP in UP during those days. Prime Minister Indira was in touch with him through his party MLA Satya Pal Malik, but he played a key role in Opposition unity. He delivered a very long speech in the assembly where he lambasted the Congress leadership. He said:

> I have been jailed 3–4 times during the British period and I remember everything of those days; those days nothing happened like what is happening today… Congress wants to remain in power forever… Judiciary is in a bad condition, Magistrates have no courage and the Press and Radio are in your hands. News agencies are under your control and we can't address public meetings. Whatever I am saying here today will not be published in newspapers. Why? Why are you afraid? Whoever you wanted, you arrested. This is dictatorship… But you think you can collect steam in a boiler and nothing will happen. Something will happen; there will be an explosion.[21]

He criticized the slogans being raised, such as '*Aaj ki neta Indira Gandhi, yuvakon ka neta Sanjay Gandhi, kal ka neta Rahul Gandhi*' (Today's leader Indira Gandhi, leader of youth Sanjay Gandhi, and leader of future Rahul Gandhi).

Charan Singh merged the BKD with some small parties and formed the Bharatiya Lok Dal (BLD) in 1974. He entered

---

[20] *Statistical Report on General Elections 1971*, Election Commission of India, New Delhi.

[21] *Vidhan Sabha ki Karyawahi*, 23 March 1976, UP Assembly Secretariat, Lucknow, pp. 96–128.

the Lok Sabha in 1977 from Baghpat on a BLD ticket (Janata Party candidates had contested on BLD tickets) and joined the Morarji Desai government as the minister of home affairs. But amid growing differences between different factions within the Janata Party, Desai removed him from his post on 1 July 1978. On 23 December 1978, his seventy-sixth birthday, Charan Singh organized a huge rally of farmers in Delhi. This *kisan* rally was an awe-inspiring spectacle, with an estimated 8 lakh farmers from all over India thronging the Boat Club and the many surrounding roads leading up to it. This was Charan Singh's way of demonstrating the mass support he enjoyed across India. Desai took him back in his cabinet on 24 January 1979, this time as the deputy PM and finance minister. He presented the Union Budget on 28 February 1979. But things continued to be uneasy in the Janata Party, and, on 16 July 1979, he defected from the Janata Party, resigned from the Desai government and formed the Janata Party (Secular). Then, he took oath as the PM of India on 28 July 1979 with outside support from the Congress. But just before he was set to take a confidence vote in the Lok Sabha, Indira Gandhi withdrew support. After a mere 23 days as the PM, he was forced to resign. He has the 'distinction' of being the only PM of India who did not attend Parliament while on post.

Charan Singh had created his support base very tactfully. In 1939, decades before caste identity politics had become a reality, Charan Singh had suggested that 50 per cent of the higher administrative posts in the government should be reserved for children of farmers and villagers, a suggestion he reiterated time and again. In this regard, in 1939, and again in 1947, he introduced a resolution before the executive committee of the UP CLP. While Charan Singh was best known as a farmers' leader with no affinity to any particular caste, and he was often annoyed if called a 'Jat leader', years later, his son Ajit

Singh gradually reduced his party to a party of Jats and was being identified as a Jat leader, which limited his base to only some western UP districts dominated by the Jats. Paul R. Brass wrote, 'Charan Singh faced a political dilemma in relation to his identification with the upper castes'. He added, 'Charan Singh worked skilfully at the local electoral level and in state and national politics to form alliances with other castes and community groups. Although he was sometimes successful in forming such alliances, his solid and persistent political support always came predominantly from backward castes.'[22]

Charan Singh authored several books such as *Abolition of Zamindari* (1947), *Joint Farming X-Rayed* (1959), *India's Poverty and Its Solution* (1964), *India's Economic Policy* (1978), *Economic Nightmare of India* (1981) and *Land Reforms in UP and the Kulaks* (1986).

Though Charan Singh had quit the Congress, he continued to hold the Congress's stance on one issue—he established his family members in politics, which became a trend among India's political class. His wife Gayatri Devi was elected an MLA in the 1969 mid-term polls and was again elected to the assembly from Gokul in 1974. She was elected to the Lok Sabha from Kairana in 1980. Charan Singh's daughter Gyanwati won from Iglas on a Janata Dal ticket, and in 1996, she won from Khair in Aligarh on a BJP ticket in the assembly polls. His son Ajit Singh was the president of the RLD, which he had formed after several switchovers. Ajit Singh lost two consecutive Lok Sabha polls, in 2014 from Baghpat and in 2019 from Muzaffarnagar. He passed away in 2021. Ajit Singh's son Jayant Chaudhary was elected to the Lok Sabha from Mathura in 2009, but lost to Hema Malini from the same seat in 2014. He went on to

[22]Brass, Paul R., *An Indian Political Life: Charan Singh and Congress Politics 1937–1961*, SAGE Publications, New Delhi, p. 12.

form an alliance with the SP in the 2022 assembly polls, and was elected to the Rajya Sabha in June 2022 with the SP's support and joined the National Democratic Alliance (NDA) just before 2024 Lok Sabha polls.

Charan Singh patronized and promoted several leaders, but his political legacy was inherited by his son Ajit Singh, an IITian who returned from the US before Charan Singh's demise. The arrival of the Mandal Commission Report and Hindutva fundamentally changed politics in UP, and the Jats under Ajit Singh made several adjustments to remain relevant over the next decades. In 1989, when there was a wave in favour of the Janata Dal under V.P. Singh, Ajit Singh had tried all means to be considered for the CM's chair in UP, but he failed, and it was Mulayam Singh Yadav who occupied the chair. Later, the Jats started seeking reservation and got the status in UP in March 2000. They are still fighting to be included in the central list of the OBCs.

Charan Singh passed away on 29 May 1987 in Delhi. The BJP stalwart L.K. Advani wrote, 'Since 1967, being CM, being Home Minister, or being a top leader of the country, Chaudhary Sahib initiated a debate, which nobody did in 67 years.'[23]

Because of Charan Singh's love for the farmers, his memorial in Delhi is named as Kisan Ghat. In 2001, it was Atal Bihari Vajpayee's Union government that declared that Charan Singh's birthday would be celebrated as National Farmers Day every year. In 2024, the Narendra Modi government conferred him with the Bharat Ratna, the highest civilian award.

[23]Rawat, Gyanendra (ed.), *Chaudhary Charan Singh: Smriti Aur Mulyankan,* Kisan Trust, Delhi, 1995, p. 56.

6

TRIBHUVAN NARAIN SINGH

The Story of a Failed Tenure

Sixth CM: Tribhuvan Narain Singh

Party: Congress (O)

Tenure: 18 October 1970–3 April 1971

Constituency: Maniram (lost)

Days in office: 167 days

In early 1970s, the political situation of the state as well as of the country was changing rapidly. At the Centre, PM Indira Gandhi was trying very hard to reclaim her Congress base by wiping out her rival party Congress (O). She had, on the midnight of 19 July 1969, announced the nationalization of 14 banks before the split in the party, and then, on 5 September 1970, a bill was introduced in Parliament to abolish Privy Purses given to erstwhile rulers, which also became the reason why Charan Singh's second government ended. Smelling the withdrawal of Congress (R) from the coalition government, some parties, including the BJS, had already met Governor

B. Gopala Reddy to express their support for CM Charan Singh; PM Indira had also spoken to the governor. Charan Singh did not switch allies to continue on the chair but resigned on 1 October 1970, and President's Rule was imposed the same day.

However, Charan Singh's party allied with others, like the BJS, and managed to be part of the next government, but who to choose as leader of the coalition was the big question. After over a fortnight, the BKD, the BJS and some other parties decided on Tribhuvan Narain Singh as their leader. T.N. Singh was a Rajya Sabha MP at that time, and had aligned with Congress (O) after the split in the Congress. His name cropped up as a compromise candidate out of the deadlock created by the infighting among state leaders of coalition partners. Singh was specially called by his well-wishers from the Centre to head the coalition government. He staked claim to the new government with the support of 257 MLAs.

Singh was sworn in as the sixth CM of UP on 18 October 1970. His short-lived government saw three cabinet expansions.[1] Some ministers of the erstwhile Charan Singh government were taken in T.N. Singh's government as well. This was the second time that the BJS got a taste of power.

Born in Banaras, Singh had been a class fellow of Lal Bahadur Shastri and took part in the freedom movement on the appeal of Mahatma Gandhi. Singh had been a member of Provisional Parliament in 1950 and was elected to the first Lok Sabha in 1952 from the Banaras East seat on a Congress ticket, defeating the Socialist Party stalwart Prabhu Narain Singh. In 1957, he

---

[1]*Uttar Pradesh mein Mantrimandalon ka Gathan, January 1921–September 1988,* Vidhan Sabha Sachivalay, Lucknow.

won from the adjoining Chandauli seat on a Congress ticket where his rival candidate was again a socialist legend, Dr Ram Manohar Lohia, who had fought as an independent candidate. Singh was nominated as member of the Planning Commission in 1958. After the demise of PM Nehru, when Lal Bahadur Shastri was sworn in as the PM, he took Singh in his cabinet as the minister of heavy engineering in the Ministry of Industry and Supply. He was elected to the Rajya Sabha on 8 January 1965 as a member of the Congress. He was the minister of steel and minister of mines and minerals in the Indira Gandhi Cabinet. After the split in the Congress, he was again elected to the Rajya Sabha on 2 April 1970, this time as a member of the Congress (O).

From the very outset, T.N. Singh's government had to face criticism in the assembly as well as a legal battle because he was not a member of either House of the state legislature when he took oath as the CM. While an incident like this is not an issue today, the story in those days was completely different.

After his oath-taking, when the assembly first met on 7 December 1970, Narayan Dutt Tiwari of Congress (R), who was the finance minister in the outgoing BKD–Congress (R) government, stood up and said, 'The gentleman [T.N. Singh] who is sitting in the chair of Leader of the House was a member of the Rajya Sabha and he is still a member of the Rajya Sabha... First it should be decided who is to be the Leader of the House.'[2] When Speaker A.R. Kher asked Tiwari if he considered Singh as the CM, he replied, 'The Governor has administered him oath of CM's post, therefore, for the time being he is the CM of his government. [But] we don't recognize him as the CM.'[3] After heated arguments in the

[2] *Vidhan Sabha ki Karyawahi*, 7 December 1970, UP Assembly Secretariat, Lucknow, p. 12.

[3] Ibid. Author's translation.

assembly on both sides, Speaker Kher ruled the next day, on 8 December 1970, that T.N. Singh was Leader of the House as well as the CM.

That was not Singh's only problem he had to face while on this post. As the CM, he continued to be a member of the Rajya Sabha during his entire tenure. However, it was mandatory for him to become a member of either House of state legislature within six months of taking oath as the CM, so his well-wishers were on the lookout for a safe seat for him.

A major achievement of the T.N. Singh government was that it abolished lagaan for farmers having up to 6.25 acres of land. Some bills that had been brought in during the previous BKD–Congress (R) government and termed as dictatorial by SSP and BJS members were cleared by the assembly with the support of members of the same parties. In spite of that, Singh found it increasingly difficult to manage his coalition partners. But since Charan Singh's BKD was in his government, he carried forward programmes started by Charan Singh. Prominent among them was a bill to control the goonda elements in the state.

In the midst of the battle of prestige and ego between PM Indira and her rivals, Singh was fielded in a by-poll from Maniram (now renamed as Gorakhpur Urban) in March 1971, a seat under which the Goraksh Peeth also comes. Yogi Adityanath's predecessor Mahant Avaidyanath had won from this seat in 1962 as a Hindu Mahasabha candidate, in 1967 as an independent, and in the mid-term polls of 1969 again as a Hindu Mahasabha candidate. Avaidyanath's guru, Mahant Digvijay Nath, was elected to Lok Sabha from Gorakhpur in 1967, but he passed away in October 1969. In the Lok Sabha by-polls on 17 May 1970, Avaidyanath won and thereafter resigned from the assembly seat on 26 May 1970. Since the assembly seat for Maniram had been vacant, T.N. Singh accepted the suggestion of his friends to contest the by-poll from there, but this decision proved unwise later. The by-poll for the Maniram Assembly seat was held along with mid-term polls for the fifth Lok Sabha in March 1971. The Lok Sabha was meant to last up to March 1972, but PM Indira decided to dissolve it in December 1970, over a year ahead of schedule. Avaidyanath contested the Lok Sabha seat as an independent candidate from Gorakhpur, and under his Lok Sabha constituency, Singh was fielded from the Maniram Assembly segment for by-poll. The battle for seats in Gorakhpur took an interesting turn as PM Indira went there to campaign for Congress's Lok Sabha candidate Narsingh Narain and Maniram by-poll candidate Ram Krishna Dwivedi. When the results were announced, Dwivedi was declared elected and Singh lost his by-poll. Not only that, Avaidyanath also lost his Lok Sabha seat to the Congress nominee.

That historic by-poll win, by defeating a sitting CM, gave a much-needed boost to the Indira Gandhi faction of the Congress after the split. The 1971 Lok Sabha mid-term polls—in which PM Indira, influenced by leftist ideology and eyeing mass support, gave the 'Garibi hatao' (Remove poverty) slogan and aggressively publicized her decision of the nationalization of banks—proved to be a big victory for the Indira Gandhi faction of the Congress. From UP's 85 Lok Sabha seats, it won 73 seats, which included all 18 seats reserved for the SCs.

On 30 March 1971, discussions on the motion of thanks to the governor's address were going on. Results of the by-polls in Maniram had already been declared; Singh had lost. Surprisingly, in the assembly, the Singh government was defeated on N.D. Tiwari's amendment to the motion of thanks on the governor's address. Singh announced in the assembly on 30 March 1971, 'I have decided and I am sending my resignation to the Governor. My submission is that it will be better if the assembly's sitting, which is scheduled for tomorrow, is postponed.'[4] He returned to Delhi as he had retained the membership of the Upper House of Parliament. He remained in the CM's post as an interim arrangement until 4 April 1971, when a new CM was sworn in. During Singh's tenure as the CM, Kamalapati Tripathi of the Congress was the LoP and N.D. Tiwari had also emerged as one of the prime faces of the Congress in the state.

Incidentally, in the period from February 1969 to March 1974, UP saw five CMs (C.B. Gupta, Charan Singh, T.N. Singh, Kamalapati Tripathi and H.N. Bahuguna) and two brief stints of President's Rule. This is a record in any of the assemblies of UP. Second to it is the period between 1996 and 2002, which saw a brief stint of President's Rule and four CMs (Mayawati, Kalyan Singh, Ram Prakash Gupta and Rajnath Singh).

Singh's party, the Congress (O), was later merged with the Janata Party along with several other parties. When the Janata Party government of Morarji Desai was formed, it appointed Singh as the governor of West Bengal in November 1977 where he continued until 12 September 1981, when the new Indira Gandhi government at the Centre removed him. When he was appointed as the governor, West Bengal CM Jyoti Basu was opposed to him, but later came around after Morarji Desai convinced him.

As governor, he developed a good relationship with the ruling Communist Party of India-Marxist (CPI-M) leaders, and when he was removed, he continued to enjoy respect from the party. The CPI-M gave him a grand farewell when he was relieved from the post. Chief Minister Jyoti Basu, along

[4] *Vidhan Sabha ki Karyawahi*, 30 March 1971, UP Assembly Secretariat, Lucknow, p. 544; author's translation.

with the ailing party secretary Promode Dasgupta and other cabinet colleagues, were there at the Howrah Railway Station to see him off on the train to Varanasi.[5]

T.N. Singh passed away in Varanasi on 3 August 1982. Among his two sons and four daughters, none joined politics. There is no one in politics from his third generation either. On his demise, then CM of UP Sripati Mishra said:

> He was always above all types of ego. I worked as a minister in his government, and he always directed us to do only good work. He was always a giver. I met him once at the Raj Bhavan in West Bengal, and I found that, at the back of the palatial Raj Bhavan, he was living in a two-room set like any ordinary person, wearing a white *kurta-pyjama* washed with his own hands. He was among those who had created a certain decorum for a human being.[6]

---

[5]Sen, Sumanta, 'Warm Farewell to Outgoing West Bengal Governor Tribhuvan Narayan Singh', *India Today,* 15 October 1981.

[6]*Vidhan Sabha ki Karyawahi*, 19 August 1982, UP Assembly Secretariat, Lucknow, p. 97; author's translation.

7

KAMALAPATI TRIPATHI

The CM Ousted by His Own Party

Seventh CM: Kamalapati Tripathi

Party: Congress

Tenure: 4 April 1971–12 June 1973

Constituency: Chandauli

Days in Office: 2 years and 69 days

T.N. Singh's debacle in the by-poll that he contested from Maniram in March 1971 was unexpected and quite inconceivable in those days when rigging, booth-capturing and misusing government machinery were also quite easy. The obvious fallout of Singh's defeat was his resignation as the CM on 30 March 1971, after which the state was again caught in the grip of political instability. But the morale within the Congress was very high, as its young leader had defeated a CM in such a crucial state. Prime Minister Indira's hold on the Congress base was only getting stronger.

It was then the turn of Kamalapati Tripathi, a former journalist from Varanasi, who had been eyeing the post for a few years by then. He was the LoP when T.N. Singh was the CM. Tripathi was sworn in as the seventh CM of the state on 4 April 1971. His seven-member cabinet (including himself) took oath that day; it was later expanded on 21 May 1971.

Tripathi was born on 3 September 1905 in Banaras and educated at Kashi Vidyapeeth. He was also a freedom fighter and was imprisoned multiple times for participating in the freedom struggle. He was a member of the Constituent Assembly and of the Hindi Translation Committee of the Constitution of India. Tripathi started his career as a journalist and was the editor of the daily newspaper *Aaj* and later *Sansar*. He is the author of books such as *Maurya Kaleen Bharat, Islami Duniya Ka Sartaj, Cheen Aur Chiang, Bapu Aur Manavta, Bapu Aur Bharat, Bandi Ki Chetna, Patra Aur Partakar,* and *Yug Purush Bapu Ke Charanon Mein*.

Tripathi was elected to the United Provinces Assembly for the first time in 1937 and again to the UP Assembly in 1952, 1957, 1962, 1967 (by-election) and 1969. When the G.B. Pant government was formed after the first assembly elections in 1952, Tripathi was appointed as the minister of information and irrigation. He had these portfolios in Dr Sampurnanand's first government as well. When the second government of Dr Sampurnanand was formed after the 1957 assembly polls, Tripathi was appointed as the minister of home affairs and police, and thereafter, for over a year, he was the minister of education and information, besides heading the state's estate and harijan welfare departments. However, Dr Sampurnanand was gradually losing his grip on state politics and C.B. Gupta was emerging as one of the most dominant leaders. At that time, Charan Singh and Tripathi were considered close to Gupta. When Gupta was sworn in as the CM on 7 December 1960, he did not take Tripathi in his team, but after the 1962 polls, when Gupta continued as the CM, he appointed Tripathi as a minister and allotted him the crucial portfolios of finance, sales tax, registration, stamp and court fee from 22 March 1962. He retained these portfolios in the Sucheta Kripalani government as well until 13 March 1967. Gupta did not take him in his team in his third term of 19 days in March 1967 as Tripathi had lost his own assembly seat, Chandauli.

However, between April 1967 and February 1969, many crucial political developments took place in UP. Charan Singh left the Congress and many other senior leaders were either sidelined or had aligned with Charan Singh. As a result, Tripathi emerged as one of the prominent Congress leaders besides Gupta. But before the mid-term polls in 1969, relations between Gupta and Tripathi had begun to deteriorate—serious differences had been developing between them. Gupta's hold was over the government, and Tripathi had become dominant in the UPCC. However, Gupta has written that while Tripathi was annoyed with him during the 1967 polls, it was the help provided by him to Tripathi in his by-election from Jaunpur in 1967 that ended Tripathi's annoyance towards him.[1] But there is another version of this episode. Senior leader H.N. Bahuguna, who became the CM later, was the one who tried to broker peace between the two leaders. He conveyed to Gupta how it would be impossible for the latter to become the CM if the Congress lost the assembly polls, and at the same time, asked Tripathi if Gupta becoming the CM once the Congress won

---

[1]Gupta, Chandra Bhanu, *Safar Kahin Ruka Nahin, Jhuka Nahin*, Naman Prakashan, Lucknow, 2021, p. 210.

the election would be very costly for him.[2] The Congress won 211 of 425 assembly seats in the 1969 polls, just two seats short of a simple majority. When Gupta came to power for the fourth time on 26 February 1969, he appointed Tripathi as his deputy CM, holding charge of the ministries of irrigation and power; post the split in the Congress, Tripathi resigned from the Gupta government on 20 November 1969 as both had joined different factions. Even before the split in the Congress, Tripathi had aligned with the faction led by PM Indira and had earned the blessings and patronage of the Gandhi family.

As a minister, Tripathi was the target of his opponents not only for alleged corruption but also for encouraging casteism and nepotism. During Dr Sampurnanand's government, several allegations were made against Tripathi (then minister) and his family members, and there were many heated debates in the assembly as these issues were raised again and again by the socialist leaders. In fact, years before Tripathi allied with Charan Singh in 1970 to form a BKD–Congress (R) government, the latter had written a long letter to the then Union home minister, G.B. Pant, against Tripathi, in which he had demanded that Tripathi be not only sacked from the state cabinet but also barred from contesting assembly elections.[3] But nothing could stop the rise of Tripathi, and his family grew rapidly as an important political family of UP; it continues to be in politics even now.

Tripathi had been eyeing the CM's post even during the 1967 polls, but unfortunately, he lost his own assembly seat Chandauli to the SSP's Chandra Shekhar by a narrow margin of 397 votes. This was such a big setback that he even considered

---

[2]Joshi, Rita Bahuguna and Ram Naresh Tripathi, *Hemvati Nandan Bahuguna: Bharatiya Janchetna ke Samvahak,* Vani Prakashan, Delhi, 1999, p. 101.

[3]Gupta, Chandra Bhanu, *Safar Kahin Ruka Nahin, Jhuka Nahin*, Naman Prakashan, Lucknow, 2021, p. 248.

leaving politics at the time. But before polling was held in Jaunpur in the 1967 assembly elections, the Congress candidate Hargovind Singh, who was then a Member of Legislative Council (MLC) and home minister of the state in the Sucheta Kripalani government, passed away, and the election to this seat was postponed. Soon after the general elections, a by-election for Jaunpur was held, and Tripathi was fielded by the Congress from there. He won by defeating the BJS's Jang Bahadur Yadav.

Tripathi's stint as the CM of UP did not receive much plaudits. Political developments and the situation in the state in the following two years proved that his experience of working in different capacities was not of much help. Tripathi was criticized for unnecessary wastage of money from the state exchequer, an example being constructing a circuit house in Varanasi when one was already there. Ministers in Tripathi's government were criticized for corruption. During a discussion on a no-confidence motion against the Tripathi government, Charan Singh alleged that MoS (Home) Ram Krishna Dwivedi had to resign because he did not succumb to pressure to transfer an honest police official and instead transferred a corrupt one. There were also allegations of weak leadership of ministers. On 23 July 1971, the BJS MLA, Madhav Prasad Tripathi, said in the assembly, 'Since ministers have no control on officials [of their departments], generally people say that ministers tell them *le de kar kaam kara lo.*'[4]

A major controversy arose when Tripathi, himself a former journalist, dissolved the Press Accreditation Committee, and the government stated in the assembly on 28 July 1971 that the decision was based on a note prepared by the Charan Singh government in 1967. During his own regime, Charan Singh

---

[4] *Vidhan Sabha ki Karyawahi,* 23 July 1971, UP Assembly Secretariat, Lucknow, p. 1182; author's translation.

had been annoyed with the media and had abolished the post of district information officer from many districts. The Charan Singh government had also stopped giving advertisements to certain newspapers as they had been publishing articles critical of his government. It was also criticized for trying to please the central government of PM Indira.

The no-confidence motion against the Tripathi government was brought in by the BKD's Jairam Verma (MLA from Tanda), the BJS's Madhav Prasad Tripathi (MLA from Bansi), the Congress (O)'s Kalpnath Singh (MLA from Chillupar) and the SSP's Anantram Jaiswal (MLA from Nawabganj). Charan Singh, during the discussion, criticized the government for riots in Firozabad and Varanasi, which he alleged, the Tripathi government had failed to control. Recalling some incidents of Dalit atrocities, Charan Singh attacked the caste system and said, '[People] believe in caste by birth, and caste by birth means one person is not equal to another; some are inferior and some are superior. The inferior one is superior to another and the superior one is inferior to someone else. It means, everyone is either inferior or superior to someone. How can democracy survive [in this]?'[5]

The extent to which PM Indira trusted Tripathi became clear when, after his oath-taking ceremony as the CM, she said at a public meeting in UP in 1971 that the 'cold war' between the Centre and UP would end. She is also believed to have said that since UP had a government that had cordial relations with the Centre, it would get all assistance and help for the state's projects.[6] Notwithstanding her promises, neither were the sick industrial units of the state revived, nor was the

---

[5] *Vidhan Sabha ki Karyawahi,* 2 August 1972, UP Assembly Secretariat, Lucknow, p. 830; author's translation.

[6] Gupta, Chandra Bhanu, *Safar Kahin Ruka Nahin, Jhuka Nahin,* Naman Prakashan, Lucknow, 2021, p. 111.

decay in the sugar, cotton and oil industries stopped. Nothing much was done for increase in electricity generation. As a result, UP's development was much slower on every front in comparison to many other states. The statement of the then finance minister, N.D. Tiwari, in the UP Assembly on 12 July 1971—that out of 112,624 villages of the state, only 20,719 were electrified up to 31 March 1971—is an apt example of the low level of development in UP at that time.[7] Industries in cities like Kanpur were rapidly on the decline; disparities in development among the different regions of the state, for example between eastern UP and Bundelkhand regions and other regions like western UP, were also very high.

What came as a major shock for Tripathi and his government was an unfortunate incident in the summer of 1973. Seeds of dissent were sown in the police forces when it was pointed out that there was disparity in pay and perks between the personnel of police and the Provincial Armed Constabulary (PAC). What proved irreparable for the Tripathi government was a revolt in the PAC in May 1973. The PAC personnel were very often being deployed wherever and whenever the police were unable to control a difficult situation. They were disgruntled about their pay packages being low compared to the work they were expected to do—they had been demanding better pay scales for a long time. In order to negotiate with the government to fulfil their demands, some PAC personnel formed an organization called Police Parishad, the membership of which kept increasing.

In Lucknow, on 11 May 1973, when the assembly session was adjourned sine die, over 100 kilometres away in Kanpur, preparations were going on for the PM's visit, and an officer

---

[7] *Vidhan Sabha ki Karyawahi,* 12 July 1971, UP Assembly Secretariat, Lucknow, p. 100.

of the PAC was addressing its personnel regarding preparations. Suddenly, the personnel started raising slogans of 'Police Parishad zindabad'. Then, on 20–21 May, there were incidents of fire in some offices in the campus of the University of Lucknow, allegedly ignited by PAC personnel. The Indian army had to be called in to control the situation. The PAC personnel defied army orders to lay down their weapons. There were such crossfires at other places as well, like Kanpur and Ramnagar. In all, 35 PAC personnel were killed in the firing, with some casualties and damages to the army. A report stated that by 23 May 1973, the casualties had risen to 40. Since the revolt began, 600 men had been reportedly arrested and many others disarmed and/or confined to the barracks.[8] Later, the situation was brought under control and several PAC personnel were dismissed from service, which led to litigations in courts for decades to come.

Hemwati Nandan Bahuguna was always considered Tripathi's man within the UPCC. Veteran journalist Janardan Thakur wrote that the PAC had been simmering with discontent, but people on the inside knew how the revolt had come about. Prime Minister Indira's close associate Yashpal Kapoor was elected to Rajya Sabha from UP in April 1972. Thakur wrote that the PAC revolt 'was allegedly a joint handiwork of Yashpal Kapoor and Hemwati Nandan Bahuguna.'[9] Bahuguna later became the CM after the few months of President's Rule that followed Tripathi's resignation.

However, the revolt's big fallout was on Tripathi's political career, as criticism for the failure of his government and demand for his resignation were widespread. Prime Minister Indira

[8]'Death Toll Is 40 in Indian State As Revolt by Police Continues', *New York Times*, 24 May 1973, http://tinyurl.com/5n8h2ju2. Accessed on 30 July 2022.
[9]Thakur, Janardan, *All the Prime Minister's Men,* Vikas Publishing House, New Delhi, 1977, p. 92.

asked him to resign, and he did so on 12 June 1973. Thus, Tripathi's tenure as the CM of two years and 69 days came to an end. Prime Minister Indira asking for the resignation of her own party's elected government and imposing President's Rule was an unusual step.

President's Rule was imposed under the then governor, Nawab Akbar Ali Khan. Tripathi was removed, but choosing his replacement was a challenge. Prime Minister Indira was also considering Chandrajit Yadav, a former CPI leader who was then the general secretary of the AICC and an MP from Azamgarh, for the post of the CM. President's Rule continued in the state as Tripathi's successor could not be finalized. Tripathi had also put his weight behind Bahuguna. Finally, after President's Rule of nearly five months, H.N. Bahuguna was sworn in as the CM on 8 November 1973, and assembly polls were held in early 1974. Tripathi was elected as the UP Congress president, but soon after, he moved to the Centre. He was elected to the Rajya Sabha thrice. He continued to earn the trust of the Gandhi family, and, in 1983, he was appointed as the working president of the Congress by PM Indira.

Tripathi was an old Congressman and a true secular. But when he was the CM, he was criticized for being anti-Muslim. On 10 May 1973, when some SSP leaders, including MLA Vishvanath Kapoor (MLA from Ayodhya), were on their way to the CM's residence to protest against some matters pertaining to the AMU, they were lathi-charged, and socialist leaders like Raj Narain and Kapoor were arrested. The issue was raised in the assembly on the same day, with wild allegations connecting the incident to Tripathi being anti-Muslim. On the other hand, when Tripathi was out of the government and living a retired life in Varanasi, he was a staunch critic of the movement launched by the Vishva Hindu Parishad (VHP)–RSS–BJP for the Ram temple in Ayodhya.

He continued to be involved with the Congress even after his retirement. In June 1986, when the Congress was undergoing changes under Rajiv Gandhi's leadership, Tripathi wrote a letter to Rajiv raising his concerns, 'My contention is that Congress is rapidly losing its contact with the masses and you are surrounded by a number of sycophants who are not only Indira-baiters, but most of them are Indira-haters.'[10] He seems to have sensed the problem—since then, the Congress kept losing its ground, and as of March 2024, it is reduced to only one Lok Sabha seat, two assembly seats, and no Council seats in the state, forget the entire country.

Tripathi passed away on 8 October 1990. Today, in a limited way, his legacy continues with his fourth generation. After Tripathi resigned as the CM in 1973, a year later, in early 1974, his son Lokpati Tripathi became the tourism minister and continued as a minister in all Congress governments in UP until 1989, when he lost the assembly polls, in which the Congress also lost power in the state. Lokpati's wife Chandra Tripathi was elected to the Lok Sabha from Chandauli in 1984. His son Rajeshpati was elected as a Congress MLA in 1996 from Rajgarh (Mirzapur), and Rajeshpati's son Laliteshpati was elected as a Congress MLA from Marihan in 2012. With the Congress losing its hold on UP, both Rajeshpati and

[10]Badhwar, Inderjit, 'What Were the Reasons for Kamalapati Tripathi's Mini-Revolt against Rajiv Gandhi's Govt?', *India Today*, 30 June 1986, http://tinyurl.com/3zxwbtma. Accessed on 6 August 2022.

Laliteshpati joined Mamata Banerjee's All India Trinamool Congress in October 2021.

Kalyan Singh, who later became the CM of UP, had this to say about Tripathi when he was leader of the BJP in the UP Assembly:

> He was not only Congress' leader but he was a leader of this state. It would not be an exaggeration to say that he was a leader of the country. On some of the issues my party and I had differences with Pandit Kamalapati Tripathi ji. Still, he was committed to his ideology and we are committed to ours. We respect him a lot.[11]

[11] *Vidhan Sabha ki Karyawahi,* 19 November 1990, UP Assembly Secretariat, Lucknow, p. 4; author's translation.

G.B. Pant: Receiving then interim President of India Dr Rajendra Prasad at the Varanasi airport on 9 March 1951

Dr Sampurnanand: With Prime Minister (PM) Nehru and then Union Minister of Commerce and Industry Lal Bahadur Shastri at the Nainital Club on 17 June 1959

C.B. Gupta: Took the oath of office of the chief minister (CM) on 7 December 1960

Sucheta Kripalani: At a programme hosted at Uttar Pradesh Sainik School in Lucknow on 11 February 1966

Chaudhary Charan Singh: At a function organized by the Uttar Pradesh (UP) police

T.N. Singh: Taking the oath of office of the CM on 18 October 1970 from Dr B. Gopala Reddy

Kamalapati Tripathi: At an exhibition on 25 years of Independence on 20 December 1972

H.N. Bahuguna: At a public function in Gorakhpur on 31 December 1973 after distributing *tamrapatra* (bronze plaque) to freedom fighters

N.D. Tiwari: Taking the oath of office of the CM from Governor M. Chenna Reddy (right) on 21 January 1976

Ram Naresh Yadav: Taking the oath of office of the CM from Governor M. Chenna Reddy (right) on 23 June 1977

Banarasi Das: Taking the oath of office of the CM on 28 February 1979 from Governor G.D. Tapase (left)

V.P. Singh: With then PM Indira Gandhi at a function in Raebareli on 30 November 1980

Sripati Mishra: On Gandhi Jayanti, 2 October 1982, at Gandhi Ashram in Hazratganj, Lucknow

V.B. Singh: Addressing the Holi Milan Samaroh on 16 March 1987 at the CM's residence in Lucknow

Mulayam Singh Yadav: Taking the oath of office of the CM on 5 December 1989 from Governor Mohammed Usman Arif (extreme left) at K.D. Singh Babu Stadium in Lucknow

Kalyan Singh: Welcoming the newly appointed governor of UP, Mohammad Shafi Qureshi (centre), on his arrival at Raj Bhavan, Lucknow, on 17 March 1998

Mayawati: Taking the oath of office of the CM on 3 May 2002 from Governor Vishnukant Shashtri

Ram Prakash Gupta: Governor Suraj Bhan (left) administering the oath of office of the CM on 12 November 1999

Rajnath Singh: Taking the oath of office of the CM from Governor Suraj Bhan (left) on 28 October 2000 at Raj Bhavan, Lucknow

Akhilesh Yadav: After inauguration of the Museum of Socialism: Jai Prakash Narayan Study Centre in Lucknow on 11 October 2016

Yogi Adityanath: Taking the oath of office of the CM on 25 March 2022 from Governor Anandiben Patel at Bharat Ratna Shri Atal Bihari Vajpayee Ekana Cricket Stadium, Lucknow

8

HEMWATI NANDAN BAHUGUNA

The Congress Loyalist Who Fell Out of Favour (and Power)

Eighth CM: Hemwati Nandan Bahuguna

Party: Congress

Tenure: 8 November 1973–29 November 1975

Constituency: Bara

Days in Office: 2 years and 21 days

Following the mishandling of the PAC revolt, CM Kamalapati Tripathi resigned on 12 June 1973. His resignation was accepted and President's Rule was imposed the very next day under Akbar Ali Khan, who had been the governor of the state since 14 November 1972. A tough task lay ahead for the Congress's political managers, and Indira Gandhi's central government faced the big challenge of winning the UP elections, which were due in early 1974.

Things were not running smoothly even under President's Rule. So, after nearly five months, the Congress leadership started thinking of holding early assembly polls and was on the lookout for an efficient leader to take on the mantle of chief ministership. Tripathi also put his weight behind him, and they chose Hemwati Nandan Bahuguna. Prime Minister Indira asked him to resign from the Centre as the MoS for communications to become the CM of UP.

About the decision of PM Indira to impose President's Rule in UP after asking her own party's CM Kamalapati Tripathi to resign, Morarji Desai wrote, 'It was obvious that both actions were deliberately planned for the purpose of winning the [assembly] elections [in 1974]… The results came out as planned.'[1] In October 1972, when Desai was attending a programme in Gwalior, he was asked how long the 'misrule' of Congress (R) in the country would last, and he responded that the Congress party would not survive beyond the next 18 months. About the country's situation those days, he had this to say: 'Such a state of helplessness among the people leads to apathy, inaction and surrender which only helps those in power. In order to lend courage and hope to the people, I made this forecast [about the end of the Indira Gandhi faction of Congress] publically, especially since I believed I was correct. However, I should not have committed this error.'[2] By winning the UP elections, PM Indira established the fact that her faction was the real version of the Indian National Congress. And so, all predictions for collapse of her faction of the Congress made by seasoned politicians like Desai were proved wrong.

Meanwhile, Bahuguna was sworn in as the CM on 8 November 1973.

---

[1]Desai, Morarji, *The Story of My Life*, Volume 3, S Chand & Company Ltd, New Delhi, 1979, p. 78.

[2]Ibid. 77.

Bahuguna, who was a Garhwali Brahmin, belonged to a simple family in Bughani village, Pauri Garhwal, and was born on 25 April 1919. During his student days, he was very active in the Allahabad University union politics, and he continued to influence student politics there for several years even after joining politics of the state and the Centre. During the freedom movement, he was a member of the Congress in Allahabad and had been jailed for his role in the freedom struggle and for participating in underground activities. Later, on account of becoming a labour union leader and a dedicated Congress worker in Allahabad, Jawaharlal Nehru and Lal Bahadur Shastri got to know him well since the initial years of Independence.

After Independence, he worked as a special representative of the AICC for conducting the first general elections in Himachal Pradesh (then a union territory) in 1952. Bahuguna was elected to the first UP Assembly in 1952 from the Karchhana North-cum-Chail South seat on a Congress ticket. He was appointed as the parliamentary secretary to UP's second CM Dr Sampurnanand on 10 April 1957, and on 17 November 1958, he was elevated to the position of deputy minister. Chandra Bhanu Gupta, who always addressed him as Natwarlal, retained him as a deputy minister in his first government. In Gupta's short-lived government in March 1967, Bahuguna was the finance minister.

After only a few years since Independence, the relationships among various Congress leaders in UP started changing. The UP Congress was looking divided in groups—one group was headed by Gupta, which later got associated with Morarji Desai at the Centre, and another group was that of Dr Sampurnanand and Kamalapati Tripathi, which was favoured by central leaders like Jawaharlal Nehru, Lal Bahadur Shastri and, later, Indira Gandhi. Bahuguna connected himself to the second group. Prime Minister Indira had realized his strength during the 1969 mid-term polls of UP and the 1971 Lok Sabha polls, as he was then the general secretary of the AICC and played a key role in the UP polls. As the CM, he chose the same Bara seat in February 1974 from where he had lost in 1969, went on to win and continued his tenure as the CM. Bahuguna did not take a confidence vote in the assembly, neither was any no-confidence motion tabled in his first tenure as the CM, because the assembly session was not called and fresh assembly elections were held in February 1974.

When Bahuguna lost the UP Assembly poll in 1969 from Bara, he made an attempt to enter the Lok Sabha in 1971, won from Allahabad and was sworn in as a MoS at the Centre. That was the time when socialist parties were on the decline and PM Indira had become closer to the CPI; she was actively propagating 'Garibi hatao' slogans and trying very hard to project her pro-poor and pro-downtrodden image. The big task before the Congress was to make the Congress (O) faction led by C.B. Gupta irrelevant in the state and establish Congress (R) as the real version of the grand old party.

Prime Minister Indira was busy laying foundation stones and with inaugurations in the state, during October 1973 up to mid-January 1974. Her former principal information officer, B.G.Verghese, wrote, 'Fresh elections were due and Mrs Gandhi was determined to win... She portrayed herself as the giver of good things, and undertook whirlwind tours of UP every weekend by IAF helicopters or other official aircraft to lay the foundation stone for a vast number of projects. These clearly were sweeteners to woo the electorate.'[3]

---

[3]Verghese, B.G., *First Draft: Witness to the Making of Modern India,* Tranquebar Press, Chennai, 2010, p. 184.

Meanwhile, the Bahuguna government was trying to woo every section of the electorate. It created a welfare fund for lawyers with ₹33 lakh, ahead of the assembly polls of 1974. Large numbers of government officials were transferred before the announcement of the poll schedule. Several measures to uplift minorities were taken, and Bahuguna emerged as a leader who was most popular among the state's Muslims, next only to Charan Singh, who was the LoP. Just before the 1974 polls, a chunk of Nazool land in Lucknow was transferred to a society of Muslims for a *kabristan*, and for that, a file was processed and final action was taken within a week, though it created an uproar in the assembly.[4]

As the CM, Bahuguna started writing letters to all gram pradhans of the state. The first letter was written in December 1973 and the second in April 1974. He also introduced a legislation, among other things, to end the exploitation of villagers by private moneylenders. There were several corporations established in the state by his government. Nineteen public-sector units were announced in January–February 1974, and work on many of them started almost immediately. Universities like Rohilkhand (renamed after Mahatma Jyotiba Phule) in Bareilly, Avadh (renamed after Dr Ram Manohar Lohia) in Ayodhya, Acharya Narendra Deva University of Agriculture and Technology in Ayodhya, and Chandra Shekhar Azad University of Agriculture and Technology in Kanpur were established during his time.

Assembly polls were held in February 1974 amid allegations of massive rigging and booth-capturing across the state and misuse of government machinery for the same. Re-polls were held in at least 1,440 polling stations, and over 50 election petitions were filed in courts. Considering the demands for OBC reservation

---

[4] *Vidhan Sabha ki Karyawahi,* 25 June 1974, UP Assembly Secretariat, Lucknow.

that were being made by leaders of BCs since Independence, a commission under Chhedi Lal Sathi was constituted on 31 October 1975 during H.N. Bahuguna's tenure as the CM.

Allegations were also made that the Bahuguna government had released hundreds of dacoits from jails to help the Congress candidates, with promises that if the Congress won, their sentences would be remitted. There were accusations that criminals were used to terrorize the electorate and that arms were issued to Congress supporters without license.

However, when results were declared, the Congress was able to manage a very thin majority: it won just 215 seats out of the 425 by relegating its rival, Congress (O), to just 10 seats.[5] With the Congress's return to power and Bahuguna having proved his mettle to the party leadership, it looked like the Congress's search for an effective leader in UP had finally ended.

Bahuguna, after taking oath to continue, was in full command of the government. When the assembly session started on 18 March 1974, so did the protests against alleged rigging and booth-capturing in the polls. There were demonstrations outside the assembly as well against the alleged irregularities in the polls. So the main Opposition parties like the BKD and the BJS tried to pursue a coordinated approach once again. Charan Singh said:

> This government does not have the actual majority ... it is an example of real dictatorship... My friends are of the view that unseating a government through ballot papers is a way which the Congress does not believe in. What Congress has done and what is proved in this election is

[5]*Statistical Report on General Election 1974 to the Legislative Assembly of UP*, Election Commission of India, New Delhi. On 11 January 1971, the Election Commission of India ruled that the Congress (R) was the real Congress. After a further split, on 2 February 1978, Indira Gandhi's faction was named as Congress (I), and from 1984, '(I)' was removed.

> that, if this is going to continue, then we have to decide which way we should move now.[6]

There were demands from parties including the BKD and the BJS for an inquiry into alleged foul play.

Bahuguna was an eloquent speaker, and his speeches in the assembly were often well researched; many of them would leave the Opposition leaders on the defensive. The Bahuguna government started reserving promotions in certain departments for SCs, besides increasing the percentage of reservation for them on certain recruitments. Continuing after March 1974, his government decided to establish 26 new sugar mills in the first year. Salaries of teachers and professors were increased, and payments were made easy.

But not everything was favourable: books were not easily available for students, and the student movement was still going on. The situation on the social inclusion front was also unfavourable. In his answer to a related question, Om Prakash Singh of the BJS (MLA from Chunar) narrated the condition of the prime educational institutions in these words: 'The Sanskrit University,[7] which is the research centre for Sanskrit and ancient languages, is the biggest centre of casteism. Only Brahmins are appointed there and among Brahmins too, their *gotra* [lineage] matters. The 20 SC appointees as mentioned [referring to a response by the government on his question that day] by the government are in fact sweepers.'[8]

While Bahuguna always showed magnanimity towards his Opposition colleagues, soon enough, things started to become

---

[6] *Vidhan Sabha ki Karyawahi,* 20 March 1974, UP Assembly Secretariat, Lucknow, p. 79; author's translation.

[7] This was a university in Varanasi, which was later renamed as Sampurnanand Sanskrit University.

[8] *Vidhan Sabha ki Karyawahi*, 18 July 1974, UP Assembly Secretariat, Lucknow, p. 790; author's translation.

uneasy for him. At this time, industrialist K.K. Birla filed his nomination papers for the Rajya Sabha as an independent candidate. He was camping in Lucknow in the third week of March 1974 as elections were to be held on 28 March that year. A protest against Birla's nomination was launched by activists of the RSS affiliate Akhil Bhartiya Vidyarthi Parishad (ABVP) under its leader Vindhyawasini Kumar, on the advice of the BJS's Nanaji Deshmukh and the RSS's Bhaurao Deoras.[9] Later, others joined the protest and MLAs like Shatrudra Prakash of the BKD from Varanasi Cantt raised the issue within and outside the assembly. The BJS's Madhav Prasad Tripathi alleged in the assembly that Birla was actually the Congress's candidate and was in Lucknow to garner support by corrupt means. Tripathi said that Birla was uncomfortably close to CM Bahuguna. However, Bahuguna later clarified that K.K. Birla had neither any relation with his party nor did he want to help him in any manner.[10] On 26 March 1974, Beni Prasad Verma, then a BKD MLA from Daryabad, alleged in the House that he was offered ₹50,000 as bribe by a private person to vote in favour of Birla.

Janardan Thakur, an author and political analyst, wrote that one day, when Bauhguna was away in Delhi, PM Indira's advisor Yashpal Kapoor arrived in Lucknow and camped in the CM's residence with a mission to get Birla elected to the Rajya Sabha. This gave the impression that Bahuguna and the state government were also behind Birla's candidature. When he returned from Delhi, Bahuguna 'learnt what was going on in his house … he ordered Kapoor's luggage to be thrown out of the house.'[11] Thakur adds that Kapoor was elected to the Rajya Sabha from

---

[9]Vindhyawasini Kumar in conversation with the author.

[10]*Vidhan Sabha ki Karyawahi*, 26 March 1974, UP Assembly Secretariat, Lucknow, p. 315.

[11]Thakur, Janardan, *All the Prime Minister's Men,* Vikas Publishing House, New Delhi, 1977, p. 98.

UP in April 1972 and '[d]uring the UP elections of 1974, he [Kapoor] became the "super controller of men and money"'.[12] So, the two friends, Bahuguna and Kapoor, who were allegedly behind unseating of the Kamalapati Tripathi government, were on different sides. While state satraps had been behind the collection of political donations for the Congress, in UP the person at the forefront was C.B. Gupta. But post the Congress split, PM Indira took control of party funds, and Kapoor emerged as a controller of everything on her behalf.

Bahuguna's equation with Birla at this point was of friends turned into foes. The former was not ready to tolerate anyone trying to erode his authority as the CM. In the Rajya Sabha polls, Birla and another Congress nominee had lost, while Opposition candidates Raj Narain and Subramanian Swamy were elected. Birla had written that Bahuguna was the one behind his defeat in those polls:

> There could be no logic behind Bahuguna's open opposition towards me, more so as I enjoyed the support and confidence of Indira ji and Sanjay. But owing to personal prejudices and hostility, Bahuguna started a tirade against me and made public statements that it should be the common aim of all parties, Congress and the Opposition, to get me defeated.[13]

Bahuguna's behaviour towards Birla and Kapoor started annoying PM Indira and Sanjay Gandhi, as both of them were behind Birla's Rajya Sabha plan. This behaviour was a protest against the influence of money in Rajya Sabha polls. However, times have changed, and today, it has become a trend in almost every party to field people just because of their wealth; no one protests.

---

[12]Ibid.

[13]Birla, Krishna Kumar, *Brushes with History: An Autobiography*, Penguin Books India, New Delhi, 2007, p. 169.

There were other problems, too, that Bahuguna encountered. While parts of UP were facing shortages of *bajra* (pearl millet) and paddy, thousands of tons of these were sent to Gujarat illegally. It was based on an order of the former CM Kamalapati Tripathi. This scandal was debated hotly in the assembly on 27 December 1974. Opposition leaders including Charan Singh (MLA from Chhaprauli), Satya Pal Malik (MLA from Baghpat), Mulayam Singh Yadav (MLA from Jaswantnagar), Madhav Prasad Tripathi (MLA from Bansi), Triveni Sahai (MLA from Gonda) and Rajendra Garg (MLA from Hardwar) asked for relevant papers to be placed before the assembly.

Subsequently, the ruling party and the Opposition tried to fight each other on the corruption issue. On 2 January 1975, a no-confidence motion was moved against the Bahuguna government by the BJS's Madhav Prasad Tripathi. This was decided by a coordinated Opposition led by LoP Charan Singh and BJS leader Tripathi on 31 December 1974, when newspaper reports carried a statement by Bahuguna that if allegations against him were proved to be true, he would retire from politics. It was discussed in the assembly on 2–3 January 1975. Opening the discussion, Tripathi accused the government of misuse of power in connection with a Congress rally and alleged that transport officials were asked to arrange vehicles for the rally. He also said that ministers were involved in many scandals. Meanwhile, Charan Singh accused the government and the Congress of adopting a dictatorial attitude and not tolerating the Opposition.

Bahuguna responded that the politics of character assassination was not good for the country; it should stop as it would harm democracy. 'There is a political gang in India leading the country to demoralization,' said Madhav Prasad Tripathi.[14] Before voting on the no-confidence motion on 3 January 1975, Charan Singh

---

[14] *Vidhan Sabha ki Karyawahi,* 3 January 1975, UP Assembly Secretariat, Lucknow, p. 1080; author's translation.

said, 'Government will be run efficiently only if the public has trust in administrators and politicians. This is in your interest and in the interest of the ruling party,'[15] and walked out from the House along with his MLAs. He was followed by Madhav Prasad Tripathi and his MLAs. Evidently, the Opposition was trying to charge the atmosphere on the corruption issue as the JP Movement was already going on. Those who had brought in a no-confidence motion had walked out before voting. In the absence of Opposition MLAs, the no-confidence motion was negated, and the session was adjourned sine die.

However, with the increased reach of the JP Movement, there were sudden widespread arrests of Opposition leaders, which took the country by surprise. On 17 February 1975, Raj Narain was arrested in Faizabad. There were arrests of student leaders in several cities and university campuses. These issues were repeatedly raised in the assembly. The next few months turned out to be historic for UP and for the country. In the 1971 Lok Sabha polls, Raj Narain had stood against PM Indira for the Raebareli seat. She had been declared winner with 183,309 lakh votes, whereas Narain had come second with 71,499 votes. He had challenged the results in the Allahabad High Court. Justice Jagmohan Lal Sinha, on 12 June 1975, gave his verdict and declared Raj Narain as the winner. However, the case went to the Supreme Court, which, on 24 June 1975, stayed the judgement in part. Meanwhile, Opposition parties came together against the Indira Gandhi government. Facing all this, on midnight of 25–26 June 1975, PM Indira imposed internal Emergency in the country. The rest is history.

During Emergency, Bahuguna was not able to maintain good relations with Sanjay Gandhi, who was annoyed with him since the defeat of K.K. Birla in the Rajya Sabha polls. There

---

[15]Ibid.

was uneasiness in his dealings with PM Indira, and even more so with Sanjay Gandhi. Sanjay was attempting to bring the Congress organization under his absolute control and looking to allocate several important posts to Youth Congress leaders because he felt old leaders like Bahuguna were not paying obeisance to him. Sanjay was emerging as the chief controller of the Congress party, and Bahuguna was finding it increasingly difficult to adjust to his autocratic ways of functioning.

As a result, Bahuguna resigned on 29 November 1975, after spending just two years and 21 days as the CM. The assembly was suspended, President's Rule was imposed, and within two months, Bahuguna was replaced by his University of Allahabad junior N.D. Tiwari, who proved himself to be among the most loyal and trusted supporters of the Nehru–Gandhi family. Through Bahuguna's resignation, the Congress leadership again proved that it did not encourage any strong leadership in the states, particularly in UP, that could be a threat for the party leadership later.

After his resignation as CM, Bahuguna continued with the Congress, but when PM Indira lifted Emergency and decided to hold elections in 1977, Bahuguna quit the Congress along with Jagjivan Ram and former Orissa CM Nandini Satpathy[16] to form a new group called Congress for Democracy, in February 1977. They later joined hands with the Janata Party, which had been formed on 20 January 1977, merging parties like the BLD, the Congress (O), the BJS and the SSP. Bahuguna won the Lok Sabha polls from Lucknow in 1977 by defeating Sheila Kaul, and he was appointed as the minister for petroleum, chemicals and fertilizers in the Morarji Desai government. He later joined Chaudhary Charan Singh's short-lived government

[16]She was a staunch Indira Gandhi loyalist since 1969 but fell out of favour and was forced to resign on 16 December 1976.

as minister of finance. After the collapse of the Janata Party, when Indira and Sanjay Gandhi had been trying to revive Congress, they approached Bahuguna as well. Thus, Bahuguna returned to the Congress (I) in 1980, and this time, instead of Allahabad or Lucknow, he was fielded from his home turf Garhwal on a Congress (I) ticket; he won. But his *ghar-wapsi* to the Congress (I) did not last long as he quit the party again in 1982. Subsequently, he resigned from the Lok Sabha as well. He decided to contest the Garhwal Lok Sabha by-poll in 1982 and proved his mettle by winning it as an independent candidate, despite the best efforts of the Congress (I)'s UP government of V.P. Singh to defeat him.

Bahuguna encountered his most embarrassing electoral defeat in Allahabad in 1984. By then, he had been established and known as one of the stalwarts of Indian politics. However, as a candidate of the Lok Dal, he lost the Lok Sabha poll from Allahabad by a margin of more than 1.87 lakh votes to the Congress candidate, film actor Amitabh Bachchan, who was a novice in politics.

After his defeat in Allahabad, which reflected a new politics emerging under the leadership of Rajiv Gandhi, Bahuguna's health started to deteriorate. But he remained politically active, along with his friend Charan Singh. Charan Singh's son Ajit Singh returned from the US to carry forward his father's legacy, albeit just two months before Charan Singh's demise. Very soon, in March 1987, the Lok Dal was split into two parts—Lok Dal (A) headed by Ajit Singh, and Lok Dal (B) headed by Bahuguna. Leaders like Mulayam Singh Yadav went with Bahuguna.

Bahuguna's family entered politics after he quit the Congress. His second wife Kamala Bahuguna had won from the Phulpur

(Allahabad) Lok Sabha seat on a Janata Party ticket in 1977. His son Vijay Bahuguna had studied law and went on to become a judge of the Allahabad High Court in 1991. He was later transferred to the Bombay High Court. He resigned as a judge in February 1995 and joined the Congress, becoming a Lok Sabha MP from Tehri Garhwal after winning the 2007 by-poll and the 2009 general elections. In March 2012, he was sworn in as the CM of Uttarakhand. Vijay joined the BJP in May 2016, and his son Saurabh was elected as a BJP MLA from the Sitarganj Assembly seat in Uttarakhand in 2017 and 2022. H.N. Bahuguna's daughter Rita Bahuguna Joshi was elected to the Lok Sabha in 2019 from Prayagraj on a BJP ticket. She had joined the BJP in October 2016 and was elected an MLA from Lucknow Cantt and sworn in as a minister in the Yogi Adityanath government in March 2017, in which capacity she remained until 2019 when she entered the Lok Sabha. Rita's son Mayank joined the SP in March 2022.

Bahuguna suffered from pleurisy. On 17 March 1989, he passed away in a hospital in Ohio, US, where he had been admitted for a coronary bypass surgery. On his death, N.D. Tiwari, who replaced Bahuguna as the CM and was on the post when Bahuguna died, said:

> He always played with danger. There is hardly any other leader who had seen the kind of ups and downs that Bahuguna ji had seen. He was a shining star of UP who established his significant place in India's politics, and in UP's politics, for the last decades. He was a great politician, diligent freedom fighter, courageous administrator, and a renowned parliamentarian. He was able to recognize lakhs of workers.[17]

[17] *Vidhan Sabha ki Karyawahi,* 18 March 1989, UP Assembly Secretariat, Lucknow, p. 1; author's translation.

9

NARAYAN DUTT TIWARI

The Last Congress CM of UP

Ninth CM: Narayan Dutt Tiwari

Party: Congress, Congress (I)

Tenure: 21 January 1976–30 April 1977

3 August 1984–10 March 1985

11 March 1985–24 September 1985

25 June 1988–5 December 1989

Constituency: Member of Legislative Council, Kashipur

Days in Office: 3 years and 314 days

After H.N. Bahuguna resigned as the CM, President's Rule was imposed in the state and CM aspirants began looking towards PM Indira and her son Sanjay Gandhi for their blessings, as the mother–son duo had taken full control of the Congress by then. On account of Narayan Dutt Tiwari's vast political experience and understanding of the grassroots politics of the state, as well as because of his 'flexible' nature, PM Indira and Sanjay, in the midst of Emergency, chose him to head the government in UP. Tiwari took oath as the ninth CM of UP on 21 January 1976, after 52 days of President's Rule and in a volatile situation where thousands of people had been put in jails under the Defence of India Rules (DIR),[1] and Maintenance of Internal Security Act (MISA). He took oath as the CM of UP four times but served for less than four years (three years and 314 days) in total. Incidentally, he was the last Congress CM of UP.

Like Bahuguna, Narayan Dutt Tiwari also moved from the UP hills (now Uttarakhand) to Allahabad for his education and became a student leader at the University of Allahabad. Tiwari was the president of Allahabad University's union in 1947. During the Quit India Movement, when Bahuguna was released from Sultanpur Jail, it was Tiwari, along with a group of students, who welcomed him with garlands at the Allahabad Railway Station. He always considered Bahuguna as his *bade bhai*. In both governments of Bahuguna, Tiwari held important portfolios like finance, sales tax, stamp, registration and court fee, heavy industry, and sugar mills and sugarcane development.

Tiwari was elected as an MLA for the first time in 1952 as a member of the Socialist Party from Nainital (North), and again in 1957 from Nainital on a PSP ticket. In 1960–61, he was the LoP in the UP Assembly and also served as chairman of the Public Accounts Committee of the assembly. But in 1962, he was defeated by a Congress candidate. Around that time, based

[1]A British-era law under which the government had the power to put anybody in jail for a year without trial.

on PSP chief Ashok Mehta's belief that in developing countries, Opposition parties should cooperate with the government, a section of the PSP joined the Congress. Tiwari was one of them. He joined the Congress in 1963, and subsequently, was elected the president of the Youth Congress for four years (1965–69). He lost the 1967 assembly polls from Kashipur, though he was able to return to the assembly in the 1969 mid-term polls from the same constituency.

In 1969, when C.B. Gupta took oath as the CM, he appointed Tiwari as the minister of planning; economics and statistics; labour; and panchayati raj. In Charan Singh's second government, which he formed in alliance with Congress (R) in February 1970, Tiwari was appointed as the finance, legislative and parliamentary affairs minister. Later, in the Kamalapati Tripathi government, he was allotted departments such as finance, sales tax, stamp, registration and court fee, irrigation, power, parliamentary affairs, planning, economics and statistics, labour, and excise. All this was before he joined the Bahuguna government.

While Bahuguna had found it difficult to cope with the autocratic style of functioning of Indira–Sanjay, Tiwari successfully handled Emergency in UP with unquestioned acquiescence to the leadership's diktats, just as other Congress governments did. Besides the 20-point programme of Indira Gandhi, a five-point programme of Sanjay Gandhi had taken priority, where the main attention was on family planning. Forceful *nasbandi* (vasectomy) was a routine, and government employees at every level were given strict orders to meet the targets. There were instances of people being caught from buses, from local bazaars, from trains, from anywhere, for nasbandi. Buses were diverted to hospitals to forcibly perform the procedure on all male passengers, and things were done so hastily and with such little preparation that several people died of tetanus after their surgeries. Salaries of people employed in this undertaking were stopped and other actions were taken against many for not achieving the government targets. There was some satyagraha at a few places, but on the whole, the public was terrorized. There were police firings in places like Muzaffarnagar, Sultanpur and Basti. The bureaucracy seemed to have been given absolute power, and there were thousands of cases of misuse of the DIR and MISA. These laws were used arbitrarily against innocent people, especially those who criticized government policies, while newspapers were censored, and not even a single line was being published on the programmes of the Opposition parties.

Throughout Emergency, a competition of sorts existed among Congress leaders to see who would be more successful in making the party high command sitting in Delhi happy. Nearly 50,000 people were put in UP jails during Emergency. On 22 March 1976, the assembly was provided a list of 77 MLAs of different parties who were arrested and of those among them who were released after arrest during Emergency. Later, names of MLAs who were detained, arrested and released in different parts of the state were announced on different dates in the assembly. Tiwari continuously skipped answering questions in this regard from the members. Whenever questions about the atrocities against MLAs in jails and the facilities provided to political prisoners in jails were raised, he either replied that no complaints had been received or insisted that giving an answer to the question was not in public interest. He seemed to have made this his preferred answer to the majority of the questions on the issue, such as how many principals and teachers of intermediate, degree and postgraduate colleges were jailed; how many MISA detainees died in jails and the cause of death thereof; how many persons were arrested under MISA and DIR; how many political prisoners were getting maintenance allowances; and so on.

At this time, a quote by Jawaharlal Nehru, which had been carried daily by *National Herald* (a Congress-owned newspaper that supported Emergency) on its masthead, was removed. The quote was: 'Freedom in peril, defend it with all your might'. Interestingly, this quote has been used by Congress leaders with reference to the Narendra Modi government's actions in 2022–23 against Sonia Gandhi and Rahul Gandhi in connection with corruption charges in the *National Herald* matter.

The Tiwari government brought in a bill (tabled by the education minister Ammar Rizvi, MLA from Mahmudabad) in April 1976 that restricted the press from publishing certain things from the proceedings of the House. The bill was adopted the same day. At that time, many Opposition MLAs were leaving their parties and becoming either independent MLAs or joining the ruling Congress. Agha Zaidi (MLA from Machhlishahr) said in the assembly on 31 March 1977, 'Today I quit Congress after 45 years. The CM was not in the Congress for 17 years and during that time he could not divide it (Congress). But now he has done it.'[2]

Due to Tiwari's frequent visits to Delhi during Emergency in order to take instructions from senior Congress leaders as well as PM Indira Gandhi and Sanjay Gandhi, he was known in UP during those days as 'New Delhi (ND) Tiwari'; he was also referred to as 'Nothing Doing (ND) Tiwari'.

On Sanjay's advice, Tiwari transferred a part of UP land adjoining Noida to Delhi to resettle people from jhuggis in Old Delhi. How he developed proximity to and earned the faith of Sanjay Gandhi is believed to have been connected to an incident widely talked about in the state during those days. The incident is mentioned in a book written by the senior

---

[2] *Vidhan Sabha ki Karyawahi,* 31 March 1977, UP Assembly Secretariat, Lucknow, p. 286; author's translation.

Congress leader M.L. Fotedar. Quoting from a conversation he had with a police officer during his visit to UP for the 1977 Lok Sabha polls, the leader mentioned:

> I asked the officer for facts. He looked at me and after a long pause, he asked, 'Do you want Indira Gandhi to win and Congress to win in UP?' I said emphatically, 'Yes, Certainly, yes!' Then he requested, 'Can you do a favour to the people of the state?' I asked, 'What favour?' He said, 'The people of UP have been publicly insulted and humiliated in the eyes of the people of the country.' I asked who had done this. He said, 'I should not be quoted, but I am telling you the mood of the people. Sanjay [Gandhi] had visited Agra sometime back. When he climbed the steps to board the aircraft, his *chappal* slipped off and fell on the ground. The Chief Minister, Narayan Dutt Tiwari, picked up the *chappal* with his own hands and put it on Sanjay's feet.[3]

To his credit, as the CM, Tiwari addressed several problems, including regional imbalances. On 9 February 1976, a meeting of his UP Cabinet was held in Raebareli. Such cabinet meetings had been held in some other places as well, including Faizabad. Narayan Dutt Tiwari was soft-spoken and had friends across parties.

Emergency finally ended. On 18 January 1977, PM Indira announced holding of Lok Sabha elections. In the subsequent Lok Sabha polls held in March 1977, the Congress lost all 85 seats of UP, including PM Indira's Raebareli. The Congress had 73 seats in the state in the 1971 Lok Sabha polls; its tally was now reduced to zero. After this defeat, some Congress leaders

---

[3]Fotedar, M.L., *The Chinar Leaves: A Political Memoir,* HarperCollins, New Delhi, 2016, p. 90.

said that the bureaucracy had ensured their party's defeat. During Emergency, several Congress leaders, including PM Indira's aunt Vijaya Lakshmi Pandit, had become harsh critics of the former. The latter also campaigned against the Congress and helped the Janata Party win in UP in 1977.

Morarji Desai of the Janata Party was sworn in as the new PM on 24 March 1977, and Charan Singh also moved to the Centre as a crucial part of the Desai government. The Congress, which won 215 seats in the 1974 assembly elections, had now reached new heights with several turncoats joining it during Emergency. As per the information provided by the Speaker in the assembly on 27 April 1976, the total members of the Congress in the assembly had swelled to 237, while there were 148 Lok Paksh[4] members, 16 CPI-M members, two CPI members and 12 independents, among others, including one Hindu Mahasabha member; five seats were vacant. Just before Emergency ended, switching from one party to another had become a common occurrence in UP, as in some other states.

After the change of government at the Centre, in UP a situation of uncertainty was noticed, and a session of the assembly was called. In his address before the assembly on 25 March 1977, Governor Marri Chenna Reddy said, 'I am fully confident that despite the Central Government being from a different political party, it will assist this government.'[5] Satya Prakash Malviya, an MLA from Allahabad South, demanded that the Tiwari government step down without any delay. Tiwari did not resign, though there were reports that he had expressed his willingness to do so, but the Congress leadership asked him not to. A no-confidence motion against the Tiwari government

---

[4]On 25 March 1977, the announcement of renaming of the Lok Paksh as the Janata Party was made in the UP Assembly.

[5]*Vidhan Sabha ki Karyawahi*, 25 March 1977, UP Assembly Secretariat, Lucknow, p. 17; author's translation.

was introduced in the assembly on 26 March 1977, but it was withdrawn as Tiwari said that if the Opposition wanted voting on his government, in keeping with convention, it could do so on the motion of thanks to the governor's address. Therefore, the Janata Party moved some amendments to the governor's address, but on 31 March 1977, only 177 members voted in favour of the amendments and 222 against, and the government survived. With the change of government at the Centre, the Tiwari government faced uncertainty, but on 24 April 1977, his cabinet decided to provide 15 per cent reservation in government jobs to the OBCs, fulfilling a decades-long demand. Morarji Desai's Janata Party government at the Centre dismissed the Tiwari government on 30 April 1977.

Fresh assembly polls were held in June 1977. When the results were declared, the outcome in UP was very similar to that of the Lok Sabha polls. The Janata Party won 352 seats out of 425, and the Congress was reduced to 47 seats, which was its shortest tally since Independence.[6] However, Tiwari was able to win his Kashipur seat in an election where many Congress stalwarts were defeated.

When the Congress (I) returned to power at the Centre after the collapse of the Janata Party in 1980, Tiwari was elected to the Lok Sabha from Nainital and was sworn in as the minister of planning. He also looked after other portfolios like the ministries of labour, industry, steel, and mines and coal. He was the deputy chairman of the Planning Commission (now NITI Aayog) for over a year. Uttar Pradesh experienced several changes between 1977 and 1984. The Congress faced problems in UP under CM Sripati Mishra, a suave Sultanpur-based Brahmin. Those were months after Operation Blue Star

---

[6]The Janata Party candidates won the assembly election on the Janata Party ticket, while they won the Lok Sabha polls on the BLD ticket.

in Amritsar in June 1984, and the Congress lost the by-polls to four assembly seats and one Lok Sabha seat in the state since December 1983. Elections were due in early 1985, and PM Indira decided to send Tiwari back to the state. Thus, he was sworn in as CM for the second time on 3 August 1984 and was elected to the Legislative Council after resigning from the Lok Sabha.

Unfortunately, PM Indira Gandhi was assassinated on 31 October 1984, and India went into turmoil with anti-Sikh riots in several cities of UP as well as in Delhi and other parts of the country. General elections were held in the last week of December 1984, and in a sympathy wave, the Congress, under Rajiv Gandhi, returned to power at the Centre. In UP, the assembly polls were due in May 1985 but were held early in February that year, and the Congress won 269 of the 425 seats. Tiwari was again elected from his home turf, Kashipur, and was asked to continue as the CM. He was sworn in again on 11 March 1985.

Soon, in the true Nehru–Gandhi style of functioning, PM Rajiv also started shaking up the regional satraps. Before Tiwari could start feeling the impact of his government, PM Rajiv asked him to resign and return to the Centre. On 24 September 1985, he was replaced by Gorakpur-based Thakur Vir Bahadur Singh, who had been eyeing the post for a long time; Arun Nehru, PM Rajiv's key advisor on UP affairs, played a prime role in replacing Tiwari with Singh. At the Centre, Tiwari handled the ministries of finance, commerce and industry, external affairs, and petroleum and natural gas by turns.

But this was also not a long-term arrangement as UP had again become a concern for the Congress; the state was going through political and social upheaval and the party's support base seemed to be rapidly eroding. V.P. Singh had left the

Rajiv Gandhi Cabinet and the Congress party, and had won a by-election from Allahabad. He launched a campaign against 'Mr Clean' Rajiv Gandhi based on the Bofors scandal, though it was never proved, and several Congress leaders started leaving the party one after the other to join V.P. Singh.

On the other hand, the BJP and RSS as well as their affiliated and supported organizations were feeling triumphant on account of the Faizabad sessions court's order to open the locks of Ram Janmabhoomi in Ayodhya on 1 February 1986. They now re-launched campaigns to build a Ram temple at the site, and programmes for 'mass awakening' were being held one after the other. Prime Minister Rajiv called V.B. Singh back to Delhi and appointed him as the Union minister of communication; Tiwari was sworn in as the CM of UP for the fourth time on 25 June 1988.

Politics had become very volatile due to V.P. Singh's campaigns and his rising popularity; Tiwari was being closely watched by his leaders. In July 1989, V.P. Singh, when asked about Rajiv Gandhi's alternative in the Congress, had named N.D. Tiwari. There were rumours that Tiwari was also in touch with V.P. Singh, like several other leaders of the Congress and other parties. However, in order to save his chair and the base of the Congress, in 1989, Tiwari began to address many important pending issues, and one of them was declaring Urdu as the second official language of UP on 7 October 1989, evidently to woo Muslims. This was just a few months before the Lok Sabha and UP Assembly elections, in which Congress was going to face a tough challenge from V.P. Singh's Janata Dal at the Centre; Mulayam Singh Yadav was its prime leader in the state. It was Tiwari's idea to hold assembly polls along with the Lok Sabha polls, and that proved fatal for the Congress and for him; the results confirmed it. Tiwari resigned on 5 December 1989 and was replaced by Janata Dal's Mulayam Singh Yadav.

It is the misfortune of the Congress that under Tiwari's chief ministership, the party lost the UP Assembly elections in 1989. Since then, it has not been in power in the state. He was the last Congress CM of UP, and the party has been virtually wiped out from the state—only two of its candidates won in the assembly polls of March 2022. Since July 2022, there has been no Congress member in the Legislative Council, and in the 2019 Lok Sabha polls, the party won only one seat.

As the CM, Tiwari is remembered for establishing industrial areas like Noida in 1976 during his first stint, and Gorakhpur Industrial Development Authority (GIDA) and Sataharia Industrial Development Authority (SIDA), Jaunpur, in his last stint. In 1975–76, under the Tiwari government, the Small Industries Corporation established 21 industrial complexes in 19 districts. Noida was established so that industries that were moving to Gurgaon (now Gurugram) and Faridabad in Haryana because of their proximity to Delhi could continue to be located in UP in the new township. The Bahuguna and Tiwari governments also cancelled licenses of over 11,000 small industrial units as during a survey, they were not found at the addresses listed. Tiwari established some big industries in UP and said repeatedly that they were a must for all-round development of the state. He constantly raised concerns about the growing population. In his second and third stints as the CM, he travelled a lot, from eastern UP to Bundelkhand, UP hills and other areas, in order to understand and address the problem of regional imbalances.

The four-time CM of UP was witness to the failure of his government and that of his party. Many industrial units established in the public sector in different parts of the state—either during his regimes as CM or earlier when he was the finance minister of the state—turned into loss-making ventures due to weak willpower, lack of interest of politicians and bureaucrats, insufficient infrastructure, law-and-order problems, and corruption, nepotism and casteism. Many of them were later sold to private entrepreneurs. For the next few years after Tiwari demitted office after serving his first regime on the post, he remained one of the most prominent leaders in the state. He greatly influenced UP's politics until December 1989 and, surprisingly, continued to influence it for years after that. Mohsina Kidwai, a seasoned Congress leader who worked with both Bahuguna and Tiwari, wrote about the latter that he 'was considered a soft politician and a darling of bureaucracy. As chief minister, he was never harsh on bureaucrats, no matter what decision they had taken.'[7]

When he was sent to the Centre in September 1985, he was again elected to the Rajya Sabha. The Congress had to face a very embarrassing situation when the Kashipur seat, vacated by Tiwari in September 1985, was won by an independent candidate, Akbar Ahmed Dumpy, in a by-election held after that. In the 1989 assembly polls, Tiwari had contested from the Haldwani seat and won, and in the 1991 elections, when there was a BJP wave in the state, Tiwari again won from the Haldwani Assembly seat.

But victory in the 1991 UP Assembly elections was not important for him as he needed a Lok Sabha seat. His Lok Sabha loss from Nainital in the 1991 polls was a big setback. When PM Rajiv was assassinated in May 1991, it was widely thought that Tiwari could be a front-runner for the PM's post if the Congress was able to form the government. Tiwari lost his seat to the BJP's first-time contestant Balraj Pasi by over 11,000 votes. Thus, he was out of the race for the PM's post.

---

[7]Kidwai, Mohsina, *My Life in Indian Politics*, HarperCollins, New Delhi, 2022, p. 251.

While Tiwari was active in UP politics, the Congress witnessed many changes under P.V. Narasimha Rao as the PM and party president. When, ahead of the 1996 UP Assembly polls, Narasimha Rao decided to have an alliance with the BSP, with just 126 out of 425 seats given to the Congress to contest, Tiwari quit the Congress in protest. Along with his old associates like Arjun Singh and some other Gandhi family sympathizers like Sheila Dikshit, he formed the All India Indira Congress with himself as the president and Arjun Singh as the working president. In the 1996 Lok Sabha polls, he even won the Nainital Lok Sabha seat as a candidate of this new party.

Tiwari returned to the Congress in 1998 but lost his Nainital Lok Sabha seat to the BJP's Ila Pant (daughter-in-law of the first CM of UP, G.B. Pant). In 1999, he won from Nainital on a Congress ticket, but in 2002, the Congress decided on a new assignment for him in his new home state Uttaranchal (his government renamed it as Uttarakhand), which was carved from the old UP in November 2000. He might not have had a full tenure in UP as the CM, but he served a full five years (between 2 March 2002 and 7 March 2007) as the CM of Uttarakhand. As the CM, he entered the Uttarakhand Assembly from the Ramnagar seat in 2002, which the sitting MLA Yogambar Singh vacated for him. When the Congress lost the Uttarakhand Assembly polls in 2007, Tiwari was sent to Andhra Pradesh as its governor. He was subsequently involved in a sex scandal at Raj Bhavan and resigned in December 2009.

Tiwari's past followed him. At the age of 88, in 2014, following an order of the Delhi High Court, he was forced to marry his erstwhile lover Ujjwala Shekhar (a professor at the University of Delhi) after accepting that he was the biological father of her son Rohit Shekhar. Tiwari again quit his grand old party, the Congress, on 19 January 2017, and he, along with Rohit, joined the BJP.

After his demise on 18 October 2018, Yogi Adityanath, the UP CM, spoke of him, 'Tiwari's contribution to the development of UP and Uttarakhand was remarkable. He was always ready to resolve problems in his state. He implemented several welfare and development schemes for these two states which benefited all sections. He was a sober and soft-spoken person and an efficient administrator, and had thorough knowledge of parliamentary conventions.'[8]

[8] *Vidhan Sabha ki Karyawahi,* 18 December 2018, UP Assembly Secretariat, Lucknow, p. 22; author's translation.

10

RAM NARESH YADAV

A Champion of the Backward Classes

Tenth CM: Ram Naresh Yadav

Party: Janata Party

Tenure: 23 June 1977–27 February 1979

Constituency: Nidhauli Kalan

Days in Office: 1 year and 249 days

The post-Emergency 1977 Lok Sabha elections were historic. After the Janata Party's win, a government with Morarji Desai as PM was formed at the Centre on 24 March 1977. On 30 April, the Desai government dismissed the governments of Congress-ruled states, including that of UP, leading to fresh assembly polls in the state in June 1977.

The results of these polls were similar to that of the Lok Sabha. The Janata Party won 352 of the 425 assembly seats.[1]

[1] *Statistical Report on General Election 1977 to the Legislative Assembly of UP,* Election Commission of India, New Delhi.

Considering that the Janata Party was a myriad mix of leaders from the BJS, the BLD and others, finding a consensus candidate to head the Janata Legislature Party (JLP) was not an easy task.

Chief ministership in the state since Independence had included a Brahmin (Pant), a Kayasth (Sampurnanand), a Bengali (Kripalani, married to a Sindhi man) and a Vaishya (Gupta), all part of the Congress; from the BKD and Congress (O), there was a Jat (Charan Singh) and a Thakur (T.N. Singh), respectively. Post 1970, all three consecutive Congress CMs of the state were Brahmins (Kamalapati Tripathi, H.N. Bahuguna and N.D. Tiwari). In the 1967 assembly polls, many candidates from backward castes or OBCs won from different parties that included the BJS, socialists (particularly the SSP) and the Congress. Those were the days when, in UP and Bihar, the following slogan was famous:

SANSOPA [SSP] ne baandhi gaanth, pichhde paaven sau mein saath,
Raj-paat hai kiske haath, angrezi aur oonchi jaat,
Oonchi jaat ki kya pehchan, git-pit bole, kare na kaam,
Chhoti jaat ki kya pehchan, kare kaam aur sahe apmaan…
Angrez yahaan se chale gaye, angrezi ko bhi jaana hai,
Angrezi mein kaam na hoga, phir se desh ghulam na hoga.
Rashtrapati ka beta ho, ya chaprasi ki ho santaan,
Birla ya garib ka beta, sabki shiksha ek samaan.
Karkhaniya damon ki keemat, aane kharch se dyodha ho.
Ann ke daam ki ghatati-badhti, aane ser ke bhitar ho.
Jo jameen ko jote hai, vo jameen ka malik hai,
Julm karo mat, julm saho mat,
Jeena hai to marna seekho, kadam kadam par ladna seekho.[2]

---

[2]Late Ram Vilas Paswan used to recite this often. I was a part of two IdeaExchange programmes, a space for newsmakers to interact with journalists at *The Indian Express*, where Paswan recited it.

[It is SSP's firm resolve that OBCs should get 60 per cent (of all opportunities),
Who is in power these days, these are English-speaking people and upper castes,
The upper-caste people talk much and don't work,
Those belonging to the lower castes work hard and face humiliation...
The Englishmen left India, and the English language must also go,
No work will be done in English, the country will not be a slave again.
Whether it is the son of the president of India or a child of a peon,
Whether a son of Birla or that of a poor man, everyone should get uniform education.
Products of factories should be one and half times of cost.
Grain price should be less than ₹1 per kg.
Land should be owned by those who cultivate it,
Don't commit atrocities, don't tolerate atrocities,
If you want to live, you learn to die, you learn to fight at every step.][3]

The OBCs had found a voice in Charan Singh as they were his main support base. These communities were never comfortable in the Congress, and in the 1977 victory of the Janata Party, they played a key role. Notably, 1977 was the first assembly where some old faces were not there. There was no Charan Singh and no C.B. Gupta (the former had moved to the Centre and the latter did not contest after his debacle in the 1974 assembly elections, though he was with the Janata Party); H.N. Bahuguna had moved to the Centre and Kamalapati Tripathi was also not in the assembly.

[3]Author's translation.

For the leader's post in the UP Janata Party, there were many aspirants, but the party leadership zeroed in on two names: Ram Naresh Yadav and Ram Dhan. Yadav was a first-time Lok Sabha MP from Azamgarh, whereas Ram Dhan was a Lok Sabha MP from the adjoining Lalganj (SC) seat who had been elected to the Lower House as a member of the Congress twice previously. After several rounds of discussions, it was clear that Janata Party President Chandra Shekhar (who later became the PM) was in favour of Ram Dhan, but Charan Singh and Raj Narain preferred an OBC candidate from the same region. Thus, Ram Naresh Yadav was chosen, and he took oath as the tenth CM of UP on 23 June 1977.

Before he joined electoral politics, Yadav had been a practising advocate in Azamgarh since 1953. He was widely respected for his simplicity and honesty and was known as the Gandhi of Purvanchal among his supporters. Born on 1 July 1928 to a school teacher's family in Azamgarh, Yadav was an MA in Hindi and an LLB from BHU. He went to jail many times, participating in movements of socialists like Acharya Narendra Dev and Dr Ram Manohar Lohia. He was also in jail for 19 months during Emergency. In order to enter the assembly and become the CM, he resigned from the Lok Sabha and moved from the Azamgarh seat in eastern UP to contest from the western district of Etah's Nidhauli Kalan seat in a by-election. Nidhauli Kalan is a Yadav-dominant area.

When the Janata Party came to power, the expectations of people were very high. Considering the rhetoric of the constituents of the Janata Party since decades and the call of Lok Nayak Jayaprakash Narayan for sampoorn kranti, people in the state had big hopes from the new government. The series of misrule and atrocities faced by the UP electorate since Independence was another reason why people were hoping for a positive change in the state. When the assembly session started on 12 July 1977, the governor said in his address: 'This session of the assembly is a result of the country's second historic revolution. The first revolution was in 1947 on 15 August and the second revolution is now in two phases in the year 1977, when UP's people voted against dictatorship and in favour of democracy in the Lok Sabha and UP assembly, respectively.'[4]

The new Yadav government seemed keen to immediately get down to some serious work. On the very first day of the assembly session, the UP Lokayukta Act came into force, under which every public servant except the CM was covered. Over a month later, Justice Bishambhar Dayal, who had retired as the Chief Justice of the Madhya Pradesh High Court in September 1972, was appointed the first UP Lokayukta. Several other big promises were made by the Janata Party government, and one of them was that it would increase the literacy rate of the state to 90 per cent in the next 10 years (in the 1971 Census, this rate was just 21.70 per cent in UP).[5] During one year of Yadav's tenure, 360 dacoits were killed in 2,000 encounters and 7,616 were arrested.[6]

But the decision for which the Yadav government is best known and which had a far-reaching impact on society was implementing the 15 per cent reservation for OBCs in government services and for admissions in educational institutions of the state. For communities that were mainly dependent on

---

[4]Governor's address, *Vidhan Sabha ki Karyawahi,* 12 July 1977, UP Assembly Secretariat, Lucknow, p. 12; author's translation.

[5] Sinha, D.M., *Uttar Pradesh: A Portrait of Population,* Director of Census Operations, UP, Lucknow, 1973, p. 93.

[6]*Vidhan Sabha ki Karyawahi,* 27 March 1979, UP Assembly Secretariat, Lucknow, p. 1067.

agriculture and some artisan communities that had negligible representation in government jobs despite their high numbers, this decision of the Yadav government proved to be a game-changer. The cabinet decision for this was already taken by Yadav's predecessor N.D.Tiwari on 24 April 1977 a week before he was dismissed, and the Yadav government implemented it.

A majority of OBC communities had earlier been considered supporters of socialists, who had wooed them with slogans like Lohia's 'Pichhde paaven sau mein saath', but after his demise, they had aligned with Charan Singh when he quit the Congress in 1967 and gained prominence as the two-time CM. Reservation for OBCs had been an ongoing demand in UP since decades. Demands and questions regarding OBC reservations and an increase in their representation in government services had continued to be raised in the assembly and outside. For instance, during the second assembly in 1961, Shyamlal Yadav, a Congress MLA from Mughalsarai who later became the deputy chairman of Rajya Sabha and a Union minister, had brought in a private-member resolution to give a three-year relaxation in the age limit for OBC candidates in recruitment at government and semi-government organizations, like in the police.[7] While the debate had been going on, the Congress issued a whip to its members that if Shyamlal Yadav did not withdraw the resolution, all Congress members should vote against it. Criticism from the Opposition had been that the resolution was politically motivated and introduced keeping in mind the approaching elections, and also perhaps with the intention to delay other pending businesses of the House. The members of the PSP and Raj Narain's Socialist Party

[7] *Vidhan Sabha ki Karyawahi,* 5 May 1961, UP Assembly Secretariat, Lucknow, p. 36; author's translation.

and the BJS members had walked out.[8] The issue was raised repeatedly in the assembly by many other members such as Ram Swarup Verma, Ram Sewak Yadav, Beni Prasad Verma, and Roopnath Singh Yadav.

A commission was constituted on 31 October 1975, during Emergency, when H.N. Bahuguna was the CM. It was headed by Chhedi Lal Sathi, and it recommended 29.5 per cent reservation for OBCs with a rider that 17 per cent of that should be reserved for the 'most backward'.[9] The commission also said that if any candidate of a BC is selected on merit, they should not be considered under the reserved category.

The level of representation of OBCs in government was of some concern, as government services were not reflecting inclusiveness of all social groups and were dominated by only a handful of communities. With Ram Naresh Yadav at the helm and with the Janata Party appearing to have captured the sentiments of those communities, on 20 August 1977, the government implemented 15 per cent reservation for OBCs in Groups A, B and C posts, and 10 per cent in Group D. Reservation was also granted to medical college teachers and local bodies from 15 February 1978. There were protests across the state against the decision. Public properties were damaged, and there was judicial intervention as well. A petition was filed by Chotelal Pandey before the Allahabad High Court against the government's decision on reservation for OBCs; the court quashed the reservation notification on 2 February 1979. However, on a special leave petition filed by the government of UP, after over a month, on 5 March 1979, days after Yadav had stepped down as the CM, the Supreme Court stayed the

---

[8] *Vidhan Sabha ki Karyawahi*, 11 August 1961, UP Assembly Secretariat, Lucknow, p. 854.

[9] *Social Justice Committee Report*, 31 August 2001, UP Government, Lucknow, p. 10. The committee was headed by Hukum Singh.

Allahabad High Court order, and reservation for OBCs became a reality. That was a new beginning in UP as this decision resulted in a gradual increase in representation of OBCs in government services. At a social level, he was criticized by those against reservation. A slogan was sung those days:

Ram Naresh wapas jao
Lathi lekar bhain charao

[Ram Naresh, go back and take care of your buffaloes.]

The Congress, which had lost power for the first time by such a vast majority, was trying very hard to make a comeback. On 17 March 1978, when the assembly session was in progress, N.D. Tiwari led a protest in Lucknow, and he was arrested with 20 other MLAs of his party. He had been arrested earlier as well on 2 October 1977, at Kachhla Ghat in Etah. Such protests and subsequent arrests of Congress leaders were happening quite frequently across the state. Congress leaders, workers and their allies were being accused of atrocities against Dalits at many places. One of the most public and damaging of these incidents happened in the assembly. On 17 March 1978, some MLAs disrupted Governor G.D. Tapase's address by coming in front of the governor's dais, breaking mics, throwing chairs and sticks, etc. Some MLAs and guards were injured. Some objects were thrown towards the governor's dais as well.[10] Governor Tapase was a Dalit, and several members (including Rajendra Kumar Gupta of Sitapur and Kanhaiyalal Sonkar of Chail) alleged that the lower castes were being targeted by workers of Congress (I) and its associates, and that the governor was also targeted for that reason.[11]

[10] *Vidhan Sabha ki Karyawahi*, 17 March 1978, UP Assembly Secretariat, Lucknow, p. 20.

[11] Ibid. 30.

After his oath as CM, the Azamgarh Lok Sabha seat was vacated by Ram Naresh Yadav, and in the by-poll held on 7 May, the Janata Party candidate Ram Bachan Yadav lost to the Congress's (I)'s Mohsina Kidwai, giving a big boost to the grand old party that had been wiped out from the Lok Sabha and the assembly only a year earlier. A few months later, Indira Gandhi won in the Chikmagalur Lok Sabha by-election, beating the Janata Party contender Veerendra Patil.

Both these victories gave a thumbs-up to the Congress, and its workers started the slogan, '*Azamgarh se Chikmagalur, nahi rahi ab Dilli door*' (From Azamgarh to Chikmagalur, now power at the Centre is not far away).

Circumstances would suggest that for Azamgarh, Yadav sowed the seeds for the party's defeat. He had expanded his cabinet on 2 May 1978 and dropped his minister of local bodies Satya Prakash Malviya (MLA from Allahabad South) without prior intimation. Malviya made a statement in the assembly that he was 'pained' and 'humiliated' by Yadav's decision. 'If he [CM] was unsatisfied with me, he should have indicated it, I would have resigned,' he said.[12] A day before, Janata Party General Secretary Madhu Limaye had visited Lucknow and, sensing dissidence in the party, had requested party MLAs to keep calm until the Azamgarh by-poll. The Azamgarh by-poll was held just a week after that. On 9 May, the MoS, Mukhtar Anis (MLA from Behta), resigned, criticizing the dropping of Malviya. The impact of all this mess was seen in the Azamgarh by-poll results.

That loss in Azamgarh made Charan Singh a little annoyed with his protégé CM Yadav, whom he had chosen ignoring other aspirants. A year after the formation of the Yadav government,

---

[12] *Vidhan Sabha ki Karyawahi*, 17 May 1978, UP Assembly Secretariat, Lucknow, p. 743; author's translation.

a different struggle started in the Janata Party as socialists like Madhu Limaye began raising the issue of dual membership of BJS members in the Janata Party, as many of them were associated with the BJS's parental organization RSS, and the repercussions were seen in the Yadav government as well. Ministers who had come from the BJS to the Janata Party after the merger were told that they could be members of either the RSS or the Janata Party. Then rose the question of Janata Party's RSS-associated MLAs being ministers. When the acrimony escalated, it was decided that Yadav would seek a vote of confidence within the JLP on 4 June 1978. With 273 votes on his side, Yadav continued as the leader. Still, all was not well within the Janata Party, not only in UP but also in Delhi.

One of the popular schemes initiated by the Yadav government was called Antyoday. Inaugurated on Gandhi Jayanti, 2 October 1978, it was to provide easy loans and grants to nearly 5 lakh poor people in the state. The scheme was launched by the then president of India, Neelam Sanjiva Reddy, in Lucknow. However, Yadav's enemies were increasing within the Janata Party, which had never behaved like a party of people sharing the same ideology. It was perhaps not possible because it was, in fact, not a party but a conglomeration of several parties formed against Emergency. Hence, these conflicts were inevitable, and there was no consensus on many issues.

In a surprise move, Yadav sacked two ministers in January 1979 on the grounds that they were RSS members. This resulted in a signature campaign against Yadav. The issue seemed to have gone beyond his control, as he advised the governor on 11 February 1979 to dismiss 13 more ministers who had earlier been with the BJS before formation of the Janata Party. Yadav repeatedly said that there was a battle going on between 'progressive' and 'communal' forces. The ministers' dismissal led to a demand for fresh trial of strength within the legislature party.

To make matters worse, on 14 February 1979, an order[13] was issued by Prakashchand Jain, the home secretary of UP, that without prior permission of the legal owner/custodian of common places, no drill, physical exercise, rally or demonstration could be organized by any person, community, group or organizations like the RSS. There occurred another voting within the JLP on 15 February 1979, in which Yadav lost the majority of MLAs and, on the advice of Charan Singh, resigned as the CM the same day. He continued until his successor Banarasi Das was sworn in on 28 February 1979. Yadav was appointed as one of the two deputy CMs in the Banarasi Das government; the other deputy CM was Narain Singh from Bijnor. Additionally, once, Yadav was attacked by a 27-year-old youth Gajendranath Mishra at the CM residence.[14]

From day one of Yadav's oath-taking as the CM, his image emerged as one of a soft-spoken gentleman who respected his officials but lacked leadership qualities. He had an opportunity to ride the wave, but he tumbled and lost his way. After that he never got that kind of a high-profile seat, nor could he play any significant role in politics. When the Janata Party was divided, he went with Charan Singh and contested from Nidhauli Kalan again in 1980 on a Janata Party (Secular) ticket but lost. In 1985, he won the Shikohabad Assembly seat as an independent candidate. On 28 March 1988, he was elected to the Rajya Sabha from the Lok Dal (A), but that was a victory that happened after Charan Singh's demise, and the new leaders were merely trying to capture the legacy of the former PM. The Lok Dal factions were eventually merged with V.P. Singh's new formation, Janata Dal, in October 1988.

---

[13]Quoted by N.D. Tiwari during a discussion in the assembly. See *Vidhan Sabha ki Karyawahi,* 19 March 1979, UP Assembly Secretariat, Lucknow.

[14]Yadav, Ram Naresh, *Sankshipt Jeevan Parichay*, Janm Divas Ayojak Samiti, New Delhi, 2008, p. 16.

At one stage, Balram Singh Yadav, Chandrajit Yadav, Ram Naresh Yadav and, a little later, Mulayam Singh Yadav were the four prominent Yadav leaders in UP and were often rivals in electoral politics. However, among them, Ram Naresh had no support base. When Balram Singh was appointed as the UPCC chief in the late 1980s, Mulayam Singh was heading the Janata Dal in UP. Annoyed with the appointment of Mulayam Singh as the chief of UP Janata Dal, Ram Naresh resigned from the party and Rajya Sabha, and joined the Congress in 1989, which promptly sent him to the Rajya Sabha too. In the 1996 assembly polls, he was elected from Phulpur in Azamgarh on a Congress ticket, defeating the SP candidate. In 2002, he entered the assembly by defeating his rival BSP candidate from the same Phulpur seat, again on a Congress ticket. In 2004, he contested from Azamgarh for the Lok Sabha on a Congress ticket, but he lost, securing only third place. Yadav was appointed as the governor of Madhya Pradesh in August 2011 by the UPA government of Dr Manmohan Singh.

Yadav was known for his simplicity and was easily accessible to his workers, supporters and ordinary people. But he could not maintain his image of an honest politician in the later years of his life. As the governor of Madhya Pradesh, his tenure ended with allegations of corruption in the much-talked-about Vyapam Recruitment Scam, and he had to resign due to that. Among his two surviving sons, one, Ajay Naresh Yadav, contested the 2012 assembly elections from Phulpur on a Congress ticket, but lost. Just before the 2024 Lok Sabha polls, Ajay joined the BJP.

Ram Naresh Yadav passed away on 22 November 2016 in Lucknow. After his demise, Suresh Kumar Khanna, a senior

BJP leader who has served as a minister in UP a number of times said:

> I knew him personally. When he was the CM and after that as well, I kept meeting him. His life was an example of simplicity and innocence. When he took oath as the CM, there was a country-wide perception that in UP an honest CM has taken oath. He continued this tradition of honesty throughout his entire life. There was nothing like ego in his life.[15]

[15] *Vidhan Sabha ki Karyawahi,* 21 December 2016, UP Assembly Secretariat, Lucknow, p. 34; author's translation.

11

BANARASI DAS

Dismissed in Disgrace

Eleventh CM: Banarasi Das

Party: Janata Party

Tenure: 28 February 1979–17 February 1980

Constituency: Khurja

Days in office: 354 days

When Ram Naresh Yadav resigned as the CM on 15 February 1979 due to intense conflicts within the Janata Party, the search for a new leader started. A majority of MLAs in the Janata Party were originally from Charan Singh's BLD, and so his role was crucial. There were many aspirants, but Charan Singh chose Banarasi Das, who was an MLA from Khurja, as the next CM. Das was widely considered as a surprise choice for the CM's post. He resigned from his incumbent post as Speaker of the Legislative Assembly on 26 February 1979, and the next day, he was elected as the leader of the JLP. To contest against Banarasi Das, people in the leadership who were pro-change nominated Raj Mangal Pande. Though Pande had a large support base of MLAs who were erstwhile members of the BJS before the formation of the Janata Party, he lost to Banarasi Das by a margin of 35 votes. Pandey was, in fact, ditched by H.N. Bahuguna, who had visited Lucknow from Delhi for the JLP meeting—at the last moment, Bahuguna supported Banarasi Das.

Born on 8 July 1912 in Bulandshahr, Banarasi Das entered politics at a very young age and took active part in the freedom struggle. At the age of 15, he spoke up against British rule. He was jailed many times for his role in the freedom movement. On the night of 5 February 1943, he was tied to a jamun tree in the jail compound and brutally beaten by the collector and his sepoys. After Independence, he was elected as a member of the first assembly in 1952 from Bulandshahr Central and was appointed as the parliamentary secretary to Minister Chandra Bhanu Gupta in Govind Ballabh Pant's and Dr Sampurnanand's governments. He was known as a trusted man of C.B. Gupta and particularly assisted him in fund collection for the Congress. When Gupta passed on the baton to Sucheta Kripalani, Das was appointed as a cabinet minister for cooperation and parliamentary affairs. In 1967, he was again elected from the Sikandarabad seat, and in the short-lived third government of C.B. Gupta, he was given the more important portfolios of power, irrigation, labour and parliamentary affairs.

When the Congress was divided in November 1969, Banarasi Das aligned with the faction led by K. Kamaraj called Congress (O), which was managed by C.B. Gupta in UP. From 1970 to 1973, Banarasi Das was the president of the Congress (O) unit of UP. In 1972, he was sent to the Rajya Sabha and continued there until 1977, when the Janata Party was formed. He contested the post-Emergency assembly polls in 1977 as a member of the Janata Party from Khurja in his district and was elected to the assembly again.

In Parliament, Banarasi Das has a unique record of officiating Rajya Sabha proceedings in one aspect of Article 91 of the Constitution of India, which has incidentally been invoked only once so far. This particular article states that if the posts of chairman and deputy chairman of the Rajya Sabha fall vacant, 'the duties of the office shall be performed by such a member of the Council of States as the President may appoint for the purpose'.[1] In 1977, when the then vice president (and chairman of Rajya Sabha) B.D. Jatti was appointed as the officiating president of India, and the then deputy chairman of the Rajya Sabha, Godey Murahari, was elected to the Lok Sabha on the president's order, on 20 March 1977, Banarasi Das was appointed to perform the duties of the chairman of Rajya Sabha until 30 March 1977, a situation that had never arisen before and never has since then.

As a CM handpicked by Charan Singh, like Ram Naresh Yadav, and witnessing his predecessor's unceremonious departure, Banarasi Das played it safe, while dealing with issues affecting the BJS members in the Janata Party. For instance, whenever he was asked to clarify on the government order restricting RSS activities, the CM said that restrictions were not just on the RSS's activities in public places but also on other organizations. He categorically expressed his view in the assembly by saying, 'I have differences of opinion with the RSS, it can be so, but I consider it cowardliness to crush any ideology by a ban through a government order. Ideology can be countered by ideology.'[2]

---

[1]Article 91, Constitution of India.

[2]*Vidhan Sabha ki Karyawahi*, 27 March 1979, UP Assembly Secretariat, Lucknow, p. 1063; author's translation.

Confrontations and differences of opinion had become routine among the sundry groups within the Janata Party, and problems within the party were on a steady rise. Chaudhary Charan Singh took oath as the PM on 28 July 1979, after a division in the Janata Party. There was already a petition pending before the Election Commission of India regarding a dispute between the Janata Party and Janata Party (Secular). Their impact on Charan Singh's home state was only to be expected. On 28 August 1979, Raj Mangal Pande, then Janata Party MLA from Bhatpar Rani in Deoria, submitted a list of 160 MLAs to Deputy Speaker Jagannath Prasad and claimed that they had formed a separate party. The deputy Speaker gave them a tentative name in the House—Janata Party (R)—and designated the rest of the party as Janata Party (B), where 'R' stood for Raj Mangal Pande and 'B' for Banarasi Das,[3] and clarified that he named the two groups just for the convenience of House proceedings.

Pande tabled a no-confidence motion against the Banarasi Das government on 29 August 1979. The deputy Speaker accepted the motion as Banarasi Das had no objection to that.[4] Answering the concerns, he categorically denied all allegations. However, there were reports of horse-trading until the last moment, and the no-confidence motion was not adopted as only 192 members voted for it and five votes were declared as invalid, while 218 members voted against the motion.[5]

Banarasi Das faced some serious challenges and was accused of corruption. In spite of everything, he did manage to take some significant decisions. During his chief ministership, he

---

[3] *Vidhan Sabha ki Karyawahi*, 29 August 1979, UP Assembly Secretariat, Lucknow, p. 74.

[4] Ibid.

[5] Malhotra, G.C., *Cabinet Responsibility to Legislature*, Lok Sabha Secretariat, New Delhi, 1998, p. 896.

had to deal with floods and then drought, which affected large parts of the state. Due to floods, kharif crops were damaged to the extent that production of paddy was only one-third of the previous year's, and due to drought, there was inordinate delay in sowing of the rabi crops, if at all they were sown. In several parts of the state, people were seriously impacted by the shortage of food and water. The previous government had started a scheme named 'Antyoday' in 1978 to provide easy loans and grants to nearly 5 lakh poor people in the state, but the real benefit of the scheme reached the people during Banarasi Das's time.

However, there seemed no end in sight to the intra-party turmoil. At the Centre, Charan Singh resigned as the PM before facing Lok Sabha because Congress (I) had withdrawn its support. The Lok Sabha was dissolved and fresh elections were announced. Polls ended on 6 January 1980. In UP, the Indira Gandhi faction of the Congress had lost all 85 seats in 1977, but in 1980, the party won 51 of them. The Janata Party (S) of Charan Singh got 29 seats, while the other factions got only three. The new Lok Sabha was constituted on 10 January 1980, with Indira Gandhi once again taking oath as the PM on 14 January 1980.

While Banarasi Das's party had received a rude shock in the polls, 14 January would prove to be a bad day for him in more ways than one. On 11 January, in Narainpur village in Deoria district, a vehicle had crushed a 65-year-old woman and villagers had demanded compensation, but no agreement was reached between the bus owner, local police and villagers. On the night of 14 January, the police and PAC personnel attacked the villagers and committed multiple atrocities, including looting, beating, and raping women. They killed at least two people. Most of the inhabitants in the village were Dalits and Muslims. The new PM had taken oath the same day.

The unpardonable blunder of the Banarasi Das government was that the CM told the assembly on 8 February—which would prove to be the last day of the session under his chief ministership—that he came to know about the rapes and other atrocities in Narainpur only on 23 January, nine days after the incident, and that too through a newspaper report. He said that he had directed Mohan Singh, an MLA from the nearby Barhaj constituency, to visit the village. On 25 January 1980, Bankey Lal, Janata Party MLA from Ramkola, and Hari Keval Prasad, Janata Party MLA from Salempur, both in the same district back then, raised the issue in the House. Bankey Lal even expressed his desire to resign as an MLA because Narainpur was under his constituency and he had not been able to stop the atrocities committed by the police against his people. Mohan Singh made a detailed statement on 28 January 1980 highlighting the atrocities committed by the police of Hata and Kaptanganj police stations.

But political repercussions were heavy. Prime Minister Indira visited Narainpur on 7 February 1980. While returning from the village, she said in Gorakhpur that the Banarasi Das government had no right to exist and that 'instead of going to Narainpur and seeing things, the UP government had accepted the version of the police,' who were responsible for the outrage.[6] Since the Janata Party had dismissed the Congress's state governments in April 1977, with Indira Gandhi coming back to power again, Banarasi Das was expecting the same and was losing confidence. On 8 February 1980, he said in the House that the PM's statement had created unnecessary confusion. Satya Prakash Malviya, the transport minister in his government, said that it should be seen as interference in the

[6]'Forty Years Ago, February 8, 1980: Indira Criticism', *The Indian Express,* 8 February 2020, http://tinyurl.com/4e4ry3ms. Accessed on 29 February 2024.

state government's work as law and order was a state subject. The issue of the Narainpur incident was discussed thrice in the assembly.

On 7 February, a total of 43 MLAs changed their party loyalties. Of them, 32 joined the Congress (I), and so the party's total number in the assembly reached 75. This was an unmistakable sign that the Janata Party was losing ground, and the party MLAs quite clearly discerned the peoples' changing mind towards the Congress (I).

There was not much time left for Banarasi Das. The Indira Gandhi government at the Centre was now ready with its action plan. On 18 February 1980, governments of nine states ruled by non-Congress (I) parties, including UP, were dismissed and their assemblies dissolved. After that, the Janata Party saw many more splits. As for the BJS, its members came together to establish the BJP on 6 April 1980. When the assembly elections were held afresh in May 1980, the Congress (I), which was reduced to 47 seats in 1977 and had even lost the LoP status in the assembly due to the split, now returned to power with 309 seats. The Janata Party (S) won 59 seats, and its other two factions won just four seats each. The newly formed BJP, now sensing a new beginning, had contested 400 seats but shockingly won just 11. That was the end of the Janata Party experiment that had created much hope in the minds of people just three years ago. Charan Singh's Janata Party (S) was renamed as Lok Dal on 9 July 1980 in the assembly.

In the 1980 assembly elections, Banarasi Das contested from Anupshahar but lost to the Congress (I)'s Previn Kumar. However, he gained his influence in Bulandshahr again, and in December 1983, won the Lok Sabha by-poll from this seat, which had been vacant due to the demise of the incumbent Mahmood Hasan Khan. This Lok Sabha by-poll at the end of 1983 had become very prestigious for Banarasi

Das. Furthermore, he won the seat defeating Sarwar Hussain, a candidate of Charan Singh's Lok Dal. Charan Singh had a tie-up with the BJP at that time, so his party leaders felt that the BJP supporters voted for Banarasi Das and not for the Lok Dal candidate because he was Muslim.[7] In later years, Banarasi Das started inching towards the Congress (I) from where he had started, and on 22 November 1984, within a month of Indira Gandhi's assassination, he rejoined his old party.

Two of Banarasi Das's sons followed him into politics. The elder, Harendra Agrawal, was a member of the Legislative Council in UP. He contested the 2019 Lok Sabha polls from Meerut on a Congress ticket but lost. Das's youngest son, Akhilesh Das, was a Rajya Sabha member from the Congress, but he joined the BSP in May 2008 after the party came to power in UP. Later he joined the Congress again, was elected to the Rajya Sabha, and became a Union MoS in Manmohan Singh's UPA-I government. Banarasi Das's family has a chain of institutions named after him and is one of the richest political families in the state.

When Banarasi Das was the CM, he faced allegations that one of his sons was misusing his father's authority to influence government officials. Like C.B. Gupta and Sucheta Kripalani, he too did not stay at the palatial CM residence during his tenure.

Banarasi Das passed away on 3 August 1985 in Lucknow. On his demise, Kalyan Singh who later became CM, said:

> [Das] kept moving on, he was never tired. His personality was multifaceted, and he had amazing organization skills. His decision-making capacity was unparalleled. My constituency is adjoining to his home district and when

---

[7]Chawla, Prabhu, 'Charan Singh Takes Firm Stand over Continuing Alliance with BJP Despite Tempting Offers', *India Today*, 31 January 1984, http://tinyurl.com/mrxjwj45. Accessed on 31 August 2022.

I talk to the villagers, every one of them realizes that he loved them so much. When I spoke to people in the city, each one felt he loved him so much. That was his amazing capacity to get everyone to realize that he loved them a lot.[8]

[8] *Vidhan Sabha ki Karyawahi*, 5 August 1985, UP Assembly Secretariat, Lucknow, p. 7; author's translation.

12

VISHWANATH PRATAP SINGH

The Stint Before Becoming the PM

Twelfth CM: Vishwanath Pratap Singh

Party: Congress (I)

Tenure: 9 June 1980–18 July 1982

Constituency: Member of Legislative Council, Tindwari

Days in Office: 2 years and 39 days

With the Banarasi Das government dismissed, the assembly was dissolved and the Janata Party regime ended. The Congress (I) was on its way to recovering from the losses it had suffered in the previous three years. In UP, President's Rule was imposed on 18 February 1980, making way for fresh polls.

A development of some surprise at this time was that H.N. Bahuguna, who had been elected to the Lok Sabha from Garhwal on a Congress (I) ticket in 1980, left the party in the first week of May 1980, only a few months after joining it back, and declared that he would support the rebels against the Congress (I) in the UP polls. At that time, the campaign and management of UP assembly polls for the Congress (I) were controlled by a team under 34-year-old Sanjay Gandhi, who was then the Lok Sabha MP from Amethi. The assembly polls turned violent under these circumstances, and there were 13 murders in the state.[1]

When the results were announced, the Congress (I) returned to power with 309 seats, while Congress (U), which was formed by D. Devaraj Urs in July 1979 after breaking away from Congress (I), won 13 seats. The Janata Party was fragmented into four parts besides the BJP: Janata Party (SC), headed by Charan Singh, contested 399 seats and won just 59; Janata Party (JP) contested 239 seats and won just four; Janata Party (SR), headed by Raj Narain, contested 302 seats and won just four; and Janata Party, which contested two seats and lost both. The newly formed BJP contested 400 seats and won 11. The Congress (I) was buoyant on its triumphant return, with its tally being the second highest since Independence.

The Congress was on the lookout for promising candidates as it had lost several leaders post the1967 defection by Charan Singh. Months before the split, in the mid-term UP polls of 1969, Vishwanath Pratap Singh, or V.P. Singh as he was later known, was fielded from the Soraon Assembly segment of Allahabad on a Congress ticket. It was Bahuguna who had insisted on V.P. Singh contesting the assembly elections, and that is how he had been fielded in the 1969 mid-term poll. He had chosen to contest from Soraon under the Phulpur Lok Sabha segment, as his home constituency Meja was reserved for SC candidates. The other claimant for the ticket was Sangram Singh, who was a prominent leader in Soraon. V.P. Singh had

---

[1] *Vidhan Sabha ki Karyawahi,* 5 August 1980, UP Assembly Secretariat, Lucknow, p. 706.

been told by his well-wishers in the Congress that he would need to meet important leaders for his ticket. When he met Indira Gandhi just before the 1969 mid-term assembly polls, he told her, 'The ship may sink or the ship may sail, you have to take the risk and all I can say is that I will not let down the trust you repose on me.'[2] Referring to his rival Sangram Singh, V.P. Singh said to Indira Gandhi, 'I respect him, but if the younger generation has to come up it can ask for opportunities only from the elder generation.'[3] He got the assembly ticket, and when results were declared, his was the only assembly seat the Congress won among all five under the Phulpur Lok Sabha segment.

Born on 25 June 1931 in Allahabad, V.P. Singh was from the royal family of Manda in the southern part of Allahabad. Active in campus politics during his student days, he was president of the students' union of Varanasi's Udai Pratap Intermediate College in 1947–48[4] and vice president of the Allahabad University union in 1951–52. After completing his education, he involved himself in social work, and during this period, he founded a school named Gopal Vidyalaya at Koraon in Allahabad. In 1957, he was associated with Vinoba Bhave and donated a bulk of his land to the latter's Bhoodan Movement for landless people. Being in Allahabad, he got opportunities to become close to leaders like Jawaharlal Nehru and Lal Bahadur Shastri and earn their trust.

---

[2]Mustafa, Seema, *The Lonely Prophet: V.P. Singh, a Political Biography,* New Age International Publishers Limited, New Delhi, 1995, p. 22.

[3]Ibid.

[4]'Shri Vishwanath Pratap Singh', *PMIndia,* https://tinyurl.com/wpz588nm. Accessed on 5 March 2024.

With the 1969 victory, V.P. Singh gradually got importance within the Congress. When PM Indira decided not to support Neelam Sanjiva Reddy, the Congress's official candidate for the president of India, and fielded her own candidate, V.V. Giri, in the July 1969 presidential poll, V.P. Singh supported her decision and voted for Giri. In November 1969, when the party was split into two factions, Congress (R), and Congress (O), he went with Indira Gandhi's Congress (R), which was later declared as the real Congress and renamed as Congress (I). During 1970–71, he was the whip of the CLP. In 1971, PM Indira had finalized the name of another Congressman from Allahabad, Jagpat Dubey, for the Phulpur Lok Sabha seat, but Bahuguna, then one of the key leaders in UP in the Indira Gandhi faction of the Congress, considered him as his competitor and sent him to Kanpur for some party work, from where he could not return to file nomination before the deadline. Bahuguna moved V.P. Singh's name at the last moment, and that is how he was fielded for and won the Lok Sabha seat from Phulpur in 1971. In October 1974, he was a deputy minister in the Ministry of Commerce, and in November 1976, during Emergency, he was elevated to the position of MoS for commerce. In the 1977 Lok Sabha polls, he was fielded from Allahabad where he lost—the Congress lost all 85 seats in the state. While several others from top to bottom reached out to the Janata Party during Emergency, he remained with the Congress. He kept his loyalty towards PM Indira intact during the two major setbacks the party faced in 1969 and 1977. When Lok Sabha polls were held in December 1979, V.P. Singh was fielded from Allahabad again, and this time he won. But when PM Indira formed her cabinet, Singh got a hint about the coming days. The new cabinet was formed on 14 January 1980, and V.P. Singh's name was not in the list of cabinet members.

While he was not part of the government, he was put in charge of the core team of the Congress (I), which was managing the UP Assembly polls in May 1980. The assembly election results were declared on 2 June 1980, and the CLP unanimously elected Sanjay Gandhi as its leader in a meeting held on 5 June. Prime Minister Indira was not willing to send Sanjay to UP. Sanjay, who was of the view that the UPCC must be liberated from the grip of Brahmin leadership, had suggested V.P. Singh, a Thakur, and PM Indira had agreed to it. Arun Nehru was also in his favour. V.P. Singh was called by PM Indira, and when he met her, she told him that he was the new CM. When he tried to convince her that he was not fit for state politics, she asked him, 'Was I fit for politics?' After that, V.P. Singh left for Lucknow and took oath as the CM on 9 June 1980. Everything was done in a haste, and he ended up being the first CM of UP who was sworn in without the formality of being elected as the leader of the CLP. All this is well recounted by V.P. Singh in his oral autobiography, *Manjil se Jyada Safar*, as narrated to and written by veteran journalist Ram Bahadur Rai, as well as in *The Lonely Prophet: V.P. Singh, a Political Biography* by Seema Mustafa. Rajendra Singh, who had won from Iglas under Charan Singh's Janata Party (S), was elected as the LoP.

V.P. Singh resigned from the Lok Sabha on 26 July 1980 and was elected to the Legislative Council on 21 November 1980, but within seven months, on 14 June 1981, he resigned from the Council and decided to contest the assembly by-poll from Tindwari in Banda district, which was vacated for him by Congress (I) MLA Shiv Pratap Singh. In the by-poll, V.P. Singh got more than 95 per cent of the polled votes, defeating his main opponent, the BJP's B.B. Brahmchari.

However, V.P. Singh's tenure started with a big loss for him. Just two weeks after he took oath as the CM on 23 June 1980,

Sanjay Gandhi, who had played a key role in Singh's chief ministership, died in an air crash. When the first session of the eighth assembly started on 3 July 1980, it condoled the death of Sanjay, who was a Lok Sabha member from Amethi when he passed away. What V.P. Singh said reflected their relations: 'Life in one hand and death in the other, this was called Sanjay Gandhi. After his demise, heroism is trying to find a body. Sanjay had a certain strength; whichever side he stepped, that became the way. Whichever stone he touched, that became a triumphal arch. When he breathed, it became a storm.'[5]

Days before Sanjay Gandhi's death in the air crash, V.P. Singh's government had to face another setback. On 18 June 1980, Maya Tyagi, her husband Ishwar Tyagi and his two friends Rajendra Dutt and Surendra Singh were going from Ghaziabad to Baghpat in a white Ambassador car when the car's tyre got punctured; they had stopped near a railway crossing to fix it. While Maya kept sitting in the car, the other three had moved towards a tea stall, but when they saw two men trying to molest her, they ran back and pushed both of them. Both were policemen from a nearby police station. Within minutes, nearly a dozen policemen had come and shot all three of them dead. Maya, six months pregnant, was dragged to the police station naked, raped and beaten, and subjected to other atrocities. The police tried to explain the incident away as an encounter and said the three men were trying to loot the Syndicate Bank branch located near the spot. The UP Assembly and Parliament proceedings were disturbed for many days, a judicial inquiry was ordered, and finally, the policemen were booked. Later, four of them were sentenced with life term and six with capital punishment. However, the

[5] *Vidhan Sabha ki Karyawahi*, 5 July 1980, UP Assembly Secretariat, Lucknow, p. 21; author's translation.

capital punishment was converted to life term by the Allahabad High Court. This incident occurred only nine days after V.P. Singh took oath as the CM and it became a big blot on his government from the very beginning. The first session of the eighth assembly commenced with Governor C.P.N. Singh's address to members, where he presented an observation by the V.P. Singh government: '*Aane wala samay bada kathin hai*' (The coming days are going to be very difficult).

As the CM, V.P. Singh was known for his massive campaign against dacoity. His government's first such campaign against dacoits was launched for a month, from 17 June to 16 July 1980 (within just over a week of his taking oath). Police encounters with dacoits made newspaper headlines almost daily, as also the allegations of fake encounters and killings of some 'innocent people' from certain communities, particularly Dalits and members of BCs. Proceedings of the assembly during his regime reflect that the issues of fake encounters and killing of innocent people from deprived sections were repeatedly being raised in the House under different rules of procedures (of the assembly).[6]

Within three months of him taking the oath, there were communal riots in Aligarh, Moradabad and his own city Allahabad.[7] Following widespread criticism of his government, that it could not prevent the riots, he sent his resignation to PM Indira on 14 September 1980, which was released to the press, and he did not attend assembly proceedings for a few days. He wrote that his resignation 'arises out of both

---

[6]Singh, Vishwanath Pratap, *Manjil se Jyada Safar*, Ram Bahadur Rai (ed.), Rajkamal Prakashan, New Delhi, 2006, p. 115.

[7]The Moradabad riot was among the deadliest. For more details, see Seth, Maulshree, 'After Four Decades, Moradabad Riot Report Tabled in UP Assembly: RSS, Officials Exonerated', *The Indian Express*, 9 August 2023, https://tinyurl.com/3ubvjku9. Accessed on 5 March 2024.

personal conviction and political propriety.'[8] The next day, on 15 September, the issue was raised in the assembly as a question of propriety by Mohan Singh, the Lok Dal MLA from Barhaj. He said that if the CM was actually willing to resign, he should have written to the governor. The Speaker did not admit it as a propriety issue, which resulted in most Opposition members walking out. Prime Minister Indira did not accept V.P. Singh's resignation, so he started attending the assembly proceedings from 22 September 1980. This incident made him stronger within the UP Congress (I), but the coming months were to prove more challenging.

His style of working created a storm. On 8 October 1980, police sleuths entered the Legislative Council, and there were allegations that they dragged some Opposition members, including Sarju Prasad Tyagi, out of the House and misbehaved with some journalists. In the assembly, Opposition members criticized the government for sending the police into the Upper House. But Deputy Speaker Yadavendra Singh ruled that the police was permitted to enter the House with the permission of the Chair.[9] Almost all members of the Opposition walked out of the proceedings of the Lower House as the government did not issue a statement on the situation.

But the really difficult time started after the V.P. Singh government completed nearly 10 months in office. While the CM increased his government's efforts to eliminate dacoits through encounters, there was a massacre that tarnished his image and created a political storm that continued for several decades. On the afternoon of 14 February 1981, in Behmai, a village nearly 85 kilometres from Kanpur, Phoolan Devi (a

---

[8]Thakur, Janardan, *V.P. Singh: The Quest For Power,* Warbler Books, New Delhi, 1989, p. 41.

[9]*Vidhan Sabha ki Karyawahi,* 8 October 1980, UP Assembly Secretariat, Lucknow, p. 777.

gang-rape victim-turned-bandit) and her gang brutally attacked and killed 20 people and injured four.[10] It was alleged that the senior officials responsible for anti-dacoity operations had been away in Delhi to handle security arrangements for the Congress (I)'s proposed farmers rally scheduled on 17 February 1981.

When the assembly's budget session started on 20 February, less than a week from the massacre, Bhagwandin Kushwaha, the Lok Dal MLA from Derapur, demanded that the CM should resign forthwith. This matter was discussed in the assembly on 23 February. Mohan Singh said, '[The CM] must resign on moral grounds after this heinous crime in Behmai.'[11] He added, 'It is unfortunate that it is a result of the policy of fake encounters ... there are efforts to divide the state administration on caste lines by deploying officials of a caste in last four-five days... Chief Minister has no moral right to remain on his chair.'[12] However, V.P. Singh requested members to keep away caste from the killings as 'blood of every human being has the same colour'.[13]

After the Behmai massacre, V.P. Singh, on 13 March 1981, announced that he might contest the Lok Sabha polls (by-polls were due for the Allahabad seat vacated by him). His announcement was seen as a ruse to create political instability in the state. However, he did not contest. Intensive efforts to capture Phoolan Devi and her gang members were underway, and on the night of 31 March 1981, there was an encounter between the police and the dacoits near Jalaun, but the police failed to arrest her on that occasion. Phoolan Devi finally surrendered in February 1983, two years after the Behmai

---

[10] *Vidhan Sabha ki Karyawahi,* 23 February 1981, UP Assembly Secretariat, Lucknow, p. 148; author's translation.

[11] Ibid. 151.

[12] Ibid. 149.

[13] Ibid. 178. Author's translation.

massacre, and that too in Madhya Pradesh and after V.P. Singh had already resigned as the CM.

Protests against 'fake encounters' were reported across the state at regular intervals. The Lok Dal launched a Jail Bharo movement against V.P. Singh's policies; its leaders and workers were beaten up at several places by the police. On 21 September 1981, some Opposition leaders brought Radhey Shyam Patel, an MLA from Soraon, on a stretcher to the assembly, alleging that he was beaten by the police. Patel was said to have been beaten soon after his release from Naini Jail. The House was adjourned repeatedly that day due to the pandemonium created by Opposition members.

There was crisis after crisis for the V.P. Singh government. In Dehuli, a village in Mainpuri district, on 18 November 1981 around 4.30 p.m., a gang of 16 people, dressed in fake police uniforms and led by two Thakur youths, attacked the villagers. For four hours, they gunned down every Jatav (SC community) in sight. Later, 24 bodies were recovered from the area, which included nine men, six women and nine children, and seven people were critically injured. When asked whether he would resign, this time V.P. Singh responded with, 'I don't want it said by history that two murderers threw out my government.'[14] This massacre prompted him to issue a statement on 23 November that he would give himself one month to improve the law-and-order situation in the state and eliminate certain dacoit gangs, which meant that he would resign if he failed to deliver. The UPCC, then headed by Bishambhar Nath Pande, offered its full support to V.P. Singh. Rajiv Gandhi, who was elected to Lok Sabha from Amethi after Sanjay Gandhi's death and was looking after UP on behalf of PM Indira, was

---

[14]Kalbag, Chaitanya, 'India Reacts to Dehuli Bloodbath with Shock, Horror and a Sense of Fatalism', *India Today*, 15 December 1981, http://tinyurl.com/3467kxnu. Accessed on 18 September 2022.

also against his resignation. But his frequent announcements of resignations were becoming a joke in UP, and his opponents and critics referred to them as mere histrionics.

Shortly afterwards, four suspects behind the Deoli massacre were killed in an encounter with the police, and 16 suspects were arrested. But these efforts did not stop the massacres. Merely six weeks after Deoli, another such attack on the SC community was reported in Sadhupur, in the same district, on 30 December 1981, where 10 more Jatavs were killed. The image of the V.P. Singh government was badly tarnished; it was termed as being anti-lower caste, going against the very people who were considered among the Congress (I)'s core vote banks those days. It was a huge embarrassment for the Congress (I), whose Union government had sacked the Banarasi Das government in February 1980 citing atrocities against the lower castes in Narainpur, Deoria.

There were several gangs of dacoits, but V.P. Singh had identified the three most dreaded ones, headed by a Yadav, a Thakur and a Mallah (boatman). A major success was achieved on 3 March 1982, when, in an encounter with the police, 14 dacoits belonging to Chhabiram's (Raghubir Singh Yadav's) gang, including him, were killed in Mainpuri. In V.P. Singh's words, 'Chhabiram had built up his image like that of Robin Hood. He used to raid the houses of only rich people. It was said that he never attacked women. He used to help people in marriages. His influence had increased and even politicians had started taking his help.'[15]

Only 17 days after Chhabiram's encounter, V.P. Singh's brother Justice Chandra Shekhar Prasad Singh, a judge in the Allahabad High Court, along with his 14-year-old son, was

---

[15]Singh, Vishwanath Pratap, *Manjil se Jyada Safar*, Ram Bahadur Rai (ed.), Rajkamal Prakashan, New Delhi, 2006, p. 115; author's translation.

killed by dacoits on 20 March 1982 in Bargarh forest at the Allahabad–Banda border, while they were on their way to a hunting expedition. This not only came as a huge shock to the CM but was also a definite proof of the rampant, unmitigated hold the dacoits had over UP. One of the main accused in the case, Jagatpal Pasi, was killed in an encounter with the police in Banda district on the night of 8 April 1982.

V.P. Singh's government, apart from fighting the menace of dacoity, took several praiseworthy measures too. He started a system of preparing an index of development for all *vikas khand*s (development blocks) based on 36 parameters, and the fund allocation was decided based on that. He is said to have narrated that some ministers were against it and that those dissenting voices were organized by Vir Bahadur Singh.[16] As CM, he tried to convince the MLAs not to recommend people for transfers; when recommendations were received, he mostly did not accept them. Due to this, he became unpopular among the MLAs. He decentralized monitoring of development programmes, and ministers were given charge of different divisions and districts. His government was criticized for its high dependence on the bureaucracy and police and for ignoring public representatives. However, during his regime as the CM, V.P. Singh did not face any no-confidence motion.

While budget proceedings were going on, on the day of presentation of the budget, 5 April 1982, some pamphlets were thrown by someone from the visitors' gallery and slogans of '*inqlab* zindabad' were raised. Phirangi Prasad Visharad, a Lok Dal MLA from Maharajganj (SC), said that the person was from Varanasi, and he had given notice to the CM that his life was under threat from all those who belonged to the Thakur

[16]Ibid. 108.

castes in Varanasi.[17] As it turned out, 5 April 1982 was the last day in the assembly for V.P. Singh as the CM.

On the night of 27–28 June 1982, a gang of dacoits headed by a man named Muslim gunned down 10 people in Kanpur's Dastampur village; another such killing happened in Mainpuri. V.P. Singh was completely shaken that day. On 28 June, his 500-word resignation, which was definitely 'histrionic', was sent to the governor instead of the PM. In his resignation, he stated: 'People want results and not alibis and they cannot go on waiting for results indefinitely. The people of Uttar Pradesh have waited long enough. They could not get the desired results. Why should the people pay the price of my failure?'[18]

Earlier, on his way to Lucknow to take oath as the UP CM, he had asked Sanjay Singh, an MLA from Amethi who was close to Sanjay Gandhi, about the biggest problem of the state. When he was told that it was dacoity, he had decided to take it on in all earnestness. His tenure had started with the Maya Tyagi case and ended with a dacoity. However, his decision was well appreciated at a time when accountability among those at the helm of public affairs was widely disowned, and this trend continues to this day.

V.P. Singh returned to the Centre and was elected to the Rajya Sabha in July 1983. As a Union minister of commerce, on 29 January 1983, he was also given additional charge of the Department of Supplies. When Rajiv Gandhi took oath to continue as the PM on 31 December 1984, he appointed V.P. Singh as the minister of finance, and in June 1987, he moved to the post of minister of defence. After that he moved in a surprising new direction when he made

---

[17] *Vidhan Sabha ki Karyawahi,* 5 April 1982, UP Assembly Secretariat, Lucknow, p. 135.

[18] Mustafa, Seema, *The Lonely Prophet: V.P. Singh, a Political Biography,* New Age International (P) Limited, New Delhi, 1995, p. 52.

allegations against PM Rajiv regarding the Bofors scam, and on 17 July 1987, he resigned as the defence minister but continued with his role in the Rajya Sabha. Later, he quit the Congress, and in June 1988, he was elected to the Lok Sabha from the Allahabad seat in a by-poll as an independent candidate, as this seat was vacant due to the resignation of Amitabh Bachchan. On 11 October 1988, he formed a new party, the Janata Dal, merging various Janata Party factions. In 1989, he entered the Lok Sabha again on a Janata Dal ticket from Fatehpur. In those days, there was a popular slogan in his favour: '*Raja nahin faqir hai, desh ki taqdeer hai*' (He is not a king but a monk, he is the destiny of country). He was sworn in as the PM of India on 2 December 1989 with the support of the BJP and the Left Front. But as PM, he could continue for only 343 days, as the BJP withdrew support to his government when the *rath yatra* from Somnath to Ayodhya of the then BJP president L.K. Advani was stopped in Samastipur on 23 October 1990 and Advani and several other leaders of his party were arrested.

As the PM, V.P. Singh is remembered for his decision to implement the Mandal Commission Report's suggestions to grant 27 per cent reservation to OBCs in central government jobs. This decision resulted in the empowerment of OBCs in the entire country as their representation in the government increased. Later, his party fragmented into many groups, and his politics was consolidated by his associates like Lalu Prasad Yadav, Mulayam Singh Yadav, Sharad Yadav, Nitish Kumar and Ram Vilas Paswan, among others. The V.P. Singh government conferred the Bharat Ratna, the country's highest civilian honour, on Dr B.R. Ambedkar posthumously in 1990.

V.P. Singh entered the Lok Sabha once more in 1991 from Fatehpur on a Janata Dal ticket, but he did not contest the 1996 Lok Sabha elections or any elections after that as he decided to bid adieu to active politics. However, he was quite active on the issues affecting the downtrodden and deprived sections of society. His son Ajeya Singh was offered a Lok Sabha ticket from Fatehpur in 2009 by the Lok Jan Shakti Party (LJP) of the late Ram Vilas Paswan, but it was denied to him at the last moment. He contested on a Jan Morcha ticket but lost.

V.P. Singh passed away on 27 November 2008 in New Delhi. He was cremated in his home district of Allahabad. On his demise, Lalu Prasad Yadav, then minister of railways, said:

> [V.P. Singh was] a truly secular nationalist who was committed to people's welfare and national development. Throughout his life [he] constantly strove for the betterment of poorest among poor people, especially those who belong to the deprived sections of the society and minorities. His service to the people with utmost dedication and his contribution for the upliftment of downtrodden will be remembered for generations to come.[19]

[19]Message released through Press Information Bureau, Government of India, New Delhi, on 27 November 2008.

13

SRIPATI MISHRA

The Placeholder

Thirteenth CM: Sripati Mishra

Party: Congress (I)

Tenure: 19 July 1982–2 August 1984

Constituency: Isauli

Days in Office: 2 years and 14 days

V.P. Singh sent his resignation to Governor C.P.N. Singh on 28 June 1982 and later held a press conference to announce his decision. Since election to the office of the president of India was due at that time, PM Indira Gandhi asked V.P. Singh to continue as the CM until the results were declared. The Congress (I) had chosen Giani Zail Singh as its candidate.

In those days, the top leadership of the UP Congress was confined between two caste groups—Brahmins and Thakurs. V.P. Singh wrote in his biography, 'Caste-based groups emerged during the 1980s. The leader of one such group was Vir Bahadur

Singh and the leader of the other group was Lokpati Tripathi... Their competition was for the CM's post.'[1] This caste-based change in politics was primarily taking place among a generation that had not taken part in the freedom movement. While groupism within parties existed earlier as well, V.P. Singh, in his book *Manjil se Jyada Safar*, said that the central focus of those groups was not caste; it was mostly based on the personality of the leaders, be it Dr Sampurnanand, C.B. Gupta, Charan Singh, Kamalapati Tripathi or H.N. Bahuguna. When V.P. Singh resigned, the Congress (I) was looking for a new leader for UP. While the aspirants were many, the Congress (I) was reluctant to look beyond Brahmins and Thakurs. One of the concerns of the Congress (I)'s high command appeared to be that the CM should not be a satrap who could control UP politics. Since the assembly polls were nearly three years away, the party was not unduly worried.

Sanjay Gandhi, who had played a key role in the selection of V.P. Singh, had died in an air crash, so the Congress (I) was not averse to electing a Brahmin. In the Brahmin lobby, the name of N.D. Tiwari was again being talked about, whereas the strong Thakur lobby floated the name of Vir Bahadur Singh. The Congress (I)'s high command preferred a Brahmin but not Tiwari, as it did not want heavyweights to succeed V.P. Singh. The man chosen after hectic lobbying was Sripati Mishra, a dark horse whose name was initially not considered in the race for the party's CM candidate. A low-profile politician from Sultanpur, Mishra was then the Speaker of the assembly and changed his party affiliations frequently.

Mishra resigned as the Speaker and was elected as the leader of the CLP on 18 July 1982. Next day, on 19 July, he

---

[1]Singh, Vishwanath Pratap, *Manjil se Jyada Safar*, Ram Bahadur Rai (ed.), Rajkamal Prakashan, New Delhi, 2006, p. 64; author's translation.

was sworn in as the thirteenth CM of UP at the age of 58. Among the nine Congress CMs till that time, Sripati Mishra was the fifth Brahmin. None of the previous Congress CMs had been from SC, OBC or Muslim communities, which made up a large chunk of the state's population as well as its support base. The only CM from the OBCs till then had been Ram Naresh Yadav from the Janata Party. Sanjay Gandhi had tried to weaken the grip of Brahmin leaders on the party, but with his untimely demise, his desired social engineering could not happen across all levels.

Sripati Mishra was not a hard-core Congressman. He started his political career as a member of the Socialist Party like N.D. Tiwari, but unlike Tiwari, who joined the Congress in 1963 and remained with the party for several decades, Mishra was in and out of the Congress. After leaving the Socialist Party, he joined the Congress, but left it to join Chaudhary Charan Singh's BKD. He joined the Indira Gandhi faction of the Congress in 1971. Thus, he was not even a party loyalist unlike other claimants. When his name was announced for the CM's post, it became clear that the Congress (I)'s high command needed a CM to whom it could dictate anything from Delhi. The Congress Party had already lost, sidelined or shunted several stalwarts, and Indira Gandhi and Rajiv Gandhi and their associates like Arun Nehru had now taken full control of the UPCC and UP legislature party as well as the state government.

Mishra, while studying at BHU, joined the student movement. After completing his education from Lucknow University (LLB), he started preparing for the judicial services exam. In the meantime, he contested the Lok Sabha polls in 1952 from the Sultanpur District (North)-cum-Faizabad District (South West) seat on a Socialist Party ticket, but he lost, securing the third place.[2] He joined the government as a judicial magistrate in 1954 after clearing the exam conducted by the State Public Service Commission, but resigned in 1958 to practise law in Sultanpur. He entered active politics in 1962, when he joined the Congress and was elected to the UP Assembly from Kadipur in Sultanpur. In 1967, he was re-elected to the assembly from the nearby Jaisinghpur seat, again as a Congress candidate. In June 1967, when Charan Singh was the CM, Mishra was elected as the deputy Speaker of the UP Assembly.

However, when the Congress faced problems from within and outside in the late 1960s, Mishra joined the BKD. He was fielded in a Lok Sabha by-poll from Sultanpur and won. He resigned from the Lok Sabha and was sworn in as a minister in Chaudhary Charan Singh's second UP government when it was formed on 18 February 1970, and was allotted the portfolios of food and civil supplies, revenue, social welfare, harijan welfare, education and sports, and labour. At this time, he was elected to the Legislative Council. When T.N. Singh replaced Charan Singh as the CM, Sripati Mishra was appointed as the minister of education and technical education.

But after the collapse of the T.N. Singh government in 1971, Mishra again changed his path and quit the BKD to join the Congress (R). In 1976, during Emergency, CM N.D. Tiwari of the Indira Gandhi faction of the Congress appointed Mishra as deputy chairman of the state's Planning Commission. In the 1977 assembly polls, when there was a wave in favour of the Janata Party, Mishra lost from the Chanda seat of Sultanpur as a Congress candidate. But in 1980, when Indira Gandhi's

---

[2] *Statistical Report on General Elections 1951 to the First Lok Sabha,* Election Commission of India, New Delhi.

faction, named Congress (I), returned to power, Mishra was elected to the assembly from Sultanpur's Isauli seat and was made the Speaker of the assembly in July 1980 when V.P. Singh was the CM.

That Mishra was a remote-controlled CM was evident from the very beginning of his tenure. He did not have much say even in the selection of his ministers, and more than half of the ministers of V.P. Singh's cabinet were retained. The Lok Dal leader and its chief whip in the assembly, Mohan Singh, stated after Mishra's oath-taking that the latter was the 'captain of a defeated army'.[3] He stated that V.P. Singh had made a promise to eliminate dacoit gangs that had not been fulfilled, and, therefore, Singh had resigned, which should have meant the resignation of his entire cabinet. Hence, it was not proper to retain most of the ministers in the new government. Even Governor C.P.N. Singh raised the matter in August 1982. This led to the Opposition members demanding in the assembly that since there appeared to be a deadlock between Raj Bhavan and the CM, Mishra should resign.[4]

Regardless of the fact that a majority of the ministers were not chosen by the CM, the Sripati Mishra government started its work. It tried to placate journalists by sending cheques of ₹500 each to 13 journalists.[5]

When Mishra took over, there were apprehensions among the deprived communities because of the V.P. Singh government's encounter campaign against dacoits, in which a large number of innocent people were also allegedly targeted.

---

[3] *Vidhan Sabha ki Karyawahi*, 20 August 1982, UP Assembly Secretariat, Lucknow, p. 216; author's translation.

[4] Ibid.

[5] Sagar, Anand, 'Uttar Pradesh Govt Makes Concerted Attempt to Buy State's Journalists', *India Today*, 15 September 1982, https://tinyurl.com/ychkhj45. Accessed on 5 March 2024.

New groups of SCs were emerging and demanding their rights and share in power, and, therefore, the SCs had become an important focus of the Sripati Mishra government. Additionally, in 1982, it started Ramayana Mela in Ayodhya, which has become an annual four-to-six-day event sponsored by the state government since then.

The Congress leaders sitting in Delhi were constantly trying to dictate, and sometimes even destabilize, Mishra and his government. On 16 March 1983, conveners of the UP parliamentary body of the Congress, Rudra Pratap Singh (MP from Barabanki) and K.P. Tiwari (MP from Allahabad), asked Mishra to present before them a detailed review of the functioning of his government. Then, in mid-1983, Kashi Nath Mishra, a Congress (I) MLA from Ballia, started a signature campaign to remove Sripati Mishra. Both camps (of Kashi Nath and Sripati) began giving out statements to newspapers. Kashi Nath said, 'There is not even a semblance of a government in our state. Nothing seems to be moving... While every decision is implemented in files, nothing happens in the field.'[6] In the meantime, on 3 September 1983, when Sripati Mishra reached nearly an hour late for a CLP meeting, several MLAs threatened to walk out. It was alleged at the meeting that in the one year since July 1982, over 60 political murders had taken place in various parts of the state, including Lucknow, and that advocates in Allahabad, Moradabad, Banda, Etawah and Azamgarh had been lathi-charged by the police for protesting against police atrocities.[7]

Such problems continued amidst regular interference by the high command and by other leaders of the party. That

---

[6]Chawla, Prabhu, 'Uttar Pradesh CM Sripat Misra Hauled Up for Ruining Congress(I)'s Image', *India Today*, 30 September 1983, https://tinyurl.com/395235u6. Accessed on 6 March 2024.

[7]Ibid.

Indira Gandhi's close associates like Arun Nehru and her son Rajiv Gandhi were not happy with Mishra was becoming clear day by day, with both of them monitoring the performance of Mishra as the CM. Incidentally, his cabinet ministers like Balram Singh Yadav (MLA from Jaswantnagar), Brahm Dutt (MLA from Mussoorie) and Vir Bahadur Singh (MLA from Paniara) moved closer to Arun and Rajiv and started taking decisions without consulting the CM. All three were among the senior-most ministers in the Sripati Mishra government. Brahm Dutt held several crucial portfolios, including finance; Yadav held the portfolios of panchayati raj and rural development; and Singh was the minister of industry, export promotion and irrigation. Rumours that the Congress (I)'s high command was going to replace Sripati Mishra started spreading.

Observing the weakness of the Mishra government, Opposition leaders tried to exploit the situation. A motion of no confidence was brought in by LoP Choudhary Rajendra Singh (Lok Dal MLA from Iglas) on the grounds of 'corruption and inefficiency' of the government and the 'poor fiscal condition' of the state.[8] He demanded an inquiry by a high court judge into allegations of corruption against some ministers. Mishra replied that the Lokayukta had sent its report about only one minister, and no charges were proved against him, though an inquiry was in progress against another minister. Cane growers' problems were also raised during discussions on the motion. However, the motion was negated by a voice vote and the government survived. But what was notable during the discussions was that ministers like Lokpati Tripathi, who spoke on behalf of the ruling party, did not focus on the achievements of their government but seemed more interested

[8] *Vidhan Sabha ki Karyawahi*, 2 September 1983, UP Assembly Secretariat, Lucknow, p. 266.

in criticizing the Opposition. All this seemed to reflect the fact that all was not well with the CM, especially regarding his relations with his cabinet.

In the meantime, Mishra's comments on the Mandal Commission Report annoyed sections of the OBCs that were already displeased with the Congress (I). On 24 March 1983, PM Indira called a meeting of CMs to discuss the Mandal report, where Sripati Mishra criticized it.[9] In the assembly, MLAs criticized Mishra and said that he should have consulted his cabinet before commenting on the report, as was promised by the state's parliamentary affairs minister, Ammar Rizvi, in the House a few days before this. Interestingly, Pradeep Yadav, an MLA from Rudauli of Janata Party's Raj Narain faction, tabled a resolution on the Mandal report on 12 September 1983 and requested the CM: '*Jaate jaate ek achchha kaam karte jaiye*' (Do one good thing before you leave).[10] The resolution stating that 'the state government should take action as soon as possible'[11] on the Mandal Commission Report was adopted. Around this entire fracas, there were widespread rumours that Mishra's days on the chair were numbered.

At this time, while Charan Singh's Lok Dal still had an influence and impact in rural areas as the party had its reach across the state, the BJP was emerging as a strong challenger to the Congress (I) in urban areas. Prime Minister Indira was proving her tenacity on global forums and establishing herself internationally, what with the Asian Games held in Delhi in November–December 1982 and the 7th Summit of the Non-Aligned Movement held in New Delhi in March 1983, but

[9] *Vidhan Sabha ki Karyawahi,* 6 April 1983, UP Assembly Secretariat, Lucknow, p. 1324.

[10] *Vidhan Sabha ki Karyawahi,* 12 September 1983, UP Assembly Secretariat, Lucknow, p. 150.

[11] Ibid. 146.

she was equally concerned about her own state as Lok Sabha and assembly polls were due in early 1985.

Sripati Mishra was busy trying to manage the affairs of the state, but the party was losing its ground and looking for his replacement. In December 1983, the Congress (I) had lost by-polls of two assembly seats—Fazilnagar and Pilibhit—and one Lok Sabha seat of Bulandshahr. In May 1984, there were assembly by-polls for Jakhania (SC) and Malihabad (SC) seats, and the Congress (I) had to face a humiliating defeat in both. One of the most embarrassing incidents for the Congress (I) was the defeat of its candidate Shanti Kureel in Malihabad, where Brij Lal, a village pradhan from Amethi who had been selected by Maneka Gandhi's Rashtriya Sanjay Manch (RSM), contested and won. Chief Minister Mishra had addressed two rallies in Malihabad during campaigning, and when the party candidate lost, Mishra said that some leaders of his own party sabotaged the elections; his party high command was not impressed with his statement.

Mishra, on his part, was making every effort to consolidate his position. He transferred the heads of police of 30 districts, mostly in those districts that were seen as hostile to the Congress (I). The Mishra government was also trying to become media-friendly. On 1 May 1984, it allocated a 20-acre residential complex named Patrakar Puram for nearly 200 journalists in the state capital of Lucknow at a rate that was nearly 40 per cent lower than the market rate.[12] The idea of having an exclusive complex for journalists had been there since 1969, but it was finalized by the Sripati Mishra government. But within his party and government, things were beyond Mishra's control. Fortunately for him, the instatement

[12]Chawla, Prabhu, 'Residential Complex Project for Journalists in Uttar Pradesh Kicks Up a Row', *India Today*, 31 May 1984, https://tinyurl.com/2s3nc788. Accessed on 5 March 2024.

of his replacement got delayed somewhat as PM Indira was deeply embroiled in Punjab, where Operation Blue Star was started by the army on 1 June 1984.

Post Operation Blue Star, the Congress (I) began preparing for the next general elections, due in early 1985. It was in August 1984, nearly seven months before the end of tenure of the eighth state assembly, that the party high command asked Sripati Mishra to resign, and he did so on 2 August. He was replaced by none other than N.D. Tiwari, another Brahmin leader, who had already served as the CM during Emergency. To control the sliding support for the Congress (I) among the masses, while Tiwari was sworn in as the CM, V.P. Singh was soon appointed as the president of the UPCC, replacing Sukhdeo Prasad. Such was the desperation of the Congress (I) that both these leaders, Tiwari and Singh, who were away in Vienna to attend the fourth General Conference of the United Nations Industrial Development Organization at that time, were called back to take on their new responsibilities immediately.

One of Sripati Mishra's sons, Rakesh Mishra, joined the BJP in 2016. Before this, he was an MLC from the Congress in the late 1980s and a UPCC office bearer for a few years. Another son, Pramod, is with the Congress.

N.D. Tiwari took oath as the CM on 3 August 1984, and Mishra left state politics. In 1985, he was elected to the Lok Sabha again, this time from the Machhlishahr seat on a Congress ticket, and continued until 1989. Thereafter, he decided to leave politics forever. Mishra passed away on 8 December 2002 in Lucknow after a prolonged illness. Commiserating over his demise, one of the senior BJP leaders in the state, Harish

Chandra Srivastava, also known as Harish ji, said in the UP assembly on 3 March 2003, 'Mishra was a progressive leader of socialist thinking. He had a deep understanding of parliamentary subjects, rules and conventions and was an eloquent orator. He served this state from different positions. The state has lost a wise politician and a philanthropist.'[13]

[13] *Vidhan Sabha ki Karyawahi*, 3 March 2003, UP Assembly Secretariat, Lucknow, p. 3; author's translation.

14

VIR BAHADUR SINGH

A Balancing Act

Fourteenth CM: Vir Bahadur Singh

Party: Congress

Tenure: 24 September 1985–24 June 1988

Constituency: Paniyara

Days in Office: 2 years and 274 days

In a surprise move, the Congress, under Rajiv Gandhi's leadership, decided to replace N.D. Tiwari in the third week of September 1985, barely six months after he was sworn in as the CM. To formalize the replacement process, Harkishan Lal Bhagat, the Union minister of parliamentary affairs; Govindaswamy Karuppiah Moopanar, the AICC general secretary; and Sitaram Kesari, the AICC treasurer, were sent to Lucknow as observers. They spoke to 296 MLAs and MLCs at the state guest house in Lucknow, and the majority of them suggested the name of Vir Bahadur Singh. When the CLP met in Lucknow, Singh's name was backed by another contender for the CM's post, Lokpati Tripathi from Chandauli, son of ex-CM Kamalapati Tripathi, as well as by Baldev Singh Arya from Uttarkashi, a prominent Dalit leader, and Said-ul-Hasan from Bulandshahr, a well-known Muslim leader.

Prior to that, on 21 September, PM Rajiv had visited the state's flood-affected areas and, in the process, had also met and spoken to some party leaders, including Singh. Two days later, on 23 September, Tiwari had written to PM Rajiv of his willingness to resign and announced this decision.

For the 1985 assembly polls, CM Tiwari and state president of the party V.P. Singh had dropped a large number of sitting MLAs due to their bad image and unpopularity, among other factors. Vir Bahadur Singh, on his part, had successfully secured tickets for nearly 150 of his supporters, of whom almost 100 had won; the majority of them shared his caste, that is, Thakur. He had been eyeing the post of CM since June 1980, but back then, V.P. Singh was chosen by the Sanjay Gandhi–Arun Nehru team, and in August 1984, N.D. Tiwari was chosen by PM Indira to replace Sripati Mishra. Finally, Singh's time was here, and he took oath as the fourteenth CM of the state on 24 September 1985 at the age of 50.

Vir Bahadur Singh was born on 18 January 1935 in a village called Harnahi in Gorakhpur district. An MA in Geography from Gorakhpur University, Singh's electoral journey started in 1967 when he was elected to the assembly on a Congress ticket from the Paniyara seat in Gorakhpur (now in Maharajganj) district. He was elected to the assembly again in 1969, 1974, 1980 and 1985 from the same seat, each time on Congress (R) and Congress (I) tickets.

Singh served in various capacities before taking over as the

CM. When Chaudhary Charan Singh became CM for a second time in alliance with the Congress (R), V.B. Singh was sworn in as a deputy minister and allotted the public works department (PWD) on 19 April 1970. He remained the deputy minister of the irrigation department in Kamalapati Tripathi's government. Later, in H.N. Bahuguna's government, he was a part of the departments of heavy industries, sugarcane development, finance, parliamentary affairs and cooperatives as well. In 1976, when N.D. Tiwari took oath as CM for the first time, Singh was elevated to the post of MoS for excise and revenue. In the V.P. Singh government (1980–82), he was the minister for irrigation and flood control as well as transport, and in the Sripati Mishra government (1982–84), Singh continued as the minister of irrigation and flood control. He was sworn in as a cabinet minister in N.D. Tiwari's government during 1984–85 and handled the departments of industrial development, export promotion, and irrigation and flood control, just before his elevation to the post of the CM. Unlike Tiwari, who was known for being accommodating and not taking unpleasant decisions, Singh was considered to be a strict administrator and a straightforward person who took some tough steps as the minister of transport, industry and irrigation in successive governments, which included suspension of several errant officials.

The main force behind V.B. Singh was Arun Nehru, Rajiv Gandhi's cousin and close advisor. Singh also had the trust of his predecessors N.D. Tiwari and V.P. Singh, who were powerful Union ministers and had considerable influence in UP politics. Chief Minister Singh had served as a minister in the governments of both Tiwari and V.P. Singh. So, while claimants for the post were many, V.B. Singh's coronation happened smoothly. However, his relationship with V.P. Singh started deteriorating as he felt that some of his ministers who were close to V.P. Singh were trying to disorganize his government. Later, his relationship with Arun

Nehru also changed. One of the close advisors of the Gandhi family termed V.B. Singh as a man 'with power', and that 'when he was told Arun Nehru would be made Chief Minister and he would be Deputy Chief Minister [after he had resigned], Vir Bahadur declined. He said that he was not ready to work under Arun Nehru.'[1]

On his first day in office as the CM, Singh passed an order stating that all ministers should be present in their offices by 9.45 a.m. It was not just a formality, as he ordered the guards to close all entries to the state secretariat at 10.15 a.m. every day. He authorized the guards to stop even the cabinet ministers if they were late to office. In the first week, health minister Lokpati Tripathi was among those who could not get to work because the gates were closed and the keys were with the CM.[2] He advised his ministers not to rush to Delhi unless it had to do with official work. Singh told department heads that he wouldn't tolerate any excuse for delay in the implementation of government schemes and in the weekly reviews of all programmes that had been started. Hours were fixed in the daily schedules of ministers for meeting the public. From the very beginning, Singh started suspending officials, among them the district magistrate of Barabanki, for failing to take preventive measures against floods. When he took over, floods in some districts had been a problem. This prompted Singh to issue specific instructions to his ministers in charge of flood relief in respective affected areas not to leave their place of duty without his prior approval. He also started evaluating on a regular basis the work done by the departments and

[1]Fotedar, M.L., *The Chinar Leaves: A Political Memoir,* HarperCollins, New Delhi, 2016, p. 170.

[2]Chawla, Prabhu, 'Uttar Pradesh CM Veer Bahadur Singh Cracks the Whip on Ministers, Bureaucrats, Officals', *India Today*, 15 November 1985, https://tinyurl.com/3tuwcm9j. Accessed on 6 March 2024.

directed the vigilance department to file criminal cases against several senior officials, including Indian Administrative Service (IAS) officers, on charges of corruption.

During Singh's regime, UP faced communal violence in over 35 districts, including the Meerut massacre that claimed over 180 lives. It was during his tenure that the gates of the Ram temple in Ayodhya were opened after a court order. This period also saw long strikes (twice) by state government employees; the worst drought situation in the state; and the farmers' movement led by Mahendra Singh Tikait that had an impact on rural areas of almost the entire state. Singh's time as CM witnessed the decline of the Congress in UP, the rapid emergence of new leaders like Mulayam Singh Yadav of the Lok Dal (B) and Kalyan Singh of the BJP, and the rebellion of V.P. Singh at the Centre. Mulayam Singh and Kalyan, just like V.B. Singh, had become first-time MLAs in 1967, and were trying, after 20 years in politics, to play a prime role in state politics.

Within months of taking over as the CM, Singh's government, in order to break the nexus of politicians and criminals in the state, promulgated the Uttar Pradesh Gangsters and Anti-social Activities (Prevention) Ordinance in January 1986. To make this a law, a bill was tabled in the assembly, which was implemented after it got the assent from the President of India on 19 March 1986. As a follow-up to this ordinance, directions were issued to the state police to arrest anyone carrying even licensed arms in public—a move that annoyed many of the ruling party's MLAs as well as Opposition leaders who alleged misuse of this law against themselves. In the first six months of the promulgation of the ordinance, 771 gangsters were arrested, though 475 of them got bail.[3] His government

---

[3]Awasthi, Dilip, 'UP Government Orders Freeze on Use of Gangsters Act Saying It Is Full of Legal Loopholes', *India Today*, 15 August 1986, https://tinyurl.com/nwk6eyyd. Accessed on 6 March 2024.

also imposed restrictions on arms licenses to private persons.

It was but expected that V.B. Singh would have felt the need for the Gangsters Act. In those days, his Gorakhpur region was known for violent clashes between gangs of Brahmin and Thakur goons, which had reached their height in the 1980s. One group was headed by Hari Shankar Tiwari, a Brahmin, and the other by Virendra Pratap Shahi, a Thakur. Their dominance extended from eastern UP districts like Deoria, Gorakhpur, Basti, Ballia, Azamgarh, Gonda and Behraich to the state capital Lucknow and other districts bordering Nepal and parts of Bihar. Both Shahi and Tiwari had many friends and patrons among politicians. For years, Tiwari had earned the faith of the then CM Sripati Mishra, while V.B. Singh himself, who had been a senior minister in the Mishra government in those days, was seen batting for Shahi.[4] The Shahi–Tiwari battle had mainly been to acquire government contracts and keep their caste clout intact. In the process, several people were killed on both sides, and the government administration had proved highly ineffective in dealing with the problem. Shahi, who had been elected as an independent MLA in a by-poll from Lakshmipur in 1981 and again in general elections in 1985, was killed on 31 March 1997 in Lucknow by Shriprakash Shukla, a sharpshooter who was killed in an encounter with the UP police on 22 September 1998 in Ghaziabad. Meanwhile, Tiwari, who served six times as MLA from Chillupar in Gorakhpur—first as an independent and later from different parties, was a minister in different regimes of UP (of Kalyan Singh, Ram Prakash Gupta, Rajnath Singh, Mayawati and Mulayam Singh Yadav) and died on 16 May 2023.

During V.B. Singh's tenure as the CM, both Tiwari and Shahi were members of the assembly. The Gangsters Act, 1986,

---

[4]Bhartiya, Santosh, *Nishane Par Samay, Samaj aur Rajneeti*, Radhakrishna Prakashan, New Delhi, 2005, p. 166.

along with the U.P. Control of Goondas Act, 1970, initiated during Chaudhary Charan Singh's second regime as the CM, had become big 'weapons' in the hands of law enforcement agencies in UP, amid widespread allegations of misuse. Section 14(1) of the Gangsters Act had become an effective instrument in the hands of these agencies as it provisioned that '[i]f the District Magistrate has reason to believe that any property, whether moveable or immovable, in possession of any person has been acquired by a gangster as a result of the commission of an offence triable under this Act, he may order attachment of such property whether or not cognizance of such offence has been taken by any Court.'[5]

While Singh was trying to deal with the goons in a strict manner, the Hindu–Muslim riots that broke out in Barabanki soon after in May 1986 dented the CM's emerging image as a tough administrator. Undeterred, he carried on with his job. His equation within the party leadership was also affected. His image was severely hit by the Hindu–Muslim riots in June 1986 in Allahabad, barely a month after the Barabanki riots, and that started a rift between him and then Allahabad MP Amitabh Bachchan, who had been among the closest friends of PM Rajiv in those days. On 18 July 1986, the day Bachchan was scheduled to meet him, some newspapers carried an advertisement on the former's behalf, which said, 'There are many questions in my mind for which I shall be seeking answers when I meet the Chief Minister today, namely: Insufficient financial compensation to affected property and people; administrative lapses, vis-a-vis timely intervention, indiscriminate arrests of innocents and their subsequent care while in custody.'[6] Considering Bachchan's close friendship

---

[5]Article 14 (1), The Uttar Pradesh Gangsters and Anti-social Activities (Prevention) Act, 1986.

[6]Chawla, Prabhu, 'Half of Congress(I) CMs Face Revolt from Dissidents, Rajiv

with PM Rajiv, in political circles this seemed to indicate that all was not well between the PM and the UP CM.

Singh had not completed even a year in office before the anti-Arun Nehru faction in the state unit of his party started creating trouble for him. Some of these troublemakers included his ministers. Along with rising intra-party problems for Singh, the Opposition, though it was fragmented, was also actively trying to topple his government. However, in the three regimes (two of Tiwari and one of V.B. Singh) of the ninth UP Assembly, only one motion of no confidence was admitted and debated on, and that was against the government headed by V.B. Singh. The motion was moved by Lok Dal leader and LoP Mulayam Singh Yadav on 8 September 1986. Mulayam Singh alleged that while ministers were busy with transfers and postings of officials, policy decisions were being taken by the bureaucracy.[7] He emphasized that innocent people were being killed in fake encounters and communal tension had reached disturbing levels, but the government was doing nothing about either. Chief Minister V.B. Singh intervened and said that he had made every effort to provide a clean government after taking over the reins of the state. Ultimately, the motion was defeated with 108 members voting in favour and 250 members against.[8]

But problems for V.B. Singh seemed to not end; they kept coming one after the other. In November 1986, there was a 19-day strike by state government employees. It was called off on 29 November 1986 after an agreement was reached between the employees and the state government; CM Singh was forced to accept many of their demands. This was the

---

Gandhi Unable to Stem the Rot', *India Today*, 15 August 1986, https://tinyurl.com/mr2zbafc. Accessed on 6 March 2024.

[7] *Vidhan Sabha ki Karyawahi*, 8 September 1986, UP Assembly Secretariat, Lucknow, p. 83; author's translation.

[8] Ibid. 179.

biggest strike since 1966–67, during Sucheta Kripalani's days as the CM. Similar to how Charan Singh and C.B. Gupta had tacitly provoked employees against Kripalani on that occasion, this time it was Lokpati Tripathi, a long-time contender for the CM's chair, whose intervention aggravated the situation. The CM had to finally accept the employees' demands.

V.B. Singh's assertive measures did not continue for long, as senior ministers and MLAs began to openly defy his orders and make frequent trips to New Delhi to meet central leaders. Several MLAs and MLCs were found to be camping in New Delhi for days to meet leaders, Union ministers and prominent MPs to lobby for ministerial berths. The infighting in the Congress was at an all-time high, and so were efforts to sabotage the smooth functioning of the V.B. Singh government. The CM became aware of all this and started holding meetings with health minister Lokpati Tripathi and other dissident leaders in the state. Moreover, despite the order concerning carrying of arms, violence, in one form or the other, continued to make the headlines.

V.B. Singh is also known for drastically curtailing the number of sittings of assembly sessions. Soon after he became CM, Opposition members kept disrupting the proceedings of the assembly and raised slogans against his government within the House. One way in which Singh dealt with the situation was to face the assembly as infrequently as possible. In 1986, the winter session of the assembly was not summoned, and in 1987, the budget session was convened for only 10 days. At the end of December 1987, the Vidhan Sabha recorded the lowest number of sittings in a year since Independence: only 32 sittings in the entire year. In 1952, this number was 79. However, it has been decreasing over the years. In 2023, there were just 20 sittings.

In the midst of all this, on 6 March 1987, the Lok Dal was split into two parts: Lok Dal (A) headed by Ajit Singh, son of its founder Charan Singh; and Lok Dal (B) headed by ex-CM H.N. Bahuguna. In the assembly, Satyapal Singh Yadav, an MLA from Tilhar in Shahjahanpur, became leader of Lok Dal (A), while the other faction was headed in the assembly by Mulayam Singh Yadav. But since Lok Dal (A) had a larger number of MLAs, Yadav, being the head of the single-largest party in Opposition, replaced Mulayam Singh as the LoP in the assembly. It was then that CM Singh and Mulayam Singh allegedly formed a tacit understanding, and the CM used Mulayam Singh to divide the Opposition on several issues. Though divided, the Opposition kept trying to utilize every opportunity to pull down V.B. Singh's government.

On another front, since the gates of the Ram temple in Ayodhya had been opened as per a court order on 1 February 1986, protests and reactions were seen in several parts of the country. In Meerut and certain other districts, the situation became tense from April 1987. But what happened in Meerut's Hashimpura and Maliana on 22–23 May 1987, later known as the Meerut massacre, was sufficient to tarnish CM V.B. Singh's image. The PAC killed several Muslims in Hashimpura and Maliana, and the resultant communal riots, including in other places, took the lives of more than 180 people. Disturbed by these incidents, PM Rajiv summoned V.B. Singh to New Delhi. Subsequently, thousands were arrested. Among them, nearly 2,500 were arrested from Meerut alone, but this did not improve the image of Singh and his government in any way. Instead, V.B. Singh was accused by Congressmen of following a pro-Hindu line on the Ram Janmabhoomi–Babri Masjid issue. The CM repeatedly denied the charge by saying, 'This is an absurd allegation.'[9]

Soon, V.B. Singh's problems caused by people within his

---

[9]Chawla, Prabhu, 'We Believe in the Protection of the Rights of the Minorities: Bir Bahadur Singh', *India Today*, 15 June 1987, https://tinyurl.com/4trz5t3h. Accessed on 6 March 2024.

own party also started getting aggravated. Sunil Shastri, the minister of power in his government, resigned on 21 July 1987. Two days earlier, two ministers of state—Surendra Singh who was in the Department of Cooperatives, and Zafar Ali Naqvi who was in the Department of Forests as well as attached to the CM's office—had resigned. Shastri was so annoyed with the CM that he said, 'Such an unwarranted and irresponsible chief minister should be removed by the leadership or else the people will have to do this themselves.'[10] While V.B. Singh claimed that he had sacked them because of inefficiency, the ministers who had resigned, on their part, accused Singh of many wrongdoings, including corruption.

On 24 September 1987, V.B. Singh completed two years as CM, having already completed 20 years as an MLA. He and his family faced serious allegations of corruption. From living in a mud house and leading a poverty-stricken existence on 1.48 acres of land in his village near Gorakhpur, he and his family had now allegedly acquired more than 55 acres of land, a palatial 12-room house in the village, and some flourishing businesses; they were also involved in controversial property deals in Gorakhpur and Lucknow.[11] Chief Minister V.B. Singh had defended himself quite unconvincingly by saying, 'I can only buy it if I pay the government the market rate.'[12]

Singh made many efforts to benefit from the Hindu momentum created by the Vishva Hindu Parishad (VHP). He tried to avoid confrontation with the VHP by tacitly facilitating

---

[10]Awasthi, Dilip, and Prabhu Chawla, 'Sanjay Singh Quits, Leaves Uttar Pradesh CM Bir Bahadur Singh Shaky', *India Today*, 15 September 1987, https://tinyurl.com/ykdbkmds. Accessed on 8 March 2024.

[11]Awasthi, Dilip, 'Uttar Pradesh's First Family's Land Transactions Create Suspicion', *India Today*, 30 September 1987, https://tinyurl.com/3snzb95w. Accessed on 8 March 2024.

[12]Ibid.

its programmes in Ayodhya and other parts of the state. A three-day Ramayana Mela was held in Ayodhya from 19 December 1985 in a big way, and Singh attended this large gathering of saints and *mahants*. However, opening the locks of Ram Janmabhoomi with a court order was not the end of the dispute but the beginning of a larger movement for construction of a Ram temple at the site. Therefore, V.B. Singh's problems also started aggravating further.

Another round of by-polls was to be soon held for the Allahabad and Baghpat Lok Sabha seats—the first fell vacant due to the resignation of Amitabh Bachchan and the second due to the demise of Chaudhary Charan Singh. The by-poll for the Baghpat seat was not held as it was not mandatory in those days to hold the by-election within the stipulated period of six months after vacancy.[13] But polls were held for the Allahabad seat, and V.P. Singh, who had quit the Rajiv Gandhi Cabinet and the Congress, decided to contest from there as an independent candidate, which drew the attention of the entire country. In an effort to prevent V.P. Singh from winning in Allahabad, CM V.B. Singh undertook a *padayatra* of the Allahabad parliamentary constituency and declared that he was doing so to stop 'separatist forces'. The *padayatris* included over a dozen ministers and nearly 100 MLAs of the Congress. Along the way, at some places, there were clashes between groups of V.P. Singh's supporters and Congress leaders. The Congress had got the much-beloved Arun Govil, who played Ram in Ramanand Sagar's TV serial *Ramayan*, to campaign for its candidates.[14] The person chosen to stand against V.P.

---

[13]This provision was mandated under Section 151 of the Representation of the People Act, 1951, in August 1996 only.

[14]Recently, Govil became politically relevant again when, for the 2024 Lok Sabha polls, the BJP dropped one of its very active MPs, Rajendra Agrawal, from the Meerut seat and fielded Govil in his place.

Singh was Sunil Shastri, who had resigned from the V.B. Singh government but was called by PM Rajiv and persuaded to contest against V.P. Singh, to which he eventually agreed. The PM had convinced him by saying, 'Only you can contest here.'[15]

The actual reason why Shastri was chosen was primarily because the Allahabad Lok Sabha seat had a sizeable number of voters of his community, the Kayasths. But it did not help, and V.P. Singh won the by-poll held on 16 June 1988. Arun Govil's popularity was very high in those days, but his appeal did not work in favour of the Congress. This loss was worrisome for the Congress as this indicated the probability of losing ground in several states, but what was of greater concern was losing ground in UP, which had 85 Lok Sabha seats at that time.

The cost of loss of the Allahabad seat proved very high for V.B. Singh. His patron Arun Nehru had already joined V.P. Singh. Prime Minister Rajiv had begun looking for V.B. Singh's replacement. When the CM visited Delhi after the by-poll results, he was given an appointment with PM Rajiv after a three-day wait, and when the meeting finally took place, the conversation was very brief: V.B. Singh was asked to resign. He resigned on 24 June 1988 to make way for his predecessor, N.D. Tiwari, who once again assumed charge as the CM.

V.B. Singh used various methods to keep his ministers under check, including appointing departmental secretaries with whom they were not comfortable, a style of functioning applied by some other CMs as well. As the CM, he proposed to establish five coaching centres in 1988–89 for SC and Scheduled Tribe (ST) students preparing for provincial civil service (PCS) examinations. However, this was implemented later by Mulayam Singh Yadav's government. After his stint as the CM, V.B. Singh was sworn in as a Union minister and

---

[15]In a telephonic conversation with Sunil Shastri.

was allotted the Ministry of Communications. During Singh's occupation of crucial positions, his protégés included the late Subrata Roy, the Sahara India chief, and late Amar Singh, who later became a SP MP.

Vir Bahadur Singh passed away at the early age of 54 on 30 May 1989 in Paris, where he had gone to attend a government programme. He had started his political journey with the Congress and was among the few who remained in the party until the end. One of his sons, Fateh Bahadur Singh, was first elected as an MLA from Paniyara in 1991 on a Congress ticket. Since then, after changing to the BSP and the Nationalist Congress Party (NCP), he was elected as a BJP MLA in 2017 and 2022 from Caimpiyarganj.

After V.B. Singh's demise, when the UP Assembly session started on 25 September 1989, Satyapal Singh Yadav, the LoP in the assembly, condoled his death:

> For politicians, the age between 40 and 60 is age of youthfulness. This is not the age of demise. When he [V.B. Singh] became the CM, it was believed that he would not be able to continue for even 15 days. But he crossed several obstacles and continued. His demise is a huge loss to UP, huge loss to Indian politics, huge loss for his party, but an even bigger loss to our political class, as he never worked with animosity.[16]

[16] *Vidhan Sabha ki Karyawahi*, 25 September 1989, UP Assembly Secretariat, Lucknow, pp. 85–6; author's translation.

15

MULAYAM SINGH YADAV

The One Who Drove the Congress Out of UP

Fifteenth CM: Mulayam Singh Yadav

Party: Janata Dal, Janata Dal (S), Samajwadi Party

Tenure: 5 December 1989–24 June 1991

4 December 1993–3 June 1995

29 August 2003–13 May 2007

Constituency: Jaswantnagar, Gunnaur

Days in Office: 6 years and 274 days

The UP Assembly polls and the Lok Sabha polls of 1989 were a big setback for the Congress in UP and Bihar. In the UP Assembly polls, the Janata Dal won 208 of the 356 seats it had contested from. These were the polls in which 18-year-olds had voted for the first time, as minimum age of the voters had been reduced from 21 years. Slogans like '*Naam Mulayam Singh hai lekin kaam bada fauladi hai*' (His name is Mulayam [soft], but his deeds are like iron) and '*Thakur ki buddhi, ahir ka bal, isi ka naam hai Janata Dal*' (The wisdom of a Thakur [referring to V.P. Singh's backing] and the strength of a Yadav [Mulayam Singh], this is what the Janata Dal signifies) were raised during electioneering amid political gossips. The Congress had contested 410 seats out of a total of 425 in the state but won just 94. The BJP was in alliance with the Janata Dal, but they still had friendly contests on several seats by pitting their candidates against each other. The BJP fought 275 seats and won 57.[1] These polls were fought in the light of the alleged Bofors scandal in the Rajiv Gandhi government. Former UP CM V.P. Singh had emerged as a new hope at the Centre. Many local leaders who had been groomed by former Congressmen Dr Ram Manohar Lohia and Charan Singh during their anti-Congress agitations were ready to lead under the aegis of another former Congressman, V.P. Singh, with the help of an emerging anti-Congress force, the BJP.

In fact, when the Janata Dal was formed by V.P. Singh in UP, Mulayam Singh Yadav was appointed as the president of the party. Former CM Ram Naresh Yadav, who was with the Janata Dal, could not digest this elevation, and on 12 April 1989, he resigned and joined the Congress, where Mulayam Singh's arch opponent Balram Singh Yadav had already been appointed as the state president. Another Yadav in the fray in the Congress was Chandrajit Yadav, who was once close to Indira Gandhi and Sanjay Gandhi. The Congress's 'Yadav trio' was deployed to counter the Janata Dal and Mulayam Singh Yadav's (backed by V.P. Singh) increasing following among backward communities in the state. But for the Congress, it was too late. The day Mulayam Singh took oath as the CM, it lost the state and has

[1]*Statistical Report on General Election 1989 to the Legislative Assembly of UP*, Election Commission of India, New Delhi.

not returned to power here since. Mulayam Singh was never in the Congress and had relentlessly spoken against its dynastic politics and corruption ever since he entered politics. Targeting the Congress, he had once even said in the assembly that no political or non-political organization should use a flag similar to the national flag, as he felt that the ordinary citizen might not be able to distinguish between the national flag and the Congress flag.[2] He was a product of the first anti-Congress agitation of 1960s under Dr Lohia, actively involved in the second anti-Congress agitation of mid-1970s headed by Lok Nayak Jayaprakash Narayan, and riding the third anti-Congress tirade under V.P. Singh as the UP CM.

Born on 22 November 1939 in Etawah, Mulayam Singh became a teacher after completing his bachelor's degree of training and his MA in Political Science. He had struggled a lot to reach the CM's chair. He won his first assembly election in 1967 at the age of 28 and was the youngest member in that assembly as well as one of the 44 MLAs who won on an SSP ticket. Mulayam Singh joined Chaudhary Charan Singh's BKD before the assembly polls in 1974 as he had lost the mid-term assembly polls in 1969 on an SSP ticket. He got closer to Charan Singh, and just before the end of Emergency, when the Janata Party was formed, he established himself as one of the key leaders of the Charan Singh camp. In 1977, when Charan Singh shifted to the Centre, he preferred his other protégé Ram Naresh Yadav, then Lok Sabha MP from Azamgarh, to head the UP government, while Mulayam Singh

[2] *Vidhan Sabha ki Karyawahi*, 29 March 1988, UP Assembly Secretariat, Lucknow, p. 79.

was sworn in as the minister of cooperatives, animal husbandry and rural industries. Later, in the Banarasi Das government, he was the minister of cooperatives.

Mulayam Singh lost the assembly poll from his home turf Jaswantnagar again in 1980 as a candidate of the Janata Party's Charan Singh faction. In 1969, he was defeated by the Congress's Bishambhar Singh Yadav, and in 1980 by Balram Singh Yadav of the Congress (I). In June 1982, Mulayam Singh was elected to the Legislative Council, where he became the LoP. In the assembly, Mohan Singh was the leader of the Lok Dal, which was the new name of Charan Singh's faction of the Janata Party.

When V.P. Singh was the CM of UP between June 1980 and July 1982, police encounters with dacoits made headlines almost daily, so did the allegations of his government killing several innocent people, particularly from the backward and other deprived communities. Mulayam Singh had compiled a list of 418 people who were allegedly killed in fake encounters across the state, submitted it to the governor and raised the issue several times in the Legislative Council. Consequently, many encounters were inquired into.

Mulayam Singh's emergence as a dominant Opposition leader was clearly evident in the ninth assembly, which was elected in early 1985, post PM Indira's assassination. In the sympathy wave, the Congress won 269 of the 425 seats, while the Lok Dal won 84.[3] The Lok Dal became the main Opposition party, and Mulayam Singh was elected as the LoP. During this time, due to Charan Singh's declining health, his party was becoming increasingly faction-ridden. His son Ajit Singh was gradually taking over the party affairs, and there were conflicts among ambitious leaders: apparently Ajit and Mulayam Singh

---

[3]*Statistical Report on General Election 1985 to the Legislative Assembly of UP*, Election Commission of India, New Delhi.

were fighting to claim Charan Singh's legacy. That was how, in March 1987, the Lok Dal was split into two parts: Lok Dal (A) and Lok Dal (B). Mulayam Singh aligned with the Bahuguna faction, and on 25 June 1987, he lost his status as the LoP in the assembly and was replaced by Shahjahanpur-based Satyapal Singh Yadav of the rival faction.

Before the consolidation of OBCs under the Janata Dal and Mulayam Singh, there had been continuous attacks on the Congress alleging that the grand old party was not accommodating the OBC or SC communities, as their representation in the government was very low. As the CM, Mulayam Singh began by trying to implement the Janata Dal's promise of providing a clean and open government. He had metal detectors removed from the CM's office and then reduced the escort vehicles in his official entourage from 12 to 8. On 17 January 1990, he declared, 'I have decided that if there is a red light, my car will stop and will move only after it turns green.'[4] He stated that his government would bring the CM under the ambit of Lokayukta. He declared that he would not suspend subinspectors and constables on corruption charges or for dereliction of duty but would instead suspend top IAS, Indian Police Service (IPS) and PCS officials because corruption starts from the top.[5] He promised the citizens that with the change of government, there would be a perceptible change in the system.

Chief Minister Mulayam Singh was criticized on the grounds that political interference had increased with his ascension, but on this point, he had articulated his views very early during his first tenure by saying:

---

[4] *Vidhan Sabha ki Karyawahi*, 17 January 1990, UP Assembly Secretariat, Lucknow, p. 95.

[5] Ibid. 94.

> Every elected representative can take forward problems of the common people. It is the duty of the *daroga*, superintendent of police and collector to take follow-up measures if the issue raised by an elected representative is correct, but they should not accept if it is not correct. I will not allow officials to term any justified issue raised by an MLA as political interference. This is called *vyavastha parivartan* [change of system].[6]

Mulayam Singh repeatedly advocated education in one's mother tongue. He said, 'Poor people's children cannot get into top-class services. That is the reason why village people are flooding MLAs' houses. This is unfortunate. If we were to discuss dishonesty and honesty, it will be seen that those who have studied in public schools are more dishonest; they are traitors. People from villages are less dishonest.'[7] There was uproar in the House about him terming those who studied in public schools as traitors.

Chief Minister Mulayam Singh also increased the pension for widows and enhanced pension coverage by reducing the minimum-age criteria from 65 years to 60 years. But during his first and second regimes in particular, his image was tarnished by his open association with known criminals.

Mulayam Singh's first government was moving forward with its promises and action plans; alongside, the movement for a Ram temple in Ayodhya, the birthplace of Lord Ram, was also being intensified by the VHP-RSS-BJP trio. There were efforts to resolve the Ram Janmabhoomi–Babri Masjid dispute, but ego problems surfaced between Mulayam Singh and PM V.P. Singh. The latter said that he would talk to leaders of the Ram temple movement directly. Mulayam Singh alleged that he was being kept in the dark on such a crucial issue

---

[6]Ibid. 112. Author's translation.

[7]Ibid. 117. Author's translation.

and said that none of the three (VHP, BJP and V.P. Singh) had informed him about their discussions. In a meeting on 23–24 June 1990, the Ram temple movement leaders gave four months to the state and central governments to resolve the issue, but once again, Mulayam Singh was not kept in the loop. He started feeling alienated and gradually turned into a critic of V.P. Singh.

In the meantime, on 2 August 1990, V.P. Singh sacked his deputy PM, Chaudhary Devi Lal, who was planning to mobilize the OBCs. Though his own caste (Jat) was not in the list of OBCs, Devi Lal had enjoyed vast support among the OBCs, as had Charan Singh earlier. In a move to alienate Devi Lal from the OBCs, V.P. Singh announced in his Independence Day speech on 15 August 1990 that the suggestions of the Mandal Commission Report would be implemented and the long-pending demand for 27 per cent reservation in government jobs to the OBCs would be fulfilled. His trick worked as Jats started participating in protests against the implementation of the Mandal report.

The Mandal report and mandir issues were progressing simultaneously. Several negotiations had been going on between leaders of the VHP and other stakeholders to resolve the Ayodhya dispute, but all efforts proved unsuccessful. In a meeting of the National Integration Council (NIC)[8] in September 1990, while leaders like Chandra Shekhar and Rajiv Gandhi praised Mulayam Singh, V.P. Singh was tight-lipped. Mulayam Singh's anger with V.P. Singh increased further.

On the other hand, to counter the OBC ascendency due to the Mandal movement, then BJP president L.K. Advani

---

[8]Constituted in 1961, the NIC is a body to review all matters pertaining to national integration and to make recommendations thereon. For details, see 'Background Note on National Integration Council', *Ministry of Home Affairs*, https://tinyurl.com/ys772xej. Accessed on 13 March 2024.

launched a rath yatra from Somnath on 25 September 1990, the birth anniversary of the BJS founder Deen Dayal Upadhyay, and was moving towards Ayodhya. V.P. Singh was under pressure, and he called a meeting of all CMs on 22 October 1990, as the four-month time given by the Ram temple movement leaders had ended. By 19 October, *kar sewaks* had already started moving from different parts of the country towards Ayodhya. When the Bihar government, headed by Lalu Prasad Yadav, arrested Advani in Samastipur on 23 October 1990, the BJP withdrew its support to the V.P. Singh government at the Centre and to the Mulayam Singh government in UP. Mulayam Singh was now trapped from all sides.

The incidents that polarized the whole electorate between the BJP and Mulayam Singh occurred on 30 October 1990 and 2 November 1990. There were police firings on the kar sewaks in Ayodhya. As a result, when the UP Assembly session started on 19 November 1990, there was pandemonium, and Kalyan Singh was not allowed to raise the issue. On the same day, Advani visited Ayodhya. Slogans of '*Mulayam Singh istifa do*' (Step down, Mulayam Singh) started resonating in the House. This was the beginning of a new era of politics in UP, when the fight for secularism was gradually taken over by Mulayam Singh while the BJP consolidated itself on the other side.

When the BJP withdrew its support, the Janata Dal was split into two parts, and the new faction headed by Chandra Shekhar was named Janata Dal (Socialist). Chandra Shekhar took oath as the PM on 10 November 1990 with the outside support of the Congress. Mulayam Singh saved his government in UP with the same formula—of taking outside support of the Congress. On 20 November 1990, Mulayam Singh moved a motion of confidence in the House when both factions of the Janata Dal were attacking each other and some members were manhandled.[9] Later, Mulayam Singh alleged that V.P. Singh did not want him to continue as the CM. He said, 'This is the most difficult challenge of my political life. My chief ministership is at stake, but without the decision of the court and without *baatcheet*, I will not allow the mosque to be disturbed.'[10] During voting on the confidence motion, the BSP MLAs supported Mulayam Singh while the CPI and CPI-M members abstained; the total votes cast for the motion were 224 and those against were 146.[11] His government survived. Despite supporting the government from the outside, the Congress's N.D. Tiwari continued to enjoy the post of LoP.

With growing political instability, the enthusiasm with which Mulayam Singh ran the government in the beginning seemed to be gradually diminishing as he had to spend his energy protecting his chair. In New Delhi, sensing that the Congress was intent on withdrawing support to his government, Chandra Shekhar resigned as the PM and recommended the dissolution of the Lok Sabha on 6 March 1991; it was dissolved on 13 March. As a consequence, a similar demand was voiced in the UP Assembly—Mulayam Singh was asked to step down. On 11 March 1991, the assembly was adjourned for the day after a full day of proceedings. The budget session was scheduled to start on 4 April 1991, but it was brought forward to 12 March 1991. On 4 April 1991, a day before he was to complete 16 months as the CM, sensing that the Congress was on the verge of announcing withdrawal of support to his government, Mulayam Singh recommended to Governor B. Satya Narayan Reddy to dissolve the assembly.

---

[9] *Vidhan Sabha ki Karyawahi*, 20 November 1990, UP Assembly Secretariat, Lucknow, p. 14.

[10] Ibid. 24. Author's translation.

[11] Ibid. 79.

Fresh assembly elections were held in June 1991, along with elections for the Lok Sabha. However, when his first tenure as the CM ended, Mulayam Singh and his politics appeared to be in the doldrums. His party, Janata Dal (S), renamed before the assembly polls as Janata Party, headed by Chandra Shekhar, got only 34 seats out of the 399 seats it had contested. The BJP got the majority with 221 of the 425 seats, and the Janata Dal's V.P. Singh faction got 92 seats,[12] after which its leader Kailash Nath Singh Yadav was appointed as the LoP in the eleventh assembly. The BJP's Kalyan Singh was sworn in as the CM, and people waited for Mulayam Singh's next move. Earlier, when the Lok Dal had split into two, Mulayam Singh had ultimately emerged as a clear winner, capturing Charan Singh's legacy; this time, he planned to take advantage of the split in the Janata Dal.

Mulayam Singh separated from Chandra Shekhar on Kanshi Ram's advice and founded the SP on 4 October 1992. Interestingly, its name was suggested by the BJP leader and former UP Speaker Keshari Nath Tripathi. A little over two months after that, on 6 December 1992, the Kalyan Singh government was sacked along with the BJP's three other state governments (Madhya Pradesh, Rajasthan and Himachal Pradesh) after the Babri Masjid demolition. The BJP was expecting sympathy from voters as its four governments had been sacked, but the Congress government at the Centre, headed by P.V. Narasimha Rao, kept delaying the assembly polls and appointed Motilal Vora, former CM of Madhya Pradesh, as the governor of UP. Assembly polls were finally held at the end of 1993.

This time, Mulayam Singh aligned with another emerging force, the BSP. The SP contested 256 seats and won 109, whereas the BSP contested 164 and won 67 seats.[13] In this new

---

[12] *Statistical Report on General Election 1991 to the Legislative Assembly of UP*, Election Commission of India, New Delhi.

[13] *Statistical Report on General Election 1993 to the Legislative Assembly of UP*,

social engineering, SCs and OBCs had voted in great numbers for this new alliance, leaving the BJP utterly gobsmacked. The Congress was truly at the margins with just 28 seats. V.P. Singh's Janata Dal faction won a mere 27 seats. Heading the SP–BSP coalition, Mulayam Singh was sworn in as the CM for the second time on 4 December 1993, and with 177 seats, the BJP's Kalyan Singh was now the LoP.[14] With the SP–BSP alliance, a new slogan was born: '*Mile Mulayam Kanshi Ram, hawa mein ud gaye "Jai Shri Ram*"' (When Mulayam Singh and Kanshi Ram met, the chanters of 'Jai Shri Ram' were ousted).

In Mulayam Singh's second tenure, the BSP was a driving force behind his government's policies, which were clearly oriented to issues related to the SCs and OBCs. The birth anniversaries of Dr B.R. Ambedkar and Maharishi Valmiki were declared as public holidays. His second government, following the central government's directive, implemented 27 per cent reservation for OBCs in government jobs. This benefit was also extended to them in educational institutions. However, the BSP placed a challenge before Mulayam Singh—to keep his base intact. In order to widen his OBC base, Mulayam Singh ordered the inclusion of at least one member from SC/ST/OBC in every selection committee for Group D and clerical grades.[15] In cases pertaining to SC atrocities, it was made mandatory to file a chargesheet within 14 days of the FIR.

In a bold decision, his government withdrew all 55 cases against gang-rape victim-turned-dacoit Phoolan Devi, who was in jail for 11 years without trial. Phoolan, who belonged to the backward Mallah community, was released on 18 February 1994 and inducted into the SP. She was later elected to the

---

Election Commission of India, New Delhi.

[14]Ibid.

[15]*Vidhan Sabha ki Karyawahi*, 1 February 1995, UP Assembly Secretariat, Lucknow, p. 3.

Lok Sabha twice from UP's Mirzapur–Bhadohi constituency in 1996 and 1999. However, she was killed at her Delhi residence on 25 July 2001 while she was an MP.

Mulayam Singh's second regime's notable contribution was reforms at the panchayat level. In April 1994, the SP government made crucial amendments to the Uttar Pradesh Panchayati Raj Act and the Uttar Pradesh Kshetra Panchayat and Zilla Panchayat Acts, through which reservations were granted to SC, ST and OBC candidates in rotation in the three-tier rural and urban panchayats in the state. As there was no data on caste-wise configurations, in August 1994, Mulayam Singh directed all 67 district magistrates to carry out a 'rapid census' to estimate the OBC population at the village level.[16] While seats were reserved for women as well, a provision was made to have reserved seats for every category of women in rotation. These panchayats have played a key role in empowerment at the grassroots level for all categories of people.

But soon, the Mulayam Singh government had to face a series of protests. Because of the implementation of the Mandal Commission Report, an anti-reservation movement was launched in the hill areas of UP by the Uttarakhand Kranti Dal on 11 July 1994. When this movement had almost petered out, a new one started in support of the decades-old demand for a separate Uttarakhand state carved out of the hill areas of UP. As the protesters headed towards Delhi to hold a *dharna* on Gandhi Jayanti at the Rampur Tiraha in Muzaffarnagar, they were lathi-charged and subjected to police firing, in which over half a dozen protesters were killed. Consequently, the Congress withdrew its support to his government.

---

[16]Awasthi, Dilip, and Ashok Damodaran, 'OBCs, SCs Quotas Extended to Local Bodies Pay Off for SP as Party Sweeps UP Panchayat Polls', *India Today*, 15 May 1995, https://tinyurl.com/6duehuek. Accessed on 8 March 2024.

The conflicts between the SP and the BSP were also increasing, and on 1 June 1995, the BSP withdrew support to his government. Governor Motilal Vora asked Mulayam Singh to resign, but he refused. Meanwhile, there was a split in the BSP as 25 MLAs of the party, led by Raj Bahadur, defected and formed a new group named BSP (R). It was after this that the infamous Guest House Case happened. Several BSP legislature members, including its prominent leader Mayawati, while holding a meeting at the VVIP Guest House in Lucknow, were allegedly beaten up by SP leaders and goons. On 3 June 1995, the Mulayam Singh government was dismissed. The BSP got the opportunity to govern the country's largest state as Mayawati was sworn in as CM with the outside support of the BJP.

But within six months, the BJP pulled support from the BSP government. Fresh assembly polls were held again in the last quarter of 1996. In the ensuing assembly polls, the SP contested 281 seats and won 110.[17] Mulayam Singh had already joined the central government under the then PM H.D. Deve Gowda and continued in the government of Inder Kumar Gujral as the minister of defence, leaving the state to others by appointing his associate and party leader Dhaniram Verma as the LoP in UP. In the following years, the BJP grew rapidly by expropriating space from the OBC communities. On the other side, Mulayam Singh was busy with his own project of social engineering. While his substantial support base of OBCs was appropriated by the BJP and the BSP to some extent, he returned to the poll strategy of the Janata Dal days and tried to spread his base among Rajputs (Thakurs) by elevating leaders like Amar Singh. A well-networked person among the corporate world and

---

[17] *Statistical Report on General Election 1996 to the Legislative Assembly of UP*, Election Commission of India, New Delhi.

Bollywood, Amar Singh, by inducting other politicians across parties, soon became a part of Mulayam Singh's coterie, later becoming almost indispensable for him.

As disclosed by the CPI-M stalwart Harkishan Singh Surjeet, who had played a prime role in the formation of the UF in 1996, Mulayam Singh had once almost ascended the PM's chair, but at the last moment, Gujral beat him to it. When Deve Gowda resigned on 12 April 1997, there were just three names in the contest, and a vote was to be taken. Mulayam Singh got a majority (120 votes or more), followed by G.K. Moopanar who got just 20. Gujral was not one of the contenders. Surjeet asked the UF convener Chandrababu Naidu to announce the decision and left for Moscow. But later, some leaders—Lalu Prasad Yadav and Sharad Yadav in particular—were insistent that 'under no circumstance' should Mulayam Singh be made the PM. Gujral was served up as a compromise candidate.[18] Lalu Yadav had insisted that the PM should be from the largest constituent of the UF, that is, the Janata Dal, and had threatened to break the UF if Mulayam Singh was chosen. Amar Singh was apprised of this on the night of 18 April over a phone call by Naidu.[19] As a result, the UF was saved and Gujral took oath as PM on 21 April. Mulayam Singh lost his chance.

Mulayam Singh often went against the many calculations and predictions made by political analysts about him. One of them happened in April 1999. When the BJP-headed NDA government under Atal Bihari Vajpayee fell by one vote on 17 April 1999 and Congress chief Sonia Gandhi claimed to have the majority to form an alternative government, Mulayam

---

[18] 'Why Mulayam Hates Fronts', *The Indian Express*, 11 January 2004, http://tinyurl.com/5cm5y97v. Accessed on 29 February 2024.

[19] Singh, Ram, and Yadav, Anshuman, *Mulayam Singh: A Political Biography*, Konark Publishers, New Delhi, 1998, p. 202.

Singh, contrary to expectations, backtracked on his earlier stance by saying that he would not support a person of foreign origin for the post of PM. Sonia Gandhi lost an opportunity that was considered almost certain.

In the meantime, in November 2000, the new state of Uttarakhand was carved out from 22 assembly and five Lok Sabha segments of UP, reducing the state assembly's strength to 403 and Lok Sabha's to 80. Mulayam Singh could not return to power in 2002 when assembly elections were held in February–March that year. Poll results created a piquant situation among the SP (143 seats), the BSP (98 seats) and the BJP (88 seats).[20] Without any two of these three joining hands, the formation of a majority government was not possible. Following a spell of 56 days of President's Rule from 8 March to 2 May 2002, a BJP–BSP coalition government headed by Mayawati of the BSP was formed on 3 May 2002.

In the meantime, in July 2002, when Mulayam Singh was part of the People's Front (a non-BJP and non-Congress alliance of parties, including leftist parties), the NDA, headed by the BJP, decided to field A.P.J. Abdul Kalam, among the top scientists of the country, as its candidate for the position of president, while the leftist parties put up Netaji Subhas Chandra Bose's former associate, Captain Lakshmi Sehgal, against him. Mulayam Singh decided to support Kalam, going against the plans of his People's Front. After all, that was what he was known for.

With Mayawati becoming the CM, there eventually arose an opportunity for Mulayam Singh. Since she had taken the oath to head a BSP–BJP coalition, a section of BJP MLAs had launched a campaign against her, and, feeling too much pressure, she resigned and recommended dissolution of the assembly

[20]*Statistical Report on General Election 2002 to the Legislative Assembly of UP*, Election Commission of India, New Delhi.

on 25 August 2003. Governor Vishnu Kant Shastri accepted her resignation, but he did not accept the recommendation of dissolving the assembly.

Thus, Mulayam Singh was sworn in as the CM for the third time on 29 August 2003, in a tacit understating with then PM Vajpayee and his close associate Pramod Mahajan. Kalyan Singh's Rashtriya Kranti Party (RKP) and Ajit Singh's RLD joined the Mulayam Singh government. Within weeks of coming to power, he withdrew cases that were lodged under Prevention of Terrorism Act (POTA) by Mayawati's government previously, including those against Raghuraj Pratap Singh, popularly known as Raja Bhaiya, an independent MLA from Kunda since 1993. In this tenure, Mulayam Singh took Raja Bhaiya into his cabinet.

Mulayam Singh's most popular scheme, Kanya Vidya Dhan, was launched during this time, under which a one-time amount of ₹20,000 was to be provided to girls who would pass Class 10. This step resulted in a rapid increase in the enrolment of girls in higher classes. In 2006, he started a pension scheme and a free bus pass scheme for those who were jailed during Emergency, whom he termed as Loktantra Senani.

Mulayam Singh's third regime had the backing and influence of big corporate houses and the presence of Bollywood personalities. Amar Singh had more influence on his decisions than anyone. Some of Mulayam Singh's old associates like Beni Prasad Verma and Azam Khan quit his party; however, both returned to his side later. For years, Mulayam Singh and Kalyan Singh were considered to be poles apart in UP politics, but they joined hands twice, first in 2003, then again in 2009. Just before the assembly polls of 2007, Ajit Singh's RLD withdrew its three ministers from the Mulayam Singh government, while Kalyan Singh had already withdrawn his support before the 2004 Lok Sabha polls when he returned to the BJP. When the assembly polls were held in 2007, the SP got only 97 seats, and its staunch rival BSP got a majority with 206 seats in the 403-member House.[21] Mayawati became the CM again.

While Dr Lohia had initiated the politics of OBCs, and Ram Naresh Yadav became CM for some time, it was Mulayam Singh who had taken these communities to corridors of power in the real sense. He took over the legacy of 'Commander' Arjun Singh Bhadoria in his region instead of Nathu Singh Yadav by getting ticket from Jaswantnagar in 1967. He had to fight relentlessly with Balram Singh Yadav of the Congress (I) and with Ajit Singh and Om Prakash Chautala to capture and carry forward the legacy of Charan Singh and Devi Lal, respectively. He left them all behind in his style. In the later decades of his life, Mulayam Singh was seen making compromises. He categorically said once, 'I can't tolerate anything against Amar. Amar saved me from going to jail.'[22] He was known to go to any extent to help his friends. He was also known for his friendships across party lines and across the country, and until his demise, he remained the most prominent secular face of Indian politics. Known for quick decision-making, he promoted the use of Hindi not only as the CM but also as the defence minister.

It is ironic that as a street fighter who emerged as a leader criticizing the Congress's dynastic rule, he, like many other politicians, promoted the dynastic rule of his own family in his

---

[21]*Statistical Report on General Election 2007 to the Legislative Assembly of UP*, Election Commission of India, New Delhi.

[22]'Mulayam Singh Defends Amar Singh, Brother Shivpal Yadav as SP Meet Ends in Acrimony', *The Indian Express*, 25 October 2016, http://tinyurl.com/42d6d9k6. Accessed on 30 April 2023.

home state when he reached the top position. At one point of time, Mulayam Singh, his son Akhilesh, daughter-in-law Dimple, cousin Ram Gopal, brother Shivpal, nephews Aditya aka Ankur, Dharmendra and Anshul, and as his brother's wife Premlata were elected representatives in the Lok Sabha, Rajya Sabha, the assembly, and the panchayat, and/or occupied crucial positions in his party.

Mulayam Singh passed away on 10 October 2022 in Gurugram. On his demise, Union Minister of Home Affairs and Cooperation Amit Shah said that he 'remained active in politics for decades with his unique political skills. During the Emergency, he raised his voice for the restoration of democracy. He always will be remembered as a grassroots leader of the masses. His death marks the end of an era in Indian politics.'[23]

Until his demise, his village Saifai, in Etawah, remained a crucial place on UP's political map. On Republic Day 2023, the BJP government announced the Padma Vibhushan, the second highest civilian award, posthumously for him, which was received by his son Akhilesh.

[23]Condolence message issued through the Press Information Bureau, Government of India, New Delhi, on 10 October 2022.

16

KALYAN SINGH

The First BJP CM of Uttar Pradesh

Sixteenth CM: Kalyan Singh

Party: Bharatiya Janata Party

Tenure: 24 June 1991–6 December 1992

21 September 1997–12 November 1999

Constituency: Atrauli

Days in Office: 3 years and 217 days

To understand the journey of Kalyan Singh and the significance of the first majority BJP government in UP, it is important to understand the journey of the BJS and the BJP. The BJS was established as a separate political outfit by RSS workers on 21 October 1951 at the national level, but its UP unit had already been established on 2 September 1951, with Rao Krishna Pal Singh of Awagarh (Etah) as its president. However, in the 1952 elections, Prabhudatt Brahmachari was fielded against Jawaharlal Nehru from the Allahabad District East-cum-Jaunpur District West as an independent candidate, for which Rajendra Singh (Rajju Bhaiya) of the RSS had also filed nomination as a dummy candidate. Brahmachari stood fourth against Nehru on that two-member seat.

The BJS was a part of three governments in the state before 1991. First, in 1967, it was part of the SVD government of Charan Singh; then in 1970, it was part of the short-lived coalition government of T.N. Singh; and again in 1977, it was part of the Janata Party government. It had supported the government of Mulayam Singh Yadav from the outside in 1989. In 1991, for the first time, the BJP, which was formed on 6 April 1980 after breaking away from the Janata Party, as the new avatar of the BJS, got full majority in UP.

In 1952, in the first UP assembly polls after Independence, the BJS had won only two seats (Omkar Singh from Dataganj-North, and Ummed Singh from Utraula North East). In the 1957 assembly polls, it had done a little better, as 17 of the 236 candidates it fielded had won. In the third assembly polls in 1962, the party had fielded 377 candidates, won only 49 seats and emerged as the main Opposition party in the assembly. The LoPs in the assembly had been from the BJS—first it was Yadavendra Dutt Dubey, an MLA from Jaunpur City (28 March 1962–2 February 1964); then Sharda Bhakt Singh, an MLA from Pali in Hardoi (2 February 1964–2 April 1965); and then Madhav Prasad Tripathi, an MLA from Banganga West in Basti (2 April 1965–9 March 1967). Dubey was removed by the party based on allegations that he had a role in the defeat of the BJS founder Deen Dayal Upadhyay in the 1963 Lok Sabha by-poll he had contested from Jaunpur. In those by-polls, the BJS had allied with J.B. Kripalani and the Socialist Party, and Kripalani (as an independent candidate) and Dr Ram Manohar Lohia won from Amroha and Farrukhabad, respectively, but Upadhhay had lost.

In 1967, the BJS had won 98 seats.[1] In addition, one of its leaders had won as an independent candidate, thus bringing the total to 99. Kalyan Singh, like his predecessors V.B. Singh and Mulayam Singh Yadav, was also elected as an MLA for the first time in 1967. As part of a united Opposition, the BJS had supported Ram Chandra Vikal, an independent MLA, as the LoP, and the party had later joined the Chaudhary Charan Singh government when it was formed on 3 April that year. However, their alliance was dissolved in February 1968. Nanaji Deshmukh, one of the founders of BJS, wrote about his experience of the BJS in the SVD government, 'Our party lost the image of a party with a difference… Our people became important leaders but we were neither able to retain our image, nor was our organization able to remain the same. A party of workers became a party of leaders.'[2] However, within a year of the SVD government's oath, Dr Lohia and Deen Dayal Upadhyay, the two pillars of the first anti-Congress agitation since Independence, had passed away, the former on 12 October 1967 at the age of 57 and the latter on 11 February 1968 at the age of 52. In the 1969 mid-term polls, the BJS had fielded 397 candidates but won only 49 seats,[3] bringing the party down almost to the level of 1962. A large segment of votes, particularly of the OBCs, which had been garnered by the BJS in 1967, had shifted towards Charan Singh's new party, the BKD, and the seats and votes for the BJS were reduced to almost their earlier level.

---

[1] *Statistical Report on General Election 1967 to the Legislative Assembly of UP*, Election Commission of India, Delhi.

[2] Yadav, Shyamlal, 'Jan Sangh Founder Had Warned RSS of Losing Shine: Book', *The Indian Express*, 11 October 2014, https://tinyurl.com/38mhw2fy. Accessed on 3 April 2024.

[3] *Statistical Report on General Election 1969 to the Legislative Assembly of UP*, Election Commission of India, Delhi.

In 1974, the BJS had won 61 of 401 seats it had contested.[4] After the BJP was formed in April 1980, in the UP Assembly polls that year, out of the 400 seats it contested, it won only 11.[5] On 19 August 1984, Kalyan Singh took charge as the president of the BJP in UP because the president before him, Madhav Prasad Tripathi, had passed away. In the 1985 assembly polls, which were held after Indira Gandhi's assassination, the BJP won only 16 of the 347 seats it contested.[6] In 1989, it had contested 275 seats (most of them in alliance with the Janata Dal), won 57 seats[7] and supported the Mulayam Singh government from outside. After that, the campaign for the Ram temple in Ayodhya intensified.

After a long political journey, with the hard Hindutva campaign of the late 1980s, BJP's '*achche din*' finally seemed to have arrived, as it got a historic mandate in 1991 with a full majority, winning 221 of the 425 seats it contested.[8] This was the first time that the BJP had a majority on its own in the UP assembly. In the years when non-upper-caste communities were competing for power in the state, the BJP named Kalyan Singh—an OBC from the Lodh community who had been associated with the RSS for decades, a mix of Mandal (OBC) and Kamandal (Hindutva)—as the chief ministerial face during the 1991 polls. Kalyan Singh was sworn in as the CM, while Kalraj Mishra replaced him as president of the state BJP. If

---

[4] *Statistical Report on General Election 1974 to the Legislative Assembly of UP*, Election Commission of India, Delhi.

[5] *Statistical Report on General Election 1980 to the Legislative Assembly of UP*, Election Commission of India, Delhi.

[6] *Statistical Report on General Election 1985 to the Legislative Assembly of UP*, Election Commission of India, Delhi.

[7] *Statistical Report on General Election 1989 to the Legislative Assembly of UP*, Election Commission of India, Delhi.

[8] *Statistical Report on General Election 1991 to the Legislative Assembly of UP*, Election Commission of India, Delhi.

the Sangh Parivar's movement for the Ram temple in Ayodhya benefitted the BJP in any elections visibly, it was in the 1991 assembly poll of UP. In the 1991 elections, religious leaders involved in the Ram temple movement addressed election rallies and sought votes for BJP candidates as there was no restriction on them back then.

Born in Madholi village near Atrauli, Kalyan Singh graduated with a BA and licentiate in teaching (LT), and was a teacher prior to his election as an MLA. There were several ups and downs in his public life between the time he entered the assembly for the first time at the age of 35, and when he was sworn in as the sixteenth CM of UP on 24 June 1991 at the age of 59. Similarly, a lot had happened to the politics of the BJP and the erstwhile BJS, as can be seen in the politics of the state until this point.

Kalyan Singh was not inducted into the SVD government in 1967, in which senior BJS leader Ram Prakash Gupta was the deputy CM and Ganga Bhakt Singh was the minister of cooperatives. He was also not inducted into the T.N. Singh government, in which the prominent face from the BJS was Madhav Prasad Tripathi (minister of agriculture and scientific research). It was in the Janata Party government under Ram Naresh Yadav that Kalyan Singh first became minister and held the portfolios of health, public health and family welfare. On 11 February 1979, he resigned along with BJS-backed ministers. However, he remained active as an MLA representing his home turf Atrauli.

After being sworn in as the CM, on 21 June 1991, Kalyan Singh visited Ayodhya the very next day along with all his ministers and took a resolution at Ram Janmbhoomi that,

'Ram Lalla, hum aaye hain, mandir yahin banayenge' (Lord Rama, we have arrived here, we will build the temple here). During his first chief ministership, Rewati Raman Singh of the Janata Dal was the LoP and Keshari Nath Tripathi of the BJP was the Speaker.

The Kalyan Singh government began its stint effectively. Controlling crime and providing a clean administration were Singh's declared priorities. He started booking MLAs with criminal backgrounds one after the other. Four of them—Hari Shankar Tiwari (Congress, from Chillupar), D.P. Yadav (Janata Dal, Janata Party, from Bulandshahr), Madan Bhaiya (Janata Party, from Khekra) and Atiq Ahmed (independent, from Allahabad West)—were put in jail, among a few others; cases were registered against even more. His government also withdrew the security cover of over 200 MLAs and imposed restrictions on arms licenses to private persons. (Arms licenses had been liberalized in Mulayam Singh Yadav's government.) He tried to control frequent transfers and postings of officials. He immediately ordered the resignation of Dr Dinesh Jauhari, minister of health, medical education and family welfare, on 14 October 1991, when he came to know about the mess regarding transfers and postings in his department, which were in violation of the CM's directions.

Perhaps the most notable work that the Kalyan Singh government was known for was the control of copying in the board examinations. An ordinance called Nakal Adhyadesh (Anti-copying Ordinance), which made copying in examinations a cognizable offence, was promulgated just before the board examinations in 1992; on 24 November 1992, a bill was passed by the assembly as well. The step brought the CM and his minister of intermediate education, Rajnath Singh, praise from the educated sections but made the BJP government unpopular.

Dirty politics to unseat Kalyan Singh started within the BJP just a year after he became the CM. On 14 July 1992, two dozen MLAs, mostly Brahmins, met Kalraj Mishra at the party office in Lucknow to complain about the functioning of the Kalyan Singh government.[9] Kalraj Mishra rushed to Delhi to apprise the central leadership of the development. The then BJP chief, Murli Manohar Joshi, was in favour of replacing Kalyan Singh with Kalraj Mishra, but L.K. Advani, then the LoP in the Lok Sabha, stood firmly behind Kalyan Singh, and it was decided that there would be no change.[10] In the meantime, the VHP was going ahead with its Ayodhya agenda. On 22 July 1992, the VHP announced holding of a kar sewa at Ram Janmabhoomi in Ayodhya. Prakash Singh, a 1959-batch IPS officer, who was appointed as the director general of police by Kalyan Singh on 22 July 1991, took some remedial action, and the kar sewa was stopped. However, Prakash Singh was removed from his post on 30 September 1992, and one of the reasons for this was the conflict between him and Nripendra Mishra, principal secretary to the CM. Mishra was also later removed from the CM's office and shifted to Greater Noida Authority.

Despite all his efforts to provide clean and effective administration, Kalyan Singh's first government could not continue for long. Fighting within the BJP on caste lines had already started surfacing. In the meantime, the atmosphere in Ayodhya was also heating up, as the VHP had again announced holding of a kar sewa from 6 December 1992 and the mobilization of kar sewaks started across the country. Prime Minister P.V. Narasimha Rao was busy trying to resolve the

---

[9]Ghimire, Yubaraj, and Dilip Awasthi, 'Kalyan Singh Struggles to Subdue Revolt among Members Seeking His Removal', *India Today*, 31 August 1992, https://tinyurl.com/4n24w2sa. Accessed on 9 March 2024.
[10]Ibid.

Ayodhya dispute, and meetings of the NIC were being held one after the other. Kalyan Singh did not attend the NIC meeting on 24 November 1992, alleging that it was being used as an anti-BJP forum and did not intend to resolve the Ayodhya dispute.[11] Heated discussions were seen in the assembly on 25 November 1992, which later proved to be the last day of the eleventh assembly. Kalyan Singh said, 'I have already said this at the NIC, I have already said this here and am reiterating again that the disputed structure is completely secure… I am hopeful of a settlement within the next 10 days.'[12] He attended two meetings of the NIC, which were held in Delhi, where he gave written assurances that the disputed structure would be protected.[13] He also gave an undertaking to the same effect before the Supreme Court.

Leaders in the BJP, who were eying the CM's chair, thought that if the Ayodhya problem could not be solved and if any damage was caused to the disputed structure on 6 December 1992, Kalyan Singh would be held responsible, and as fallout, someone else might replace him.[14] But what happened in Ayodhya on 6 December proved their calculations wrong; things went beyond everyone's control. The disputed structure was demolished by the kar sewaks. The Kalyan Singh government, along with the other BJP governments of three states, were dismissed the same night. As his government failed to keep its promise and undertaking before the Supreme

---

[11] *Vidhan Sabha ki Karyawahi,* 24 November 1992, UP Assembly Secretariat, Lucknow, p. 115.

[12] *Vidhan Sabha ki Karyawahi*, 25 November 1992, UP Assembly Secretariat, Lucknow, p. 164; author's translation.

[13] *Vidhan Sabha ki Karyawahi*, 24 November 1992, UP Assembly Secretariat, Lucknow, p. 115.

[14] Based on the author's conversation with Baleshwar Tyagi, who served as the MoS for home in those days and was actively involved in the Ayodhya situation from the UP government's side.

Court of protecting the structure, contempt proceedings were initiated against Kalyan Singh. He did not make any bureaucrat a scapegoat and categorically took full responsibility. On 24 October 1994, a Supreme Court bench comprising Chief Justice M.N. Venkatachaliah and Justice G.N. Ray sentenced Kalyan Singh to a token imprisonment of one day and fined him ₹20,000, which Singh accepted. He was imprisoned for a day at Tihar Jail in New Delhi.

In light of the expected sympathy votes on account of the sacking of its governments, the BJP thought it would have a miracle in the next assembly election, whenever it was going to be held. But the P.V. Narasimha Rao government at the Centre kept delaying the election. They were held after nearly a year, towards the end of 1993. The BJP came out with a slogan, '*Aaj paanch pradesh, kal saara desh*' (We will win five state assembly polls now and Lok Sabha polls later), as elections were being held for five state assemblies.

In UP, the victory of Mulayam Singh's alliance with Kanshi Ram's BSP in the 1993 polls proved just how overconfident the BJP was. Kalyan Singh continued as the LoP in the assembly till 12 June 1995. Such was the anger among students about the Anti-copying Act that the Kalyan Singh government's minister of intermediate education, Rajnath Singh, lost his own assembly seat in Lucknow's Mahona. The BJP had to look for other options to regain power in UP. Due to cracks within the SP–BSP coalition, the BSP withdrew from the government and the BJP supported Mayawati from outside to form a new government. Consequently, Kalyan Singh lost his status as LoP to Mulayam Singh Yadav.

However, within five months the BJP withdrew its support to Mayawati's government, and after a short stint of President's Rule, fresh assembly polls were held in September–October 1996. The BJP could not secure a majority as it won just 174 seats out of 425; the SP of Mulayam Singh won 110 seats; the BSP, which contested in alliance with the Congress, won 67 seats, while the Congress won 33; and the Bharatiya Kisan Kamgar Party (BKKP) of Ajit Singh won eight seats.[15] After many rounds of backdoor negotiations between different parties, the BJP and the BSP again came up with a formula in the third week of March 1997 for jointly running the government. Ministries were divided among both parties and it was decided that the CM's chair would be shared by leaders of both parties every six months in rotation. Under this formula, Mayawati was sworn in as CM on 21 March 1997. The BJP's Keshari Nath Tripathi was elected as Speaker. The SP's Dhaniram Verma, who was Speaker during the SP–BSP government in 1993–95, was now the LoP. However, in the BJP, the message started gaining ground that Kalyan Singh was being sidelined as he was not in favour of this alliance.

As per the terms of the BJP–BSP formula, the Mayawati Cabinet resigned after six months, and on 21 September 1997, Kalyan Singh took oath as CM for the second time, with the same ministers as in the Mayawati government. But cracks within the alliance began developing when Kalyan Singh recommended a Central Bureau of Investigation (CBI) inquiry into some decisions of the Mayawati government. Within a month, on 19 October 1997, Mayawati withdrew her support to the government, and all BSP ministers resigned. The BJP, in an effort to save its government, engineered defections from other parties by indulging in alleged horse-trading. Kalyan Singh claimed that his government still enjoyed a majority, but Governor Romesh Bhandari asked him to prove his majority on the floor of the House on 21 October.

---

[15] *Statistical Report on General Election 1996 to the Legislative Assembly of UP*, Election Commission of India, New Delhi.

Hectic political activity was taking place. The Congress was divided as 22 members under Naresh Agrawal (MLA from Hardoi) had formed the Akhil Bharatiya Loktantrik Congress (ABLTC). Chaudhary Narendra Singh (Rajpur, Kanpur), along with 12 MLAs from the BSP, broke away to form the Jantantrik Bahujan Samaj Party (JBSP). The seven-member Janata Dal Legislature Party was also divided with Gadwara MLA Rajaram Pandey forming a new party named Janata Dal (Rajaram). These new parties extended support to Kalyan Singh to save his government. Independent MLAs under Raja Bhaiya of Kunda also supported his government. Amidst slogan shouting and aggressive gesticulations, someone among the MLAs flung a small mic towards the Speaker, and several other MLAs started throwing objects at each other.[16] In the ensuing bedlam, many MLAs, ministers as well as Speaker Tripathi were injured. Interestingly, after the violence, all members from the SP, BSP, Congress, CPI-M, BKKP, Janata Dal and some others walked out. Amid this, the confidence motion was tabled, with only the ruling alliance partners present to debate it and vote. After a brief discussion, all 222 MLAs present in the House voted in favour of the motion, and the Kalyan Singh government survived.[17] Governor Bhandari sent a recommendation to the Centre to impose President's Rule in the state considering the violence that had occurred in the assembly. Rajnath Singh was the state BJP president at the time. The BJP paraded its MLAs in front of the president at the Rashtrapati Bhavan, and the central government dropped the idea to impose President's Rule.

Once things quietened down, Kalyan Singh expanded his government on 27 October 1997. While pacifying several conflicting groups and their leaders, each with their own

[16] *Vidhan Sabha ki Karyawahi,* 21 October 1997, UP Assembly Secretariat, Lucknow, p. 2.

[17] Ibid. 18.

ego, at a time when the ambitions of many BJP leaders were high, Kalyan Singh's second government soon started facing a considerable amount of trouble. His relations with party leaders at the Centre started to deteriorate, particularly with the party patriarch Atal Bihari Vajpayee.

When the 1998 Lok Sabha elections approached, the stakes were high for the BJP, the main claimant to power at the Centre under Vajpayee. The party was facing tough competition on many seats. It had fielded D.P. Yadav (a gangster-turned-politician who was sent to jail by Kalyan Singh's first government) from the Sambhal seat against the SP chief and then minister of defence Mulayam Singh Yadav. D.P. Yadav had enviable influence in the area and even Kalyan Singh campaigned for him. Mulayam Singh, sensing that his chances were weakening in Sambhal, devised an unusual strategy. In order to help Mulayam Singh, Governor Bhandari sacked the Kalyan Singh government on 21 February 1998, and the same evening, Jagdambika Pal (MLA from Basti) was sworn in as the new CM after the SP, BSP and Congress wrote to the governor offering their support. Pal had earlier defected from the Congress along with Naresh Agrawal and was holding the portfolio of minister of transport in the Kalyan Singh government. Allies of the BJP were not happy about seat-sharing for the Lok Sabha polls.[18] Polling was to begin the next day, on 22 February 1998. The trick seemed to have worked in Mulayam Singh's favour as the government machinery came under the control of his supporters and well-wishers.

However, Pal's elevation was challenged before the Allahabad High Court, and on 23 February 1998, while hearing the petition filed by Kalyan Singh's minister Narendra Singh Gaur,

---

[18]Singh, Ram, and Anshuman Yadav, *Mulayam Singh: A Political Biography*, Konark Publishers, New Delhi, 1998, p. 207.

the bench of Justice Birendra Dikshit and Justice Dilip Kumar Seth declared it to be a 'wholly illegal exercise of the powers conferred on [Governor Bhandari]'.[19] With this verdict, within 48 hours of Pal's taking oath as CM, Kalyan Singh was back in the CM's chair on 23 February 1998. But Pal was yet to concede defeat. On a special leave petition filed by him, a Supreme Court bench comprising Chief Justice M.M. Punchhi, Justice S.C. Agrawal and Justice K.T. Thomas, on 24 February 1998, ordered a special session of the assembly to be convened on 26 February, where 'the only Agenda in the Assembly would be to have a composite floor-test between the contending parties [Kalyan Singh and Pal] in order to see which out of the two contesting claimants of Chief Ministership has a majority in the House'.[20] As per the Supreme Court's directive, chairs were placed for both claimants on two sides of the Speaker, with Pal sitting on the left and Kalyan Singh on the right. After voting was conducted, the Speaker announced that 225 votes were in favour of Kalyan Singh and 196 in favour of Pal, so the Kalyan Singh government survived. As it turned out, in this battle, Mulayam Singh was the only victor as he won the Sambhal seat, and Pal was the only loser. Based on the high court order, Pal was deprived of using the prefix 'former CM', making him ineligible to use the facilities of the position.

In the meantime, when results of the 1998 Lok Sabha elections were declared, out of the 182 seats in total that the BJP had won, 58 were from UP (including five of Uttarakhand, which was a part of UP in those days, and one of Maneka Gandhi, who contested as an independent candidate with the BJP's support), and Vajpayee was sworn in as the PM of the country on 19 March 1998, heading a coalition called the NDA.

---

[19] *Narendra Kumar Singh Gaur vs Union of India and Others* on 23 February 1998, 1998(1)AWC438.

[20] *Jagdambika Pal vs Union of India and Ors.* on 24 February 1998, AIR1998SC998.

Thereafter, relations between Kalyan Singh and Vajpayee (who was the Lok Sabha MP from Lucknow) started worsening day by day. After the Vajpayee government collapsed for one vote on 17 April 1999, and post the Kargil War, fresh Lok Sabha elections were held in September-October 1999. Counting was done on 6 October, and in UP, the BJP's presence was reduced to just 30 seats (including Maneka Gandhi) out of 85. However, Vajpayee managed to retain the tally of his party at 182 (excluding Maneka Gandhi) and took oath again to continue as the PM. But he was not ready to pardon Kalyan Singh. Several rounds of talks were held within the party for the next course of action. On 8 November 1999, Kalyan Singh, Rajnath Singh, Lalji Tandon and Kalraj Mishra were summoned to Delhi, and Kalyan Singh sensed that his chapter was being closed. He skipped the meeting and went to Ayodhya the next day, criticizing Vajpayee for not fulfilling the promise of the Ram temple. Considering that Kalyan Singh might leave the party, the BJP leadership decided not to replace him with a leader about whom he had reservations, like Rajnath Singh, Kalraj Mishra or Lalji Tandon, and chose the septuagenarian Ram Prakash Gupta as his successor. Kalyan Singh resigned on 11 November 1999, and the next day, Gupta was sworn in as the CM.

On 26 November 1999, Kalyan Singh had an outburst against Vajpayee, terming him as a conspirator, liar and a mask of the BJP. Soon after that, he again said, 'For the past one year, Vajpayee and a section of upper-caste leaders had been conspiring to dethrone me from the post of Chief Minister as I belong to the backward castes.'[21] The BJP had had enough. On the same day, Kalyan Singh's primary membership of the party was suspended.

[21]Mishra, Subhash, 'Kalyan Singh Becomes Reticent after His Suspension from Primary Membership of BJP', *India Today*, 13 December 1999, https://tinyurl.com/3epv689a. Accessed on 9 March 2024.

Kalyan Singh then formed the RKP. It fielded 335 candidates out of 403 seats in the 2002 assembly polls but could win only a dismal four seats, which included two of his own, as he had contested from two constituencies. Surprisingly, although his party had secured just 4.04 per cent votes on the 335 seats it contested, it ensured a loss to the BJP, which was now reduced to 88 seats in the assembly, despite high-flying claims that were made before the polls. When the Mulayam Singh government was formed in August 2003, the RKP joined it, and Kalyan Singh's son Rajveer Singh 'Raju' was sworn in as minister of health, Ayurveda and homoeopathic medicines, and Kusum Rai, a BJP corporator who had later quit the BJP with Kalyan Singh and was elected as an MLC, as minister of the PWD.

But neither the BJP nor Kalyan Singh felt happy after the separation as both had to suffer electoral losses. Vajpayee was also under pressure, in view of the 2004 Lok Sabha polls. Kalyan Singh's re-entry into the BJP became almost a certainty when he called on Vajpayee in Lucknow on 24 December 2003 at Lalji Tandon's residence to offer birthday greetings (Vajpayee's birth anniversary is on 25 December). On 21 January 2004, Vajpayee sent Pramod Mahajan to Lucknow, where he had a secret meeting with Kalyan Singh.[22] The next day, in Lucknow, Kalyan Singh praised Vajpayee and the BJP's 'feel-good factor' (the party's poll campaign in 2004) factor, and on 23 January, central leaders, including the party president M. Venkaiah Naidu, deputy PM L.K. Advani, Pramod Mahajan and Murli Manohar Joshi, met at Vajpayee's residence and approved the return of Kalyan Singh. On 3 February 2004, he finally re-joined the BJP, and Rajveer and Kusum Rai resigned from the UP government.

[22]'Kalyan's Secret Rendezvous with Mahajan', *The Times of India*, 22 Janury 2004, https://tinyurl.com/bdec98uk. Accessed on 14 March 2024.

The day Kalyan Singh re-entered the BJP, he said, 'I will make BJP number one in UP. In the 2004 polls my party will get at least 50 [Lok Sabha] seats.'[23] However, when results were announced, though he won from Bulandshahr and Vajpayee from Lucknow, the BJP could garner less than 10 out of the state's 80 Lok Sabha seats, thus losing power at the Centre.

In the 2007 assembly polls, Kalyan Singh was again the face of the BJP in UP and the Kalraj Mishra–Kalyan Singh duo, which controlled the BJP in UP for many years, was once more very actively involved in election management and campaigning, among other things. However, the party could not cross the benchmark of 51 out of the 350 seats it had contested. Both Kalyan Singh and Kalraj Mishra lost their impact and were relegated to the sidelines.

On 9 November 2008, the BJP declared Kusum Rai as one of its candidates for the Rajya Sabha biennial polls from UP. Kalyan Singh had been eyeing this chance for his son Rajveer. His detractors in the party seemed to have deliberately fielded Kusum Rai to humiliate Kalyan. Expectedly, he quit the BJP again on 20 January 2009, and on doing so, he said, 'It was a political blunder to have rejoined the party.'[24] In the 2009 Lok Sabha elections, he was elected to the Lok Sabha from Etah as an independent candidate. The SP did not field any candidate against him, and they helped each other.

But within a few months, SP leaders started distancing themselves from Kalyan Singh, thinking that the votes of his caste had not been transferred to SP candidates in some areas, and also that some sections of Muslims had distanced themselves from SP because of its association with Kalyan

---

[23]Yadav, Shyamlal, '"Main BJP ko number ek party...": Interview with Kalyan Singh', *India Today* (Hindi), 16 February 2004.

[24]'"Humiliated" Kalyan Singh Resigns from BJP', *The Indian Express*, 20 January 2009, http://tinyurl.com/ddbrcu56. Accessed on 25 December 2022.

Singh. So, in January 2010, Kalyan Singh founded a new party named Jan Kranti Party, which fielded 208 candidates in the 2012 UP Assembly polls but won none and lost deposits on 198 seats. The BJP was also in trouble, so it brought Uma Bharti, another leader from the Lodh caste from MP, to contest assembly polls in UP. She won from Charkhari seat, but the BJP was reduced to just 47 seats in the state. On his part, the ageing Kalyan Singh was getting desperate. When the BJP was gearing up for the 2014 Lok Sabha elections, he returned to the party once again. He announced this on 2 March 2014 at a rally in Lucknow addressed by the BJP's prime ministerial candidate Narendra Modi. Two days later, he was appointed as the vice president of the party. He did not contest the 2014 polls but contributed to the party through his vast experience and large vote base.

One of the most prominent faces of the Ram temple movement from among the BJP, Kalyan Singh was annoyed with the Shri Ram Janmabhoomi Teerth Kshetra trust, which was announced on 5 February 2020 after the Supreme Court's 9 November 2019 verdict in favour of the temple. He said that the OBCs should also have representation in the trust,[25] a point later endorsed by Uma Bharti.[26]

Kalyan Singh was known for wearing neat-and-clean clothes, using costly pens and speaking with logic. His handwriting

[25]'"Backward Classes as Staunch Ram Bhakts as Dalits": Kalyan Singh Demands OBC Member for Ram Mandir Trust', *News18*, 7 February 2020, http://tinyurl.com/3zvusvd7. Accessed on 22 January 2023.

[26]Yadav, Shyamlal, 'Ram Temple Trust Should Have Had OBC Face: Uma Bharti', *The Indian Express,* 7 February 2020, https://tinyurl.com/bdhxxxz9. Accessed on 9 March 2024.

was excellent, and he loved to send handwritten letters to his party workers in erudite language that several old BJS–BJP leaders-workers have preserved. His writings and speeches were always full of *tukbandi* (rhymes). Like many others who became famous for criticizing the Congress's dynasty politics but ended up helping their own family members gain a political foothold, Kalyan Singh also promoted his family in politics. His son Rajveer was a minister in the UP government and was later elected to Lok Sabha from Etah, and his grandson Sandeep was elected as an MLA and sworn in as a minister in the UP government in 2017 and 2022.

Kalyan Singh passed away on 21 August 2021 in Lucknow due to multiple-organ failure. He was posthumously conferred with the Padma Vibhushan, the second-highest civilian award, by the Modi government in 2022. Baleshwar Tyagi, a BJS–BJP leader who had known him since 1971 and worked with him very closely as MoS in his two stints as CM, said:

> He always promoted and protected hard-working party workers. More than OBCs, he was much popular among workers from upper castes. He could not mix well with politicians of other parties and that is why he returned to the BJP again and again. Leaders of SP, BSP and Congress never liked him because he never obliged them when in power. He had a clear view on complex issues, used to take quick decisions, and ensured effective implementation once a decision was taken.[27]

[27]In conversation with the author on 22 January 2023.

17

MAYAWATI

The Trailblazer

Seventeenth CM: Mayawati

Party: Bahujan Samaj Party

Tenure: 3 June 1995–18 October 1995

21 March 1997–21 September 1997

3 May 2002–29 August 2003

13 May 2007–15 March 2012

Constituency: Not a member of either House, Harora, Member of Legislative Council

Days in Office: 7 years and 10 days

The collapse of the SP–BSP alliance headed by Mulayam Singh Yadav paved way for a BSP government as the BJP had already written to Governor Motilal Vora about its decision to support it. Mayawati, a woman from an SC community and a law graduate from the University of Delhi, was sworn in as the CM of UP on 3 June 1995. It was big news not only for UP but for the whole country as well. For this day, she and the BSP had travelled a long distance. They had worked hard to mobilize the deprived sections of society to reach positions of power in the years when several changes were taking place in society and politics in North India, particularly in UP. It is important to understand the life and ideology of the BSP's founder Kanshi Ram ('Saheb' as he was called by his supporters) and his relevance to UP's politics and to the SCs, and before that, it is necessary to understand the situation SCs had to face.

Communities that faced alienation due to the social evil of untouchability were accorded the title of 'Scheduled Castes' in the Government of India Act, 1935. Mahatma Gandhi had used the term 'harijan' in 1932 for them. Post Independence, particularly after the adoption of the Constitution of India on 26 January 1950, deprived communities, including untouchables, which had been facing immense discrimination for centuries, had a lot of hope for their future as the Constitution stated: 'The State shall not discriminate against any citizen on grounds only of religion, race, caste, sex, place of birth or any of them'[1] and 'No citizen shall, on grounds only of religion, race, caste, sex, descent, place of birth, residence or any of them, be ineligible for, or discriminated against in respect of, any employment or office under the State.'[2]

With such constitutional promises, they hoped for an increase in their role and representation in power as these had been abysmally low. On the political side, reservation of

[1]Article 15(1), Constitution of India.

[2]Article 16(2), Constitution of India.

seats for SC/ST candidates was implemented to ensure their due representation in legislative bodies. The first amendment to the Constitution of India was made to legalize caste-based reservations in 1951, after considering the petitions that challenged the caste-based quota pending before courts. But in spite of this, discrimination and atrocities against the deprived sections continued unabated.

Debates in the UP Assembly in the first two decades after Independence were flooded with concern over cases of atrocities and matters raised by several members stating that people belonging to these categories were not even being appointed for Group D (Class 4) posts as the upper-caste officials and their families did not want the SCs to work with them. This was despite the fact that Article 17 of the Constitution of India declared: 'Untouchability is abolished and its practice in any form is forbidden. The enforcement of any disability arising out of "Untouchability" shall be an offence punishable in accordance with law.' To eliminate this menace, the Union government of PM Jawaharlal Nehru implemented the Untouchability (Offences) Act, which came into force from 1 June 1955, making this practice a punishable offence. Over three decades later, in September 1989, the Rajiv Gandhi government, concerned about continuing caste-based atrocities, violence and discrimination, brought in The Scheduled Castes and the Scheduled Tribes (Prevention of Atrocities) Act, defining offences and atrocities punishable by law.[3]

Besides the Acts and laws passed by successive governments, various movements and social reforms were initiated by individuals and organizations. These provided some sense of empowerment to the deprived communities. Thanks to the abolition of the

---

[3]Section 3, The Scheduled Castes and the Scheduled Tribes (Prevention of Atrocities) Act, 1989.

zamindari system, lakhs of landless people belonging to SCs had also got some part of agriculture land. The aspiration of SC communities to attain hissedari in power was but natural.

Kanshi Ram, born on 15 March 1934, in Punjab's Ropar district, joined the Pune-based Explosives Research and Development Laboratory in 1960 as a research assistant, but he quit his government job in 1964 to work towards building a social transformation movement. In 1971, he founded the All India SC, ST, OBC and Minority Employees Association, which, in 1978, became the All India Backward and Minority Communities Employees Federation (BAMCEF). Three years later, in 1981, he founded an organization called Dalit Shoshit Samaj Sangharsh Samiti (DS4).

Spreading his vision, on the fiftieth anniversary of the Poona Pact (a nine-point agreement between Mahatma Gandhi and Dr Ambedkar, which included reservation of seats for depressed castes in legislatures, signed at Yarwada Jail in Pune), on 24 September 1982, Kanshi Ram published a book titled *The Chamcha Age: An Era of the Stooges* 'to enlighten, awaken and caution the Dalit-Shoshit Samaj (oppressed and exploited society) and its workers and leaders about the large-scale existence of the element of stooges (chamchas) in our oppressed and exploited society.'[4] Chamchas, as he explained, were:

> tools, agents and stooges of the High Caste Hindus who have been increasing in numbers and varieties with the passage of time... The oppressed and exploited people of India who are about 85 percent of India's total population are a leaderless lot. The High Caste Hindus have succeeded

[4]Ram, Kanshi, *The Chamcha Age: An Era of the Stooges,* New Delhi, 1982, p. 2.

> in creating leaderlessness amongst them. Such a situation is most conducive for creating *chamchas* out of these castes and communities.[5]

Kanshi Ram and his protégé Mayawati, equating Mahatma Gandhi with Manu, repeatedly said that '[s]crews of Manuvad in the government is a legacy of Mahatma Gandhi. After Manu who divided this country into six thousands castes, it was Mahatma Gandhi who proved himself as a second Manu and destroyed *Bahujan Samaj*.'[6] They insisted that the word 'harijan' must not be used for the SCs. Although the Union Ministry of Home Affairs had issued a notification on 18 February 1982 to all concerned to ensure 'not to insert the word "Harijan" or "Girijan" in the Scheduled Caste/ Scheduled Tribe Certificates',[7] the words continued to be used in common parlance. With protests by the BSP, the word gradually disappeared, and the Gwalior bench of the Madhya Pradesh High Court also directed that 'the Central Government/State Government and its functionaries would refrain from using the nomenclature "Dalit" for the members belonging to Scheduled Castes and Scheduled Tribes as the same does not find mention in the Constitution of India or any statute'.[8] In compliance with that, the Union Ministry of Social Justice and Empowerment issued instructions on 15 March 2018 to the central government and state government functionaries requesting them that 'for all official transactions, matters, dealings, certificates, etc., the Constitutional term "Scheduled Caste" in English and its appropriate translation

[5]Ibid. 89–95.

[6]Mayawati, *Mere Sangharshmay Jeevan evam Bahujan Movement ka Safarnama*, Volume 1, Bahujan Samaj Party, New Delhi, 2006, p. 357; author's translation.

[7]No. BC. 12025/44/80-SC&BCD.I/IV, 10 February 1982, Ministry of Home Affairs, Government of India.

[8]*Dr Mohanlal Mahor vs Union of India* on 15 January 2018, WP-20420-2017 (PIL).

in national languages should alone be used for denoting the persons belonging to the Scheduled Castes'.[9]

After nearly 18 months of having published *The Chamcha Age*, on 14 April 1984, which was the birth anniversary of Dr B.R. Ambedkar, Kanshi Ram founded the BSP. He wrote that the 'Chamcha Yug' had started with the Poona Pact and predicted the end of 'the Chamcha Age within a short span of about 10 years.'[10] Before the formation of the BSP, candidates were fielded by DS4 as independents, and the first election they fought was for the Haryana Assembly of 1982, in which they secured just 1.19 per cent votes.[11]

In 1984, in the post-Indira Gandhi assassination election, Kanshi Ram contested his first election from Janjgir-Champa (now in Chhattisgarh) Lok Sabha seat as an independent candidate. Mayawati, associated with him since 1977, was fielded from Kairana in UP. Kanshi Ram secured the third place with 8.81 per cent of the polled votes. On her part, Mayawati secured 9.94 per cent of the polled votes. This was a significant percentage for first-timers and signalled that new leaders and a new party were emerging. After the demise of the sitting MP of Bijnor, Girdhari Lal, when the by-polls were held at the end of 1985, Mayawati, then just 29, contested again and got 18 per cent of the polled votes. She secured third position after Meera Kumar (daughter of Jagjivan Ram, the biggest SC leader of his time) of the Congress and Ram Vilas Paswan (another SC leader, from Bihar) of the Lok Dal that time. It was Mayawati's performance in the Bijnor by-poll

---

[9]Letter no. 12017/02/2018-SCD(R.L. Cell) dated 15 March 2018, Department of Social Justice & Empowerment, Government of India, https://tinyurl.com/trr79hyh. Accessed on 14 March 2024.

[10]Ram, Kanshi, *The Chamcha Age: An Era of the Stooges,* New Delhi, 1982, p. 3.

[11]Mayawati, *Mere Sangharshmay Jeevan evam Bahujan Movement ka Safarnama,* Volume 1, Bahujan Samaj Party, New Delhi, 2006, p. 833.

that drew the attention of political stalwarts and the media towards the BSP. An 18-month-old party and its leaders were being talked about seriously.

Due to the fact that the state has the largest SC population in the country, Kanshi Ram made UP his experiment ground. While OBCs like Yadavs, Kurmis and Lodhs (and Jats, who were not in the OBC list in UP back then) were mostly behind the two previous anti-Congress agitations—first in the mid-1960s under Dr Ram Manohar Lohia and then in the mid-1970s by Jayaprakash Narayan—the SCs and Muslims were still considered as pro-Congress segments. But when the third anti-Congress agitation was launched by V.P. Singh, Kanshi Ram was ready to grab the attention of SC voters. In the 1988 by-poll from Allahabad, Kanshi Ram contested against V.P. Singh and secured, once again, the third place with 69,517 votes.

It was obvious that the BSP would get not only SC votes in bulk but also votes from many OBC communities and some minorities. The BSP had developed leaders within the party and given tickets to them. While V.P. Singh's announcement to implement the Mandal Commission Report with 27 per cent reservation for OBCs in government jobs led other parties to include, elevate and promote OBC leaders post 1990, it was the emergence of Kanshi Ram that led other parties to give importance to their leaders from the SC community.

Coming back to Mayawati, she was born on 15 January 1956 in Delhi. Her father, Prabhu Dayal, had come to Delhi from a village called Badalpur (now in Gautam Buddha Nagar district). He was an upper-division clerk in the Department of Post. Mayawati is one of nine siblings. After graduating from the University of Delhi, she completed her BEd from Ghaziabad and was employed as a teacher under the Government of Delhi in late 1970s, where she continued to work until 1984. Alongside, she was preparing for the civil services examination and also enrolled for LLB at the University of Delhi, a degree that she completed.

Mayawati's life took a new turn when she came into contact with Kanshi Ram sometime in 1977 and became associated with the BAMCEF. Impressed with her oratory skills at a programme in Delhi, Kanshi Ram called her to his residence and told her that she could achieve much more for society by becoming a leader than by becoming a collector.[12] That is how she relinquished her dream of becoming a civil servant and started working with Kanshi Ram.

In the 1989 Lok Sabha polls, Kanshi Ram contested from Amethi against PM Rajiv Gandhi, and also from East Delhi against a powerful Union minister, Harkishan Lal Bhagat, and secured third place on both seats. Mayawati also contested from two seats of UP reserved for SCs—Haridwar (now in Uttarakhand) and Bijnor—and won from Bijnor. Her party got three seats in the Lok Sabha. Mayawati, thus, became a Lok Sabha member at the age of 33.

In the UP Assembly polls that were held in 1989 along with the Lok Sabha polls, the BSP contested 372 of the 425 seats and won 13 seats, securing 9.41 per cent of the polled votes, and supported the Mulayam Singh government from outside. In 1991, despite the BJP wave, the BSP secured 12 seats and 9.44 per cent of the polled votes in the state assembly polls. In the middle of all this, Kanshi Ram found a friend in Mulayam Singh Yadav. With his help, Kanshi Ram was elected to the Lok Sabha in 1991 after winning the Etawah seat through an arrangement where Mulayam Singh's

---

[12]Ibid. 11.

Janata Party (renamed from Janata Dal [S]) did not field a candidate there, and the BSP did not field anyone against Mulayam Singh in Jaswantnagar Assembly segment. Both won easily. By then, it was very clear that the BSP was reaching new grounds.

The big break for the BSP came in 1993 when it made an alliance with Mulayam Singh's SP. The SP contested 256 seats and won 109, whereas the BSP contested 164 and won 67 seats.[13] In the government headed by Mulayam Singh, the BSP greatly influenced policies for the welfare and empowerment of SCs and OBCs. It rapidly consolidated its position among the SCs and some backward communities. Mayawati did not contest the 1993 assembly polls.

When cases of atrocities against Dalits were being reported during the SP–BSP government in 1993–95, Kanshi Ram, on the one hand, warned CM Mulayam Singh; on the other hand, he said that those incidents, especially involving the Yadavs, were being 'blown up by the Brahminical media'.[14] In July 1994, Kanshi Ram threatened to withdraw from the government but that did not happen. However, backdoor politics were underway to unseat Mulayam Singh. Jayant Malhotra, a Rajya Sabha MP from the BSP and a businessman close to Kanshi Ram, said on 31 May 1995 that Mulayam Singh was soon going to be out of power,[15] and the BSP, soon after, withdrew support to the coalition government on 1 June 1995. Once the Mulayam Singh government was dismissed, Mayawati was sworn in as the CM on 3 June 1995 with the outside support of the BJP.

---

[13]Ibid.

[14]Ibid. 74.

[15]Agha, Zafar, 'Parde ke Peechhe ki Jod-Tod', *India Today* (Hindi), 30 June 1995, p. 52.

In the BSP regime supported by the BJP, there appeared to be an uneasy relation between the two parties from the very beginning. On 7 July 1995, in an obvious effort to intimidate both Mulayam Singh and the BJP, Mayawati wrote a letter to PM Narasimha Rao proposing 15 per cent reservation for Muslims in government jobs and admissions in educational institutions. Kanshi Ram, who was quite evidently behind this move, was clear from the very beginning on the mission of his party. Days after Mayawati took oath, he had said, 'I am not interested in the government. I am interested in a movement. I live and die for the movement.'[16] From 16 September 1995, the Mayawati government organized a three-day Periyar Mela (a fair named after Erode Venkatappa Ramasamy Periyar of the Dravidar Kazhagam movement) in Lucknow. From the BJP, the first strong reaction came from Kalyan Singh, who had been uneasy about this coalition from the beginning. For many weeks, he had stopped meeting media persons and party workers, which was against his nature. Finally, breaking his silence, he said at a press conference in Etawah, 'Mayawati is following in the footsteps of Mulayam Singh. If she will continue to do this, we will be forced to withdraw support.'[17] Kanshi Ram responded, 'We will run the government our way. If BJP does not like this, it can withdraw support.'[18] The BJP withdrew support on 17 October 1995, and the assembly was dissolved. When Mayawati took over as the CM, she was not a member of

---

[16]Agha, Zafar, 'Uttar Pradesh Is the Cradle of Brahminism: Kanshi Ram', *India Today,* 30 June 1995, https://tinyurl.com/2j2v9zn2. Accessed on 14 March 2024.

[17]Singh, N.K., and Dilip Awasthi, 'Ties between Mayawati and BJP Hit New Low as Kalyan Singh Attacks Her Government', *India Today*, 30 September 1995, https://tinyurl.com/57w88c26. Accessed on 9 March 2024.

[18]Awasthi, Dilip, 'Mayawati: Uttar Pradesh First Dalit Chief Minister Left Her Mark Despite Her Brief Tenure', *India Today*, 15 November 1995, https://tinyurl.com/2m7t5fua. Accessed on 9 March 2024.

either House of the state legislature and had continued without being a member; her government collapsed within six months.

The Guest House Case of 2 June 1995 worsened the relationship between Mulayam Singh Yadav and Kanshi Ram–Mayawati. In that scenario, for the 1996 Lok Sabha elections, Kanshi Ram, anticipating difficulties for himself in Mulayam Singh's home turf Etawah, moved from there and contested from Hoshiarpur in Punjab and Phulpur in UP. He won in Hoshiarpur but lost in Phulpur. In the 1998 Lok Sabha elections, he contested from Saharanpur but lost, securing second position with 25.97 per cent votes, and that was the last poll he contested.

For the 1996 UP Assembly polls, because their relations with both the SP and the BJP had worsened, Kanshi Ram and Mayawati aligned with the Congress. When results were announced, it turned out that the SP won 110 seats out of the 281 seats it had contested, the BSP 67 out of the 296 seats it had contested, and the Congress 33 out of the 126 seats it had contested as a BSP ally, so none of the parties got a majority again. Mayawati had contested from Bilsi in Badaun district and won. The BJP again emerged as the single-largest party, but stuck at 174 seats, it was 39 short of a majority. As no party was able to get a majority, Governor Romesh Bhandari decided to put the assembly under suspended animation. After nearly six months, the BJP and the BSP again made an alliance, but this time, the CM's post was to be shared in a rotation of six months. That is how Mayawati took oath as the CM for the second time on 21 March 1997.

Within just three months of the swearing in of the second Mayawati government, 1,500 link roads were constructed in Ambedkar villages, thousands of India Mark-II hand pumps were installed, and electricity reached 11,524 villages.[19] Mayawati

---

[19]Mishra, Subhash, and Saba Naqvi Bhaumik, 'Mayawati to Ensure Kalyan Singh

launched a drive to fill the backlog of vacancies for reserved categories in government departments in 1995 and 1997. The Mayawati government also started strict implementation of the SC and ST (Prevention of Atrocities) Act, which did not go down well with the BJP.

As per the terms of the alliance, her cabinet resigned after six months, and on 21 September 1997, the BJP's Kalyan Singh took oath as CM for the second time with the same ministers who were in Mayawati's ministry. Later, amid growing tension with its ally, the BSP withdrew from the alliance on 19 October 1997; the BSP suffered major defections after that.

After the end of the assembly tenure, fresh assembly elections were held in February 2002. Mayawati contested from Harora in Bulandshahr and from Jahangirganj in Ambedkar Nagar and won from both. But again, the outcome was a hung assembly. The BJP got only 88 seats out of the total 403, the BSP got 98 seats, and the SP emerged as the single-largest party with 143 seats. There was again a vacuum, and after waiting for nearly two months and forgetting their past misadventure, a BSP–BJP alliance was forged for the third time. Mayawati took oath as CM for the third time on 3 May 2002. Under the terms of the alliance, the Speaker's chair was given to the BJP and its leader Keshari Nath Tripathi was elected to the post. During the 2002 assembly polls (and later also in the 2004 Lok Sabha elections), Mayawati's slogan '*Chadh gundon ki chhati par, ab muhar lagegi haathi par*' (To overpower outlaws, cast vote on elephant [the BSP symbol]) had become very popular.

In the BJP, there were again differences on the issue of joining hands with the BSP for the third time. Leaders like Lalji

---

Pursues Her Policies if He Becomes UP Chief Minister', *India Today*, 1 September 1997, https://tinyurl.com/y2bssu4m. Accessed on 9 March 2024.

Tandon in UP along with L.K. Advani and M.M. Joshi at the Centre were in favour of the alliance, but leaders like Rajnath Singh, Kalraj Mishra, and many others in the state (Kalyan Singh had quit the BJP by then) were against it. Many BJP leaders raised their voice against slapping POTA on the independent MLA Raja Bhaiya. All this was affecting the functioning of the government. In her third stint, on 14 April 2003, Mayawati and her people slapped 136 criminal cases on Mulayam Singh Yadav on a single day. Cases were spread over 40 of the 73 districts. The BJP leadership was also assessing the situation and keeping a watch on Mayawati's functioning. The height of her brazenness was when, after a controversy about the Taj Heritage Corridor, she asked the central government on 28 July 2003 to remove Union Minister of Tourism and Culture Jagmohan Malhotra for alleged lapses. Although the demand was withdrawn days later, it prompted Vajpayee and the BJP to take a final call. The BJP–BSP alliance collapsed again despite slogans like '*Hathi nahin Ganesh hai, Brahma Vishnu Mahesh hai*' (It's not just an elephant, it's Ganesh, who is equivalent to the Hindu trinity) raised by then state BJP chief Vinay Katiyar. Mayawati resigned on 29 August 2003, and she was replaced by Mulayam Singh. Mulayam Singh again engineered a defection in the BSP to get a majority. This was the third major division in the BSP.

After her third coalition government collapsed, Mayawati tried to move forward, but she was faced with another challenge. The BSP patriarch Kanshi Ram had been ailing for some time, and his health was deteriorating rapidly. Kanshi Ram, after a year of hospitalization, passed away on 9 October 2006 in Delhi. He had already passed the baton to Mayawati, and on 18 September 2003, she took over as the president of the BSP. But she direly needed his mentoring and support with regard to her new strategies.

Soon after taking oath for the third time, Mayawati appointed Satish Mishra, an advocate from Allahabad who had been handling cases pending against Mayawati, as Advocate General of UP, and when she resigned in August 2003, Mishra joined the BSP and was appointed as the general secretary of the party and sent to the Rajya Sabha in July 2004. In the years 2003–07, the Thakurs had mostly aligned with Mulayam Singh Yadav's SP, and his government had the highest number of Thakur ministers. At this time, parties like the Congress, and particularly the BJP, which were mainly dominated by Brahmins, were finding it difficult to gain power in UP. Mayawati also realized the limitation of politics focussed only on SC, some OBC and some minority votes. She tried to work among the Brahmin community. The party that had earlier claimed to be a party of *bahujans* (deprived sections) now claimed to be a party of *sarvjans* (all sections). This was a U-turn for a party that was once highly critical of brahminism.

In earlier elections, whenever the BSP fielded a Brahmin candidate anywhere, a slogan made the rounds among upper-caste voters: '*Brahman nahin Chamar hai, haathi par sawar hai*' (He is not a Brahmin but actually a Chamar [SC community] who is contesting from the BSP, elephant is its symbol). But in the 2007 assembly polls, Mayawati's new strategy worked, and the BSP turned out to be a clear winner. The party contested all 403 seats on its own and got a simple majority with 206 seats. This was the first time since 1991 that a party had got majority by itself in the state, and the BSP had won for the first time with a majority. The BJP was reduced to just 51 seats and the Congress to just 22. The SP was now the single-largest party in Opposition, with 97 assembly seats. Satish Mishra was initially appointed a cabinet minister attached to CM Mayawati; from 17 November 2007 until 6 March 2012, he served as the chairman of the UP Advisory Council and given a cabinet rank. What Amar Singh was for Mulayam Singh Yadav and the SP, Satish Mishra was for Mayawati and the BSP. Mayawati completed a full five-year single tenure (2007–12) as the CM and was the first CM since 1952 to do so. During this time, the politics of the BSP and policies and programmes of the Mayawati government were powered and influenced by Satish Mishra to a great extent. She was elected to the Legislative Council twice during her tenure as the CM.

Mayawati carried out a big revamp in the bureaucracy this time around. On the very day of her taking oath, on 13 May 2007, she appointed Shashank Shekhar Singh, a former pilot, as a cabinet secretary as well as deputy chairman of the State Planning Commission, granting him the rank of a cabinet minister. The post of cabinet secretary was created for the first time in UP. Though he was not an IAS officer, during her tenure he was virtually running the show on her behalf, starting from conducting meetings of different levels of IAS and IPS officers to sorting out problems of ministers and addressing press conferences on behalf of Mayawati. This irked the IAS lobby and his elevation was challenged in courts as well, but nothing affected Shashank Shekhar's stature, and he continued on the post till Mayawati's last day in office. Reactions of her predecessor Mulayam Singh Yadav (and people of his caste) to her government were reflected and seen at every level. Among government servants, a joke was popular: '*Mayawati ke raaj mein brahman khayen kheer, saari jaat chori karen pakde jaayen aheer*' (In the Mayawati regime Brahmins enjoy rice pudding, and while crime may be committed by all castes, only Yadavs will be caught). Out of the 36 state universities of UP, 33 were established post Independence and six of them were established during Mayawati's tenures; 18 of the 75 districts in present-day UP were created during her time at office. The 165.5-kilometre-long Yamuna Expressway (also known as Taj

Expressway) from Greater Noida to Agra is considered her prime infrastructure project.

Mayawati was riding high; her confidence knew no bounds. When the Union government of the UPA headed by Dr Manmohan Singh was facing a floor test on 22 July 2008 on the nuclear deal, as four left parties had withdrawn support to the government against the deal, the United National Progressive Alliance (UNPA) had suggested her name as a prime ministerial candidate, but that did not materialize as the UPA government won the confidence motion. Undeterred, she commented on the possibility of her becoming the PM of India in these words: 'A movement has begun. When the time comes, no one can stop me from becoming the Prime Minister.'[20]

As CM, Mayawati implemented schemes like Ambedkar Samagra Grameen Vikas Yojna for overall development of over 17,000 gram sabhas; Mahamaya Gareeb Arthik Madad Yojna to provide ₹300 per month to nearly 31 lakh people below poverty line (BPL); Mahamaya Gareeb Balika Aashirvad Yojana for depositing ₹20,000 in the name of girls born after 15 January 2009; and Savitribai Phule Balika Shiksha Madad Yojana for providing ₹25,000 and a bicycle to girls of Classes 11 and 12 belonging to BPL families. But she frequently faced allegations of corruption. To implement the central government's National Rural Health Mission (NRHM), she split a ministry to give Babu Singh Kushwaha charge of family welfare, while Anant Mishra, aka Antu Mishra, a person close to Satish Mishra, was given charge of health. In five years from 2005, nearly ₹10,000 crore were granted to the state government, and construction and purchase had become a lucrative job for government doctors and officials of the department. At least seven senior doctors

---

[20]Chawla, Prabhu, '"No Force Can Stop Me from Becoming PM"', *India Today*, 18 August 2008, https://tinyurl.com/2a75pstk. Accessed on 9 March 2024.

were killed, and in the face of much criticism, Mayawati sacked both of them on 8 April 2011.[21]

The heights the BSP climbed to in 2007 and the power it enjoyed until mid-March 2012 began to see a cascading drop. In the 2012 state polls, the BSP again contested all 403 seats alone, but it won only 80 seats; the vote share came down from 40.43 per cent in 2007 to 25.95 per cent in 2012.[22] In the 2017 assembly polls, it further reduced to only 19 seats, with 22.23 per cent of the total polled votes.[23] Forgetting her animosity with Mulayam Singh Yadav, she made an alliance called 'Mahagathbandhan' with the SP, then headed by his son Akhilesh Yadav, for the 2019 Lok Sabha polls, campaigned for her bête noire, the ex-SP chief, in Mainpuri and withdrew some cases she had filed against him. Her party secured 10 Lok Sabha seats, while the SP got just five among the 80 seats in the state. However, after the Lok Sabha polls, their alliance ended. In 2022, the BSP again contested all assembly seats but won just one seat and could retain only 12.88 per cent of the polled votes, which was the lowest since 1996.[24] During the 2022 assembly polls, there were widespread allegations that the BSP was putting up candidates suited to enable a BJP victory for several seats, but Mayawati repeatedly denied it. This allegation against Mayawati continues in the 2024 Lok Sabha polls.[25]

---

[21]Yadav, Shyamlal, 'Hatyaon ka Mahkama', *India Today* (Hindi), 11 May 2011, pp. 24–8.

[22]*Statistical Report on General Elections 2012 to the Legislative Assembly of UP*, Election Commission of India, New Delhi.

[23]*Statistical Report on General Elections 2017 to the Legislative Assembly of UP*, Election Commission of India, New Delhi.

[24]*Statistical Report on General Elections 2022 to the Legislative Assembly of UP*, Election Commission of India, New Delhi.

[25]'"Falsely Called Us B-Team Of BJP": Mayawati Blames UP Loss On Media, Rival', *NDTV*, 11 March 2022, https://tinyurl.com/4b29vxbb. Accessed on 9 March 2024.

It must be admitted that Mayawati's tenure as the CM gave a lot of courage and confidence to the SCs in the state. Kanshi Ram sowed the seed and made the plant grow; Mayawati nourished it. Together, they nurtured a politics where SCs were able to assert their rights and feel empowered to seek their share in politics, power and government. Slogans started by the BSP, like '*Jiski jitni sankhya bhari, uski utni hissedaari*' (Communities should get share in power based on their population size), had high impact and gave momentum to the aspirations of the deprived sections. This was a long battle that SCs had fought since Independence.

Mayawati was elected to the Rajya Sabha thrice: in April 1994, July 2004, and April 2012. She was elected to the Lok Sabha four times.

However, Kanshi Ram's dream to organize the SCs, STs, OBCs and other minorities could not be fulfilled to the extent he would have hoped. Uttar Pradesh was the only state where the BSP got power on its own. But Mayawati also had another dream. On 14 October 2006, on the fiftieth anniversary of Dr B.R. Ambedkar embracing Buddhism, a programme had been scheduled in Nagpur by Kanshi Ram for his followers, but he passed away just five days before that. Nonetheless, the programme was still held, and Mayawati, while addressing it, declared that she would defer embracing Buddhism. She announced, 'When my party succeeds in forming the central government on its own, I will embrace Buddhism along with my crores of followers, so that, like in UP, I can establish an egalitarian society through the master key of political power and I can then spread Buddhism.'[26]

[26]Mayawati, *Mere Sangharshmay Jeevan evam Bahujan Movement ka Safarnama*, Volume

Kanshi Ram did not promote anybody from his family in the party, organizations or movement. At a time when the BSP was struggling for its existence, the party declared on 10 December 2023 that Akash Anand, nephew of Mayawati, would be her successor,[27] but this was a U-turn from her own promises. In fact, in the third volume of her autobiography, *Mere Sangharshmay Jeevan evam Bahujan Movement ka Safarnama*, released on her birthday, 15 January 2008, she said the following about her successor, 'I keep all my family members much away from politics so that I am not accused of nepotism.'[28] She later added:

> Whenever I will announce my successor, he or she will not be from my parents', siblings' or relatives' families. I will make my successor a person who will be from the most oppressed of Scheduled Castes, and among Scheduled Castes, from my *Chamar* caste. The person will be 30–35 years younger to me so that he or she can take forward this movement under his/her leadership for a long time.[29]

3, Bahujan Samaj Party, New Delhi, 2008, p. 517; author's translation.

[27]Rehman, Asad, 'BSP Supremo Mayawati Names Nephew Akash Anand as Political Heir, Keeps UP & Uttarakhand for Herself', *The Indian Express*, 11 December 2023, https://tinyurl.com/524a9z7v. Accessed on 6 March 2024. At the time of this book going to press, Mayawati removed him as her political successor.

[28]Mayawati, *Mere Sangharshmay Jeevan evam Bahujan Movement ka Safarnama*, Volume 1, Bahujan Samaj Party, New Delhi, 2006, p. 18; author's translation.

[29]Mayawati, *Mere Sangharshmay Jeevan evam Bahujan Movement ka Safarnama*, Volume 3, Bahujan Samaj Party, New Delhi, 2008, p. 391; author's translation.

18

RAM PRAKASH GUPTA

The Unexpected CM

Eighteenth CM: Ram Prakash Gupta

Party: Bharatiya Janata Party

Tenure: 12 November 1999–28 October 2000

Constituency: Member of Legislative Council

Days in Office: 351 days

Kalyan Singh was being persuaded to resign, but he did not have the authority to choose his successor. He did, however, have a say in who should *not* replace him. He was among the most prominent leaders of the BJP in UP, but his influence in the state had weakened considerably, for which both he and his party were responsible. He seemed to have lost the courage he had during his first stint as the CM. When the central leadership of the BJP called him to Delhi on 8 November 1999, along with his three known detractors—Rajnath Singh, Kalraj Mishra and Lalji Tandon—Kalyan Singh decided to skip the meeting. In this piquant situation, and considering Kalyan

Singh's mood, the BJP leadership found it difficult to oblige either of the two probable candidates—Rajnath Singh and Kalraj Mishra—with an invitation to his chair. Both Rajnath Singh and Kalraj Mishra, who had been eyeing the CM's chair, were disappointed.

On Tuesday, 9 November 1999, when Kalyan Singh was in Ayodhya to meet saints and pray to Ram Lalla, for whom he had sacrificed his CM's chair on 6 December 1992, he made an attack on his party, particularly on PM Atal Bihari Vajpayee, for ignoring the Ram temple issue. The same day, in Lucknow, septuagenarian Ram Prakash Gupta received a call from his old friend PM Vajpayee, asking him to reach Delhi by late evening to attend a crucial meeting at his residence. Gupta was then deputy chairperson of the State Planning Commission. By this time, it was clear to everyone that the successor to Kalyan Singh had already been chosen; all other things were mere formalities. Kalyan Singh resigned on 12 November 1999, and the same day, Gupta was sworn in as the eighteenth CM of UP at the age of 76. Incidentally, he remains the oldest person to take oath as the UP CM.

Gupta, a freedom fighter, was born on 26 October 1923 in Sukhwan-Dukhwan village in Jhansi, where his father worked as a government employee. Gupta did his MSc in Mathematics from the University of Allahabad. His selection as the CM was a surprise decision by his party, as his name had never been under consideration.

Gupta joined the RSS as a pracharak in Allahabad as early as 1946 in Allahabad and continued as such till 1952. In those days, Allahabad was the epicentre of politics, as it not only was the home turf of the Nehru family but also had a dynamic student politics scene. There were leaders from the Congress, BJS and RSS along with socialist leaders. Being an RSS pracharak in Allahabad, Gupta was closely connected with BJS leaders like Deen Dayal Upadhyay and Nanaji Deshmukh, and the RSS's Rajju Bhaiya, among others. Later, Gupta started working for the BJS.

After the third assembly polls in 1962, when the BJS became the main Opposition party in the UP Assembly, Gupta was sent to the Legislative Council in 1964. In the first non-Congress SVD government headed by Chaudhary Charan Singh in 1967, in which the BJS was its main partner with 99 MLAs, Gupta was chosen for the crucial post of minister of education, technical education, harijan and social welfare, cultural affairs and research, from 6 April 1967. A week later, on 13 April, he was elevated to deputy CM (he was the first person to occupy this post in the state), looking after the same departments, and from 10 December 1967, he was given charge of transport and tourism as well. After the collapse of the government, he focussed on organizational work for his party. When Vajpayee was replaced by L.K. Advani as the BJS national president in 1972, Gupta was appointed as the president of the UP unit of the party in 1973.

The first assembly election Gupta contested was in 1977 on a Janata Party ticket from Lucknow Central, which he won. He was sworn in as a minister on 23 June 1977 and given the portfolios of heavy industry, small industry, handloom and handicraft in the Ram Naresh Yadav government. Later, on 15 September 1977, he was allotted the ministry of village industries as well.

After the collapse of the Janata Party, as a candidate of the newly formed BJP, Gupta contested again from Lucknow Central in the 1980 assembly polls but lost. After that, for a while he was not actively involved in politics, but in 1993, he was fielded by the BJP from the same seat and he made it to the assembly. After dissolution of that assembly in 1995, he was considered by many to have retired from active politics. But another opportunity was on its way for Gupta, though not strictly political. He did not contest the assembly poll in 1996, though he was in constant touch with senior leaders like Vajpayee, who was representing Lucknow in the Lok Sabha. In 1998, a year after Kalyan Singh took oath as the CM under a BJP–BSP alliance, Gupta was appointed as the deputy chairperson of the State Planning Commission.

However easy his oath-taking was, his functioning as CM was proving to be quite difficult. His was not a BJP government—it was a coalition, very different from the governments of 1967 and 1977 (the Janata Party was a result of the merger of many parties) in which Gupta had worked earlier. As the CM, he found it very difficult to run a government that the BJP had constituted in 1997 after engineering defections from different parties, which also included several MLAs with criminal backgrounds. Moreover, within the BJP, some leaders had been spreading unfounded rumours about him from the very beginning, as was also being done by many in the Opposition.

When he took oath as the CM, Gupta was not a member of either House of the state legislature. He was later elected to the Legislative Council on 6 May 2000. After his oath-taking, the first assembly session started on 31 December 1999. Subhash Chandra Srivastava (Janata Dal MLA from Deoria), Rewati Raman Singh (SP MLA from Karchhana) and Pramod Tiwari (Congress MLA from Rampur Khas) raised an issue of propriety in the assembly on 3 January 2000, on the elevation of Gupta to the post of CM. Tiwari said, 'You [BJP] have put here a person who has not been in active politics since the past 15 years. If Honourable CM stands here and he is able to recognize his ministers, if he recognizes every minister, I will leave this House and will not return for the next two days.'[1] In the coming days, it became a joke among UP politicians and journalists that Gupta could not recognize most of his ministers. Also, as Gupta did not speak too much, people started calling him Mauni Baba (the mute one).

The budget session of the assembly was scheduled to start from 23 March 2000. Two weeks before that, on 10 March, through an order the Gupta government notified that Jats were to be included among the OBCs of the state as the BJP was keen on gaining the community's support in the forthcoming 2002 assembly and 2004 Lok Sabha elections. During the budget session, Gupta gave his first speech in the assembly. While participating in the discussion on the motion of thanks to the governor's address, he said, *'Main pehli baar sadan me bol raha hoon. Mujh par mauni baba hone ka aarop lagaya gaya… Aap kahte hain ki kamjor mukhyamantri hai, mera kahna hai ki kamjor mukhyamantri lokpriya hota hai kyonki aapke kaam kar deta hai. Lekin agar vah galat kaam karne se darta hai to aisa kamjor mukhymantri bade kaam ka hai'* (I am speaking for the first time in this assembly. I am accused of being a mauni baba, a mute man… You say I am a weak CM, but I think a weak CM is a popular CM as he solves your problems. But if he is afraid of doing wrong work, such a CM is most useful).[2] The same day, he also said that people had called him from various places in India and abroad and said that they were willing to invest in UP but they needed him to first make the state corruption-free and make its bureaucracy sensitive.[3] When he

[1] *Vidhan Sabha ki Karyawahi,* 3 January 2000, UP Assembly Secretariat, Lucknow, p. 93; author's translation.

[2] *Vidhan Sabha ki Karyawahi,* 7 April 2000, UP Assembly Secretariat, Lucknow, pp. 136–7; author's translation.

[3] Ibid. 137.

said this, it was in a way an acceptance of the failure of his own government. But in all due fairness, it could also mean that he recognized the problems and would make efforts to resolve them.

In the gigantic ministry of 92 members that he had, there were several groups with conflicting interests. Some of his own ministers like Naresh Agrawal (ABLTC) and Rajaram Pandey (Janata Dal [R]) made disparaging statements against government decisions. Pramod Tiwari of the Congress raised the issue that, on 12 May, in the lobby of the assembly some ministers were heard expressing strong views about the CM, including that the CM did not work.[4] There were also occasions when important issues were discussed in the House and only the CM or very few ministers were present, others skipping the proceedings. On the day when a discussion on the budget was going on, even Finance Minister Harischandra Srivastava was not present. An appeal was made by the Chair to the members, 'Honourable ministers should be present [in the House during discussions on the budget], and if there is no other engagement, the honourable finance minister should also be present here and take note of the suggestions given by honourable members.'[5] But this appeal went unheeded, and the situation continued.

Opposition members attacking and joking about him was not the only problem for Gupta; there were problems from within his party as well. Ministers in his government, particularly those who were coalition partners, behaved as if no one had control over them. Gupta was chosen as CM with the understanding that Kalyan Singh would continue in the

[4] *Vidhan Sabha ki Karyawahi,* 15 May 2000, UP Assembly Secretariat, Lucknow, p. 48.

[5] *Vidhan Sabha ki Karyawahi,* 25 April 2000, UP Assembly Secretariat, Lucknow, p. 112; author's translation.

BJP, but that proved to be a wrong calculation as the former CM suddenly quit his old party to form a new one. The BJP leadership, taken aback, started feeling that while losing Kalyan Singh was a big loss for the party, the loss would be compounded if Gupta continued as the CM.

With the next assembly polls due in less than two years and the way politics was playing out in Lucknow and in Delhi, it would appear that the BJP had realized the need to make some immediate course corrections. That the first head to roll would be Gupta's was by then a foregone conclusion. On 24 October 2000, just two days before Deepawali, when people were preparing to celebrate Dhanteras, the BJP chief Bangaru Laxman announced in Delhi that Gupta had expressed his willingness to resign as the CM and that the party had accepted it. The UP Assembly was in session when Jagdambika Pal said that if there was any change of leadership, it should be announced in the House. But Speaker Tripathi ruled that it was a party matter and had nothing to do with the procedures of the House. The same day, at his residence in Delhi, Rajnath Singh, the Union minister of surface transport, with Gupta's minister of power, Naresh Agrawal, by his side, told some reporters that he would take oath as the CM on 28 October in Lucknow. Rajnath Singh then went to 7, Race Course Road, the PM's official residence, to get the blessings of PM Vajpayee, and after that, he left for Lucknow. On the same crucial day, 24 October 2000, the UP Assembly's winter session was adjourned sine die and, as it turned out, it was the last sitting-in assembly that Gupta attended as the CM. Coincidently, that was also the last assembly session of undivided UP, as 22 members belonging to Uttaranchal (later Uttarakhand) were given a farewell that day—they were to become members of the newly created state's assembly from 9 November 2000.

Removing Kalyan Singh was one major misdoing by the BJP; the other was removing Gupta on Dhanteras, a festival widely celebrated in UP, particularly among the business communities, to which Gupta belonged. His removal, therefore, sent a wrong message. This was reflected in the 2002 assembly poll results, indicating that these communities had voted based on castes of the candidates, forgetting their party affiliation. The BJP was reduced to 88 assembly seats in 2002, and its dream to rule the state was again left unfulfilled.

Gupta, like some of his predecessors and successors to the post, also had a deep interest in astrology. His political journey underlines that luck came again and again to him when he least expected it. On 7 May 2003, the Vajpayee government appointed him as the governor of Madhya Pradesh and that proved to be his last placement on a constitutional post. None of his children are in politics.

He passed away on 1 May 2004 while serving this very post. On his demise, then CM Mulayam Singh Yadav said, 'Gupta believed in simple living and high thinking and never compromised with his principles.'[6]

[6]'Obituary Ram Prakash Gupta Was Dedicated to Social Uplift', *Organiser*, 16 May 2004, https://tinyurl.com/yxb6zd8f. Accessed on 14 March 2024.

19

RAJNATH SINGH

Stepping Stone to the Centre

Nineteenth CM: Rajnath Singh

Party: Bharatiya Janata Party

Tenure: 28 October 2000–8 March 2002

Constituency: Haidargarh

Days in Office: 1 year and 131 days

After Kalyan Singh's departure from the party to form a new one, the BJP leaders realized their dual lapses in judgement. If losing Kalyan Singh had been one of the biggest mistakes of the party high command, the error was made even bigger by the decision of replacing him with Ram Prakash Gupta at the expense of others who could have been a better choice. Therefore, the party was earnestly trying to correct its course. The BJP leadership decided to replace Gupta with Rajnath Singh, and he took oath as the CM on 28 October 2000.

The fourth person from the Thakur community to become the UP CM, Rajnath Singh was born in a village named Bhabhora near Varanasi on 10 July 1951. He completed his MSc in Physics from the University of Gorakhpur and started teaching at K.B. Postgraduate College in Mirzapur, along with working for the BJS, and later, the BJP. He contested the post-Emergency assembly poll in 1977 from Mirzapur on a Janata Party ticket and won. But, subsequently, he lost two assembly polls from the same seat in 1980 and 1985. In 1988, he was elected to the Legislative Council and continued there until 1994. During L.K. Advani's second stint as the BJP president from 1988, Rajnath Singh was the chief of its youth wing, the Bharatiya Janata Yuva Morcha (BJYM). At one point, the BJP was transforming itself through several new programmes, such as the rath yatra from Somnath to Ayodhya, while the country's politics was facing many changes. The responsibility Rajnath Singh had during this period gave him a lot of exposure.

When the Kalyan Singh government was formed in June 1991, Rajnath Singh was given the crucial portfolio of intermediate education. When the Anti-copying Ordinance was promulgated before the UP board examinations in 1992 to declare copying in examinations as a cognizable offence, being the minister of the concerned department, he was at the forefront of the implementation of Anti-copying Ordinance. This law enhanced his image among educated people, both inside and outside the state, but he became unpopular among the students as hundreds of them were arrested and several thousand students left exam halls in fear; when results were out, a huge number of students had failed. This was considered to be a big reason why he lost the 1993 assembly poll that he had contested from Lucknow's Mahona seat. In March 1997, he became the president of the UP unit of the BJP.

Rajnath Singh played a key role in saving the Kalyan Singh government in October 1997 and allowing it to continue when it was reduced to a minority after withdrawal of the BSP from the coalition. There were defections in the Congress, BSP and Janata Dal, and the defectors as well as some independent MLAs came out in support of the Kalyan Singh government.

As the CM, Rajnath Singh was looking for a safe seat as he was expected to become a member of either House of the legislature within six months of swearing in. Suddenly, the news that old Congressman Surendra Nath Awasthi, aka Puttu Awasthi (an MLA in 1985, 1991 and 1996 from Haidergarh in Barabanki), along with his wife, had met Rajnath Singh at his residence in Lucknow on 19 February 2001 came out. Awasthi later vacated his assembly seat for the CM and quit the Congress. In the by-poll on 9 April 2001, Rajnath Singh was elected as an MLA from Haidergarh seat and reached the assembly.

The first budget session of the assembly was convened from 20 March 2001. When it started, Governor Vishnu Kant Shastri's address provided a glimpse of the Rajnath Singh government's future planning. The address elaborated on the nine-point policy of his government to develop the state.

As the CM, Rajnath Singh's outreach to farmers started by hosting farmers' delegations from across the state at his official residence and talking to them for long hours. Some of his programmes of mass contact included travelling across the state; visiting a particular village in some districts and staying there the night; and organizing small rallies of several communities, mostly those that were small in numbers, in order to attract them towards the BJP. He announced that after 1 May 2001, nobody would be able to misuse red or blue beacon-lights on their official vehicles. He curtailed security covers for VIPs, and among the 9,000 policemen who were deployed for the security of those people, 7,000 were withdrawn. All these could be considered symbolic steps—he was trying everything to return in 2002 with majority so that he would a get a full term to govern the state.

A few weeks after his election to the assembly, Rajnath Singh initiated his long-term plans for dismantling the established reservation system. On 28 June 2001, Rajnath Singh constituted a committee under the chairmanship of his parliamentary affairs minister Hukum Singh to suggest reservations within reservation. Amidst this social justice exercise in UP, at the Centre, the BJP approached Ajit Singh of the RLD for an alliance. Ajit Singh agreed and joined the Union government as the minister of agriculture on 23 July 2001. To woo the farmer community, the central government declared Chaudhary Charan Singh's birthday (23 December) as National Farmers' Day from 2001.

At the same time, during the Social Justice Week organized between 30 July and 6 August 2001, the Social Justice Committee initiated the process of collecting random data of beneficiaries of welfare schemes. This random survey was similar to the one in 1995, which the Mulayam Singh government had conducted to decide on reservation in panchayats. It was conducted as there was an absence of data on populations from different communities benefitting from reservations for SCs and OBCs.

While Rajnath Singh was busy trying to control his party machinery and run the government, differences arose with some of his cabinet colleagues; at the same time, ministers from allied parties started to openly criticize BJP leaders and some of the policies of the government. This was nothing new as such issues had been raised in the assembly by Opposition members time and again, since the days of Ram Prakash Gupta and Kalyan Singh. However, Rajnath Singh decided to crack down on such dissidents. After an embarrassing statement by Naresh Agrawal, the CM called him on the morning of 10 August 2001 to inform that he had been dropped from his ministry. Agrawal was the person whose threats to leave the coalition had also paved way for removal of Ram Prakash Gupta and led to a situation where supply of electricity in the state became a cause of concern as he was the minister of power in the government.[1] Rajnath Singh's next target was Agrawal's friend and MoS in the Ministry of Power, Vikramajit Maurya (MLA from Nawabganj), who was dropped a week later on 16 August 2001. All controversial members of his ministry were now on watch. Rajnath Singh justified his actions—he was eyeing the 2002 assembly polls.

In the meantime, the Social Justice Committee submitted its report on 31 August 2001. It recommended that OBCs be subcategorized into three parts and SCs into two parts. On 13 September, at a cabinet meeting, the Rajnath Singh government accepted the report, and on 15 September, the governor approved the Uttar Pradesh Public Service (Reservation for SCs, STs and OBCs) (Amendment) Ordinance 2001. It was a highly political move to alienate communities like Yadavs and Kurmis from the OBCs, and Jatavs from the SCs. Ashok Yadav, who was a BJP MLA from Shikohabad and the MoS for tourism, was dropped from the government on 18 September 2001, as, among other allegations, he was said to be critical of the Social Justice Committee findings and was also behind a petition filed before the Supreme Court against the report.

Among the three proposed subcategories of 79 OBC communities suggested by the Social Justice Committee, Yadavs, who were considered the main force behind SP, were listed

---

[1]Mishra, Subhash, 'Andhere mein Soobe ke Soorma', *India Today* (Hindi), 28 February 2001, pp. 18–20.

under Subcategory A as it was claimed that they benefitted the most, while eight communities, including Kurmi, Jat and Gurjar, were listed in Subcategory B, and the remaining 70 communities were in Subcategory C. The committee recommendations were highly beneficial for the Jats as they were declared as OBCs in the state in March 2000, and just over a year later, they were subcategorized as second to the Yadavs. Similarly, the Jatavs, who were considered to be the main support base of the BSP, were included in the first subcategory of the most benefitted among 66 SC communities and rest 65 communities in Subcategory B. However, the report reflected that the whole exercise was to alienate Yadavs and Jatavs. *Frontline* wrote at the time, 'The entire exercise of caste enumeration was aimed at weakening the support base of the ruling Bharatiya Janata Party's major rivals in UP—the Samajwadi Party (SP) and the Bahujan Samaj Party (BSP).'[2] To seek endorsement of his social justice exercises, Rajnath Singh had met former PM (also former CM of UP) V.P. Singh. V.P. Singh is believed to have approved of his move as well as appreciated his programme of Gram Darshan as part of which he stayed overnight in some villages at frequent intervals.[3]

Around that time, the party veterans like Atal Bihari Vajpayee and L.K. Advani were getting old, and next-generation leaders like Narendra Modi, Pramod Mahajan, Sushma Swaraj, Venkaiah Naidu, and many others were trying to assert themselves. Rajnath Singh was also among them. The 2002 assembly polls were very important for his political career, so he planned everything accordingly. As CM, he was seen as a rising star, and a key role in the BJP was to be ensured for him if he was able to secure a majority for the party in 2002.

---

[2]Tripathi, Purnima S., 'A New Calculation in Uttar Pradesh', *Frontline*, 15 September 2001, https://tinyurl.com/5n7jhyr6. Accessed on 6 March 2024.

[3]Yadav, Shyamlal, 'Raj Nath ne Liya V.P. se Margdarshan', *Amar Ujala*, 30 June 2001.

But problems for Rajnath Singh persisted. While Naresh Agrawal had already been unceremoniously dropped, another minister, a prominent OBC leader (BJP) from Mirzapur, Om Prakash Singh, was not happy with many of Rajnath Singh's actions and criticized him openly.[4]

In the meantime, a three-day session of the assembly was called during 26–28 September 2001, which was the last session of the thirteenth assembly. The bill for reservation within reservation based on the recommendation of Social Justice Committee, which was the most ambitious project of the Rajnath Singh government, was tabled in the assembly on 27 September 2001. It was passed amid unaccepted amendments moved by members. This short session of the assembly was used by various parties to launch their campaign for the next assembly polls. The same day, all members of the SP resigned from the assembly.

As the state was gearing for the next elections, a spate of controversial ministers' removal started in late 2001. Ved Prakash, MoS for home guards and political pension, was removed on 30 September; Amar Mani Tripathi, MoS for institutional finance and trade tax, who was later convicted and sentenced for the murder of poet Madhumita Shukla, was dropped on 2 December 2001; and Vinay Kumar Pandey, MoS for prisons, was dropped on 4 December. Prakash (elected from Nagar East in Basti on a BSP ticket) was in the JBSP, while Tripathi (elected from Laxmipur on a Congress ticket) and Pandey (elected from Balrampur on a Congress ticket) were from the ABLTC. Later, more ministers were dropped or they resigned on their own, but that was because they sensed that they would be denied a ticket for the next assembly polls.

---

[4]Mishra, Subhash, 'Andhere mein Soobe ke Soorma', *India Today* (Hindi), 28 February 2001, pp. 18-20.

Interestingly, the thirteenth assembly, which was elected in October 1996, was the longest. In fact, for over five months, the assembly was in suspended animation. When poll dates were being fixed at the end of it, its five-year tenure was counted from the first sitting, which was on 27 March 1997. Therefore, poll dates were planned accordingly. However, by the end of 2001, all parties were in election mode, and on 16 January 2002, a three-phase poll schedule was announced. For the BJP, Rajnath Singh was on a roll. He was in control of the entire campaign for the 2002 polls, and a part of his speech, which he repeated at every election rally, became very popular in political circles in those days: '*Jeete koi, sarkaar hamari banegi*' (Whoever wins, the government will be formed by us). Initially, he was not even ready to accommodate the state BJP president Kalraj Mishra on campaign posters of the party; however, he later agreed.[5] During the campaign for the 2002 polls, several BJP leaders felt ignored.

Around this time, two important developments took place. First, a few days after the announcement of the poll schedule, on 21 January 2002, the Supreme Court stayed all appointments in the state under the formula devised by the Social Justice Committee. The other was that the VHP kept raising its demand for the acquired land around the Ram Janmabhoomi–Babri Masjid site in Ayodhya to be handed over to them, except the part on which the disputed structure had stood before it was demolished on 6 December 1992. The Atal Bihari Vajpayee government, in an effort to resolve the issue, involved personalities like Shankaracharya of Kanchi Kamakoti Jayendra Saraswati, other spiritual leaders like Sri Sri Ravi Shankar and former president of India R. Venkataraman. All efforts seemed

---

[5]Rai, Ram Bahadur, 'Raah se Bhatki BJP ke Prateek', *Jansatta*, 2 March 2002, New Delhi.

to be in vain. However, the central government as well as the state government got some respite from the Supreme Court on 13 March 2002 when it stated that no part of the acquired land should be handed over to anyone, and, thus, the tension was defused for the time being. The Vajpayee government was already of this view. Chief Minister Rajnath Singh had also repeatedly said that he would not allow anyone to take the law into their hands, and that the verdict of the Court or a consensus reached through mutual understanding, if any, would be final. Relations between Atal Bihari Vajpayee and VHP leaders, particularly Ashok Singhal, had soured because of Vajpayee's approach to the issue.

During the election campaign, the BJP workers appeared to be visibly annoyed with their leadership. In 2002, there were very few poll surveys, but one of the prominent surveys by *Aaj Tak* had predicted 147 seats for the BJP and its allies, 142 for the SP and its allies, 81 for the BSP and 22 for the Congress.[6] But party leaders who were travelling across the state, addressing rallies and meeting party workers were gradually realizing that things were not favourable on the ground.[7] When results were announced on 24 February 2002, the fourteenth assembly also turned out to be a hung assembly. The BJP got only 88 seats out of the total 403, the BSP got 98, and the SP emerged as the single largest party with 143 seats. Nothing seemed to have worked in favour of the BJP, and the caste rallies that had been organized to attract voters towards the party appeared to have helped other parties instead. On a number of seats, where previously some communities had voted for the BJP

---

[6]Malik, Ashok, and Subhash Mishra, 'Uljhe Paridrishya mein Do Nakshatra', *India Today* (Hindi), 20 February 2002.

[7]As a journalist with *Amar Ujala* in those days, I travelled a lot, accompanying BJP leaders like L.K. Advani, M.M. Joshi and state leaders to cover the election campaign. This is a personal observation.

wholeheartedly, candidates of their own caste were chosen, and those communities ditched the BJP. Driven by its ambition to run the government, the BJP again lost its self-claimed reputation of a 'party with a difference', and many individuals who were classic examples of what type of people must not be in public life, enjoyed power in this regime.

Rajnath Singh resigned as the CM on the very day of counting. But within 48 hours of his resignation, he was elected as the leader of the BJP Legislature Party 'unanimously' by just three dozen BJP members[8] out of the party's total of 130 members of both Houses of the state legislature. A senior leader of the party, Om Prakash Singh of Mirzapur, had objected to this hurried process of election.[9] The BJP's 2002 debacle had several impacts on the party, but the political career of Rajnath Singh kept moving. However, a BJP majority in those polls might have given more power to him.

Within a few weeks, on 3 May 2002 a new government was formed by the BSP's Mayawati in partnership with the BJP. Rajnath Singh, who was against a BSP–BJP government, just like his predecessor Kalyan Singh, resigned from the post of leader of the BJP Legislature Party on 22 July 2002, and Lalji Tandon, a BJP leader considered close to Mayawati, replaced Rajnath Singh on 1 August. Kalraj Mishra had also resigned as UP's BJP chief on 1 June, and he was replaced by Vinay Katiyar with in a month. Rajnath Singh resigned from the Haidargarh Assembly seat as well and was again elected to the Rajya Sabha in November 2002. Instead of staying on in the

[8]Mishra, Subhash, 'Aag Lagi Ghar ke Chiragon se', *India Today* (Hindi), 13 March 2002, pp. 40–1.
[9]Ibid.

state, his focus was on becoming a part of the central level of the BJP and joining the central government. Very soon, he was appointed as the national general secretary of his party under the then president Venkaiah Naidu.

After taking charge of the UP government, Mayawati did not go ahead with Rajnath Singh's policy of reservation within reservation that the Supreme Court had already stayed. In a meeting of her cabinet on 1 June 2002, the Mayawati government decided to revert Rajnath Singh government's decision. Once the BSP–BJP government started functioning, a number of MLAs launched a campaign against the coalition. There was no consensus among BJP leaders in UP and the Centre on the alliance, and finally it collapsed.

Repercussions of the BJP's defeat in UP were felt at the Centre as well. The party soon realized that the alliance with Ajit Singh helped only him and his RLD, which won 14 seats of the 38 it contested in alliance with the BJP. This alliance was intended as the next step in wooing the Jats, but it did not help the saffron party. Hence, talks of the breakup of the alliance started floating soon after the results of the assembly polls came out. Differences between the BJP and Ajit Singh were growing, and sensing this, Ajit Singh started openly criticizing the Union government's policies regarding the agriculture sector. In an interview, he said that if he felt that the farmers' voice was not being heard in the government, he would quit.[10] The BJP leadership took him at his word, and as pressure on him increased, he resigned as the Union minister of agriculture on 23 May 2003. The next day, on 24 May, Rajnath Singh was sworn in as Union minister of agriculture in his place.

---

[10]Yadav, Shyamlal, 'Kisanon ki Baat Sunani hi Chahiye', *India Today* (Hindi), 21 May 2003, pp. 52–3.

Soft-spoken and affable, well organized in his personal and political life, Rajnath Singh had crossed obstacles created by seasoned leaders of his party in UP and kept coming out victorious. His style of functioning reflects the style of Vajpayee. While working for the BJP, he still maintains personal rapport with certain leaders in various parties. It is easy for ordinary workers of his party and other people to meet him despite extensive security arrangements. He is also among the leaders who believe in *jyotish* (astrology).

Amidst the upheaval his party organization was facing since mid-1990s in the state, Rajnath Singh emerged as the ultimate winner. He was appointed as the president of the BJP in 2005 when L.K.Advani had to resign after his remarks on Mohammed Ali Jinnah during a visit to Pakistan. He was the BJP president in 2009 when Advani was projected as the prime ministerial candidate of the NDA, but suffered a setback as the UPA government, headed by Dr Manmohan Singh, returned to power. Rajnath Singh continued as the BJP chief until December 2009, when Nitin Gadkari replaced him. He was again elected party chief during 2013–14, and he headed it during the historic win of the party in the 2014 Lok Sabha polls. Since 2009, he has been a Lok Sabha member (once from Ghaziabad and then from Lucknow).

In those days, a succession war was going on within the BJP. Things were made crystal clear before the 2014 Lok Sabha polls, when Narendra Modi was appointed as the chief of the BJP's election campaign committee on 9 June 2013. The announcement was made by Rajnath Singh after a two-day meeting of the BJP national executive in Goa. Modi was then the CM of Gujarat. Later, he was declared as the BJP's prime ministerial candidate as well. After Modi's overwhelming victory in the 2014 polls, he emerged as a leader of the BJP and of the masses, relegating the others to be his side-players. When the BJP formed the government at the Centre, Rajnath Singh was appointed as the Union minister of home affairs. In 2019, he was appointed as the minister of defence.

The 2002 assembly poll of UP was a high-stakes event for Rajnath Singh, almost like how the December 2002 assembly polls in Gujarat had been crucial for Modi, who was sent to lead Gujarat in October 2001 by the central leadership and secured victory in all elections since then, or the way the 2022 assembly polls was significant for Yogi Adityanath in UP. But Rajnath Singh did not quite succeed as the state could not see much of his vision of development and social engineering. Questions remain: what would have happened if Rajnath Singh had not left the state but had remained there to lead the party in and outside the assembly? His original idea of dividing SCs and OBCs in UP has been taken forward by the BJP more effectively in the case of OBCs at a political level. But in the absence of proper data on the population of various castes of OBCs and their representation in government services, subcategorization is yet not finished. Justice (Rtd) G. Rohini Commission was set up by the Modi government on 2 October 2017 for subcategorization of OBCs, and it had submitted its report on 31 July 2023. On the same issue in UP, the Yogi Adityanath government had constituted a commission headed by Justice (Rtd) Raghvendra Kumar in May 2018, who submitted his report in October 2018. As of March 2024, further action on both of these reports is awaited.

Like many other leaders of BJP and other parties, Rajnath Singh's second generation is also in active politics. His elder son Pankaj Singh was elected as an MLA in 2017 and 2022 from Noida and is the vice president of the UP BJP.

20

AKHILESH YADAV

The Young Gun, the Legacy Keeper

Twentieth CM: Akhilesh Yadav

Party: Samajwadi Party

Tenure: 15 March 2012–19 March 2017

Constituency: Member of Legislative Council

Days in Office: 5 years and 4 days

When the Election Commission announced a seven-phase poll schedule for the UP Assembly on 24 December 2011, the leading parties were already well prepared for it. The BJP had re-inducted the OBC leader and former CM of Madhya Pradesh Uma Bharti into the party and tasked her with reviving the party in UP in the wake of the vacuum created by Kalyan Singh's exit from the party for the second time. The Congress was then heading a UPA government at the Centre, but in UP, among the four major players in the state, it was only a distant fourth since its organization was uprooted from the ground post the 1980s.

The BSP, under Mayawati, which had been in power in UP for five years, was facing anti-incumbency, while the SP, the main Opposition party in the state, was trying to change its old image of being a party primarily dominated by Yadavs and Muslims as well as of being a sympathizer to many unruly elements.

The BSP was facing allegations of corruption in several cases, including the NRHM. In the BJP, internal fighting was affecting the party's chances. Narendra Modi, then Gujarat CM, who had already emerged as a crowd-puller, refused to campaign in the elections because then BJP chief Nitin Gadkari had appointed Modi's bête noire Sanjay Joshi as election-in-charge of the party in UP. Akhilesh Yadav, the son of SP chief Mulayam Singh Yadav, was appointed as the UP president of the SP on 4 June 2009, and he began to gradually take over the party affairs. Before the assembly polls, he launched a bicycle yatra from Noida to Agra in October 2011. He organized a Kranti Rath Yatra to travel the entire state and covered most of the assembly constituencies. What suddenly boosted his image was a statement he gave on 3 January 2012 about his party: 'The party will not take D.P. Yadav.'[1] D.P. Yadav, having a criminal background, was brought into politics by Mulayam Singh Yadav in 1989. Mulayam Singh fielded him from Bulandshahr and appointed as a MoS in his government. After switching sides many times, including the BJP, he and his wife Umlesh were elected to the UP Assembly from Sahaswan and Bilsi, respectively, on his Rashtriya Parivartan Dal ticket in 2007. Later, the party merged with the BSP. There were reports that leaders like Azam Khan were trying to get D.P. Yadav into the SP but that Akhilesh had closed that door. D.P. Yadav later clarified that he had not approached anyone, but by that time, Akhilesh's

---

[1]'Rift in SP as Mulayam's Son Opposes D P Yadav's Entry', *IndiaTV*, 3 January 2012, https://tinyurl.com/58jx6427. Accessed on 6 March 2024.

statement had worked in his favour in public discourse. In the meantime, the BJP inducted Babu Singh Kushwaha (one of the two ministers that Mayawati had sacked due to the NRHM scam) into the party on the same day, 3 January 2012, which gave it very bad publicity. About the SP's image of being a goonda-friendly party during the earlier tenures of his father, Akhilesh said, 'Because of some outsiders who had come into the party, the party got that stamp. At that time we needed numbers as we did not have enough seats.'[2]

The SP was trying to politically cash in on every possibility. One such possibility was its promise to give allowances of ₹1,000 per month to unemployed youth aged between 25 and 40. This promise resulted in creating a huge vote bank for the party, particularly of the youth, and later, huge crowds of jobless youth emerged to get themselves registered at employment exchanges.

In an interesting incident, at an election rally in Lucknow on 16 February 2012, Rahul Gandhi, accusing the BSP and SP of only making promises and not fulfilling them, tore up a piece of paper in an attempt to explain that mere lists of assurances were of no use. Akhilesh Yadav's reaction to this incident had him saying that Rahul 'may now jump off the stage to vent his anger'.[3] He transformed the SP's election campaign machinery into a high-tech one. His image was completely different from that of his father who had wholeheartedly opposed English and once even criticized public-school-educated people.[4]

---

[2]Gupta, Shekhar, 'Rahul Asks People Questions, but Forgets They Have Questions for Him Too', *The Indian Express*, 27 February 2012, https://tinyurl.com/bdesvmjw. Accessed on 9 March 2024.

[3]'Control Your Anger: Akhilesh to Rahul', *The Indian Express*, 17 February 2012, https://tinyurl.com/2s4chfhf. Accessed on 6 March 2024.

[4]*Vidhan Sabha ki Karyawahi,* 17 January 1990, UP Assembly Secretariat, Lucknow, p. 117.

When results were announced, the SP got a historic mandate with 224 of the 403 seats in its pocket. For the first time, the SP had a majority on its own. Uttar Pradesh's electorate had given a clear mandate to a single party in the second consecutive assembly poll. The BSP, which had flooded newspapers and news channels with advertisements claiming a return to power, won just 80 seats but emerged as the main Opposition party. Despite all the hype the BJP had created, it won merely 47 seats and the Congress, which had contested as many as 355 seats, won just 28. Akhilesh was not projected as his party's chief ministerial candidate during the campaign, but the message was clear among the political circle from the very beginning—if the party got a majority, he was going to be the CM. On 10 March 2012, he was elected as the leader of the legislature party of the SP, and on 15 March, Governor B.L. Joshi administered him the oath of office as CM. Aged less than 39 years, Akhilesh was the youngest person to have taken oath as the CM of the state. He chose to enter the Legislative Council nearly two months after being sworn in as the CM.

Born on 1 July 1973, Akhilesh studied at the Dholpur Military School in Rajasthan, did his bachelor's in Civil Engineering from Mysore (now Mysuru), and obtained his master's degree in Environment Engineering from the University of Sydney. In the 1999 Lok Sabha polls, Mulayam Singh had won from two seats, Sambhal as well as Kannauj, so he vacated his home turf Kannauj for Akhilesh. In the 2000 by-poll, and in the 2004 and 2009 polls, Akhilesh was elected to the Lok Sabha from Kannauj.

When the House first assembled on 28 May 2012 after the swearing in of the Akhilesh government, the governor's speech clearly reflected the government's views: 'In the last five years, this state has witnessed the biggest corruption in its history, victimization of innocent people and *jungle raj*. People have got nothing except stones, statues and memorials.'[5] His reference was towards the memorials and statues of Akhilesh's predecessor Mayawati, her patron Kanshi Ram and other SC icons, and the BSP's election symbol of an elephant, which were installed in the state at several locations during her regime.

Kanya Vidya Dhan, a scheme Mulayam Singh Yadav had launched as the CM, but was stopped by Mayawati, was now re-launched by the Akhilesh Yadav government. He decided that every district official must be in their office for two hours, from 10.00 a.m. (except Tuesdays and Saturdays), to attend to complaints of people and resolve them.

The women's helpline number, 1090, was launched in 2012 to take real-time action in making women feel safe. Women could access the helpline number from anywhere in the state and lodge complaints without physically visiting the police station to file an FIR, and the identity of the complainant would be kept secret. His government also gave clearance for the construction of 8.3 kilometres of the Lucknow Metro in June 2013, construction for which began on 27 September 2014. From the NRHM funds during the previous government, 988 ambulances that were purchased centrally by state government officials and were parked unused in Lucknow were now sent to block level for their utilization.

At this time, things were changing rapidly. Before Akhilesh completed two years as the CM, the 2014 Lok Sabha elections were announced, which were held in nine phases from 7 April to 12 May. Modi was already appointed as the chairman of

---

[5] *Vidhan Sabha ki Karyawahi*, 28 May 2012, UP Assembly Secretariat, Lucknow, p. 24; author's translation.

the campaign committee and the prime ministerial candidate of the BJP for the 2014 Lok Sabha elections. He decided to contest from the Varanasi Lok Sabha seat, turning the state into a compelling electoral battlefield. It was an election that was preceded by communal violence during August–September 2013 in Muzaffarnagar and surrounding areas, in which nearly 60 people were killed. The SP was already facing allegations of Muslim appeasement, but the Muzaffarnagar riots charged the atmosphere in western UP to such an extent that the decades-old Jat–Muslim equation was disturbed. Earlier, aggressive statements of leaders like Azam Khan were helping the SP to garner Muslim votes in its favour, but post the Muzaffarnagar riots, the BJP and its affiliates tried to polarize Hindus as well, and statements of the SP's Muslim leaders were only helping the BJP.

During the 2014 elections, the vitiating communal divide seemed to have pervaded the entire state, and the BJP appeared to be the only beneficiary. The party that had won merely 10 seats in the state in the 2009 Lok Sabha elections won 71 seats on its own, and its ally Apna Dal (S) won two. It also got a majority in the Lok Sabha with 282 seats, and Narendra Modi formed the government at the Centre. Thus, the 2014 Lok Sabha result in UP was a precursor to the 2017 assembly polls, which were less than three years away. The BJP now had its eyes on UP.

During the 2014 Lok Sabha elections, an allegation, which had a far-reaching impact, started against Akhilesh's government—out of 86 subdivisional magistrates recruited by the Uttar Pradesh Public Service Commission (UPPSC) in a few years, 56 were Yadavs. This figure was used against his government time and again. During his tenure, the SP never clarified this issue with clear facts. Although the CBI later took over the inquiry of this matter, the real facts never came out. However, it created an anti-Yadav narrative and had a huge impact on the electoral possibilities for the SP in the state.[6] The BJP utilized it politically, and this figure, which had become like a political lexicon—an oft-repeated witticism—in the elections, made it easy for the saffron party to fulfil its old agenda of attracting non-Yadav OBCs (and also non-Jatav SCs) into its fold.

Akhilesh's problems were multifold. Besides facing heavy political opposition from outside, he was facing a crisis from within his family and party as well. Since his oath-taking as CM, there had been murmurs within the party and allegations from the Opposition that his authority as CM was compromised by his uncles Shivpal Singh Yadav and Ram Gopal Yadav, and also by his father Mulayam Singh Yadav, who had openly commented against his functioning on a number of occasions. Infighting within the party, and within the family, was the talk of the town. On 12 September 2016, the differences became public when Akhilesh, in the light of a CBI inquiry into an alleged mining scam, sacked two ministers close to Mulayam who were facing allegations of corruption. The next day, he removed the chief secretary Deepak Singhal, who was considered close to Shivpal Yadav. On the same day, Mulayam Singh, in an attempt to placate Shivpal, removed Akhilesh from the post of state president and appointed Shivpal to it.

Considering the move as an attempt to diminish his position, on 13 September 2016, Akhilesh stripped Shivpal of his key portfolios of PWD, irrigation, cooperatives, flood control, land development and water resources, wasteland development, revenue, disaster relief and rehabilitation, and public service management. Instead, Shivpal was allocated social welfare.

---

[6]Babele, Piyush, 'EXCLUSIVE: UPPCS-2011 mein Zabardast Gorakhdandha, 86 OBC Ummedwaron mein 50 Yadav', *India Today* (Hindi), 19 June 2014, https://tinyurl.com/rp9jk2te. Accessed on 10 March 2024.

However, Akhilesh returned all departments except PWD a few days later on 17 September, which hit his uncle's ego.

In a meeting of party leaders on 24 October 2016 in Lucknow, Akhilesh publicly criticized the Rajya Sabha MP Amar Singh by saying that he was behind this family feud. In the ongoing feud, Mulayam Singh, Shivpal Yadav and Amar Singh were on one side and Akhilesh and Ram Gopal Yadav were on the other. Shivpal Yadav's portfolios were changed quite frequently, and on 23 October 2016, he resigned from the Akhilesh Yadav Cabinet. Nothing short of a daily soap opera was going on in the Mulayam Singh family, and while other parties were preparing for assembly polls that were just six months away, Mulayam Singh expelled his son Akhilesh and second cousin Ram Gopal from his party. Keeping Shivpal on his side was considered a well-calculated move on Mulayam's part. Between him and Ram Gopal, Shivpal posed more of a threat to Akhilesh Yadav's political future due to the ground support he enjoyed within the party. By keeping Shivpal close to him, the SP patriarch ruled out a split from that end. Later, when Shivpal formed a new party named Pragatisheel Samajwadi Party (Lohia) with Amar Singh in May 2017, Mulayam Singh went with them, leaving Akhilesh and others aside. However, Shivpal later returned to the SP, and Akhilesh emerged victorious in the battle for the legacy of Mulayam Singh within his family and party.

Since coming to power, Akhilesh initiated measures to improve the working of his government. He distributed laptops to students of a certain level, which was greatly appreciated by the youth and increased his popularity. He tried to improve electricity generation and availability in the state.

During his stint as the CM, he avoided commenting on issues like reservation for the various social groups. His predecessor Mayawati had implemented reservation for SC and

ST employees in promotions, but the Allahabad High Court had quashed it and the Supreme Court, on 30 April 2012, upheld the decision of the High Court. The Akhilesh government, in keeping with the Supreme Court ruling, scrapped reservation in promotions order. This decision turned the SC and ST employees against him from the very beginning of his tenure.

One of Akhilesh's prime contributions to the state's infrastructure is the 302-kilometre-long six-lane (expandable to eight lanes) Agra–Lucknow Access-Controlled Expressway. It starts from Agra's inner ring road, passes through Firozabad, Mainpuri, Etawah, Auraiya, Kannauj, Kanpur Nagar, Hardoi and Unnao, and ends at State Highway 40 in Lucknow. During his government, 1,488 ambulances under the 108 scheme and 2,264 ambulances under the 102 scheme were launched.[7] These have been very helpful in rural areas of the state. Additionally, out of the 33 state universities (including technical, agriculture and medical) established post Independence in UP, five were established during Akhilesh's regime.

However, when the 2017 assembly polls were drawing near, the SP was unaware of the preparations going on in the BJP camp. Newspapers and news channels were flooded with advertisements put up by the SP, and the same officers who had controlled the public relations of the Mayawati government during the 2012 assembly polls, which the BSP had lost, were at the helm. Akhilesh was repeating the same mistakes made by Mayawati in the 2012 assembly polls—letting his coterie of selected leaders and bureaucrats convince him of an imminent win, unaware of the fact that his support base was eroding. Persuaded by Rajya Sabha MP Amar Singh and election strategist Prashant Kishore, the SP had made an

---

[7] *Vidhan Sabha ki Karyawahi*, 29 January 2016, UP Assembly Secretariat, Lucknow, p. 22.

alliance with the Congress, but it could win only 47 seats from the 311 it contested, and the Congress won just seven seats from the 114 it contested. This was despite the Union government's decision on 8 November 2016 of demonetizing currency notes of ₹1,000 and ₹500, due to which people had suffered a lot.

In fact, after Mulayam Singh took oath as CM for the first time on 5 December 1989, the upper castes in the state had lost hope of anyone from their communities becoming the CM. They, therefore, focussed their attention on supporting candidates and parties to merely secure a share in power. But by 2017, everything had changed. The BJP's massive win in the 2014 Lok Sabha polls was maintained in the 2017 UP Assembly polls, and it soon became apparent that Akhilesh Yadav's campaign slogan '*Kaam bolta hai*' (Work speaks) had not worked. As it turned out, the SP had been fighting a losing battle. Akhilesh Yadav resigned and was replaced by the BJP's Yogi Adityanath as the UP CM on 19 March 2017. There is a long list of leaders across the state who enjoyed power and government contracts during the regimes of Mayawati and Akhilesh but later moved to the BJP.

Though Akhilesh was elected to the Lok Sabha from Azamgarh in 2019, he contested the 2022 assembly polls and was elected to the UP Assembly from the Karhal seat. His party could not come to power in 2022 either, and its slogan '*Baais mein baaisikil*' (Bicycle [symbol of the SP] in 2022) did not work. Seeing that his future was actually in state politics, he quit as a Lok Sabha MP and became the LoP in the UP Assembly on 26 March 2022. He led a 109-member SP in the assembly with eight members in the Upper House. Akhilesh has over seven years' work experience in the Opposition and is the most prominent face of the Opposition in the state.

As the CM, Akhilesh Yadav had served for five years and four days. Of late, he has started raising issues that affect his party's support base, such as reservation and caste census, which he hesitated to do when he was the CM. He has also brought focus to the pichhada, Dalit and alpsankhyak (PDA), that is, the OBCs, SCs and minorities. As of 6 March 2024, his party has two members each in the Rajya Sabha and the Lok Sabha. His father Mulayam Singh captured and took forward the legacy of many, from Dr Lohia to Charan Singh to Chaudhary Devi Lal. A significant challenge before Akhilesh is to consolidate and continue the legacy of his father.

21

YOGI ADITYANATH

A New Era for UP

Twenty-First CM: Yogi Adityanath

Party: Bharatiya Janata Party

Tenure: 19 March 2017–Present

Constituency: Member of Legislative Council, Gorakhpur Urban

Days in Office: Completed one full tenure, continuing the second

Years prior to the announcement of the 2017 assembly polls, the country had gone through many political changes. The UPA government of Dr Manmohan Singh, in its second term (2009–2014), had faced widespread criticism for alleged corruption and political mismanagement due to conflicts between the PM and other leaders including the Congress's first family comprising Sonia Gandhi and Rahul Gandhi. On 9 June 2013, Gujarat CM Narendra Modi was appointed as the chairman of the BJP's election campaign committee for the 2014 Lok Sabha polls, and three weeks prior to that, on 19 May, his close confidant Amit Shah was put in charge of the party in UP. Making the most of the atmosphere against corruption, a new party named Aam Aadmi Party, headed by a former Indian Revenue Service officer Arvind Kejriwal, was born in November 2012, which unseated the Congress government in Delhi in 2013.

In the 2014 Lok Sabha polls, the BJP bagged 71 seats in UP. The BJP had been out of power in the state since Rajnath Singh demitted office as the CM in March 2002, though it had shared power with Mayawati for just over a year in 2002–03. Its tally in assembly polls had been decreasing in election after election. In the new millennium, state presidents, from Om Prakash Singh, Kalraj Mishra and Vinay Katiyar to Keshari Nath Tripathi, Ramapati Ram Tripathi and Surya Pratap Shahi, as well as leaders of the BJP from UP in central politics like Rajnath Singh, were unable to win elections for the party. Amit Shah, who had managed the BJP's electioneering and party strategy very tactfully for the 2014 Lok Sabha (the BJP's state president was Laxmikant Bajpai), which led to its landslide victory, was elevated as the BJP's national president and the chairperson of the NDA on 9 July 2014. In his inimitable style, Amit Shah snubbed several prominent leaders of the party when they tried to criticize others. His message to party leaders was very clear: '*Aapko party ne jo kaam diya hai, vahi karo*' (Do only that work which the party has assigned you).[1] Criticism of others and promotion of groups within the party were what the state BJP leaders had been spending most of their energy on for several years, and many of them were concerned about promoting their family members into the party.

After his elevation as the BJP chief, Shah was looking for a

---

[1]Based on my conversation with many BJP leaders of UP.

suitable candidate to head its UP unit. In the first week of April 2016, Keshav Prasad Maurya was appointed to the position, and he emerged as the new face of the party in the state. Now, as the state BJP chief, Maurya was full of confidence. While Mulayam Singh's family was busy with infighting and the BSP was reduced once again to its original identity of a party of SCs, the BJP (supported by the RSS machinery) was busy in laying down new roots in the state with great energy, strategy, enthusiasm and coordination. In the middle of October 2014, Dr Krishna Gopal was put in charge of the BJP in the RSS as sah-sarkaryawah (joint general secretary), a post filled by someone from UP for the first time since 1994. Kalyan Singh, who had earlier deserted the BJP twice, returned to it again before the 2014 Lok Sabha elections, and Amit Shah relied on him more than anyone while deciding the candidates and planning the poll strategy for 2017. From micro-management of electioneering, which included appointing *panna-pramukhs* (literally translated into 'page-chiefs', grassroots party-workers who were in charge of a page on the electoral roll to influence voters to vote in favour of the BJP), to intense social engineering and mass rallies, the BJP was using every tactic available in its repository.

In the midst of all this, the dust was yet to settle on the communal atmosphere created post the Muzaffarnagar riots of 2013 and new minor incidents of communal tension. As much as the anti-BJP parties tried to speak on the issue, it only resulted in polarizing the majority in favour of the BJP. Another strategy that played a key role in the BJP's favour in the 2017 assembly polls was its acceptance of anyone who was willing to leave other parties like the SP, BSP, Congress, RLD and so on. It was estimated that over one-third of the BJP candidates in the 2017 assembly polls were those who had come from other parties or were newcomers. Leaders of different parties, for example Swami Prasad Maurya and Dara Singh Chauhan, who had considerable influence, more than a few thousand votes in their pockets on several seats, and had quit their parties, were gladly accepted and given tickets by the BJP in 2017. The saffron party did not declare its chief ministerial face before the elections, and all who were hopeful were working hard and keeping their fingers crossed. During this time, there was a growing demand for Yogi Adityanath's rallies across the state.

When results for the 2017 assembly polls were declared, the BJP got a historic mandate. It went much beyond what the BJP leadership had expected. It had contested 384 seats and alone won as many as 312. Now, the primary challenge before the BJP was to choose a CM. Being the BJP president of UP, Maurya had played an important role in the state, so he was naturally eyeing the CM's chair. However, his chances were bleak as he did not have enough experience, neither in the party nor in legislature and government. Most of the prominent posters of the BJP during electioneering had joint images of the then Union minister of home affairs Rajnath Singh, Lok Sabha MP from Deoria Kalraj Mishra, former Madhya Pradesh CM Uma Bharti and Maurya himself, giving no indication about who would actually become the CM if the party was to secure a majority. In interviews given during the assembly polls, Yogi Adityanath and Maurya were equally tight-lipped on the issue.[2] There were many who were desirous of leading the government, but the decision-making process in the BJP

---

[2]Yadav, Shyamlal, 'Uttar Pradesh: SP and BSP Created So Much Imbalance, We Corrected It (by Not Fielding Muslims), Says Yogi Adityanath', *The Indian Express,* 1 February 2017, https://tinyurl.com/yed7p3et. Accessed on 7 March 2024; Yadav, Shyamlal, 'Being on BJP Posters Doesn't Mean We Are Claimants to CM Post, Says Keshav Maurya', *The Indian Express*, 9 March 2017, https://tinyurl.com/bdd7y9kn. Accessed on 7 March 2024.

under Narendra Modi and Amit Shah is such that no one knows what finally happens on such matters.

Everyone was eagerly waiting for the big news. Between the BJP and RSS leadership, many probable candidates were discussed for the post, and prominent among them were Yogi Adityanath, Keshav Prasad Maurya, Manoj Sinha, Laxmikant Bajpai and Dinesh Sharma. Decision was finally taken. After the legislature party meeting in Lucknow on 18 March 2017, former BJP chief Venkaiah Naidu told reporters that Shahjahanpur MLA Suresh Khanna had proposed the name of Yogi Adityanath, and that it was seconded by 10 others, and since there was no other name proposed by anyone, his name was finalized. That is how he took oath as the CM on Sunday, 19 March 2017.

Maurya (an OBC from Kaushambi) and Dinesh Sharma (a Brahmin, mayor of Lucknow) were chosen as deputy CMs. Yogi Adityanath and Maurya, who were Lok Sabha members from Gorakhpur and Phulpur, respectively, and Sharma, who was the mayor of Lucknow, needed to enter either House of the state legislature within six months of taking the oath. But they were faced with a bad precedent. While they were planning to be member of either House, they hesitated in trying their luck in an assembly by-poll, as, in 1971, then CM T.N. Singh had to resign within six months because he was not able to win the by-poll for his own assembly seat (then named Maniram) in Gorakhpur, a seat under which the Gorakhnath Math of Yogi Adityanath comes. Therefore, Yogi Adityanath and Maurya, who resigned from the Lok Sabha only after the presidential elections on 17 July 2017, did not contest the assembly by-polls and got elected to the Legislative Council on 18 September 2017. Dinesh Sharma, who resigned as the mayor of Lucknow, was also elected as an MLC.

Born on 5 June 1972 in Pauri Garhwal district of Uttarakhand as Ajay Mohan Singh Bisht, Yogi Adityanath was active in student politics while completing his BSc in a college under Hemvati Nandan Bahuguna Garhwal University. After his graduation, he came in contact with Mahant Avaidyanath and went to Gorakhpur. An ailing Avaidyanath decided to make Yogi Adityanath his political successor and fielded him for the Lok Sabha from Gorakhpur in 1998. Yogi Adityanath has won all Lok Sabha elections since then until 2014 from Gorakhpur. Before the demise of Avaidyanath on 12 September 2014, Yogi Adityanath had taken the reins of the whole political, social and religious legacy of the Gorakhnath Math. As per an estimate made in 2017, the assets of this math of Nath *sampraday*, which is spread mainly in Gorakhpur and the nearby districts of UP, as well as the Terai regions of Nepal, amounted to nearly ₹500 crore.[3]

Before Yogi Adityanath, Mahant Avaidyanath (born as Kripal Singh Bisht) and the Gorakhnath Math had been influencing the politics in this area for many decades. The math is known to have a following particularly among the non-Brahmins (Rajputs, SCs and OBCs) in the area. Avaidyanath and Yogi Adityanath were also actively involved with the efforts to build the Ram temple at the birthplace of Lord Ram in Ayodhya, which was finally built after the Supreme Court settled the issue in favour of the temple on 9 November 2019.

Once he had taken control of politics in the area, Yogi Adityanath formed the Hindu Yuva Vahini in 2002, which spread its network in surrounding districts within a few years. His math had always dictated the politics in the region on its own terms. When Yogi Adityanath had resigned from the BJP national executive on 15 March 2007, alleging that the party

---

[3]Harsh, Kumar, 'Ek Yogi ka Antahpur', *India Today* (Hindi), 5 April 2017, p. 27.

did not give tickets to his supporters in eastern UP, he had stated, 'I have made up my mind to float a separate party after I hold consultations with my colleagues in Gorakhpur.'[4] There have been instances in different elections when Yogi Adityanath has fielded his own candidates if the BJP candidate was not to his liking. But ideologically, the RSS and Yogi Adityanath have been on the same page, and he has enjoyed full support within the RSS, more than in the BJP.

In 2017, there was a growing demand for Yogi Adityanath during election rallies across the regions in UP, where his supporters vociferated slogans such as '*Desh mein Modi, UP mein Yogi*' (In the country it is Modi, and in UP it is Yogi). With him taking oath as the CM in UP, Yogi Adityanath's popularity started rising within and outside the BJP. On Hindutva issues, he always spoke clearly and emerged as a polarizing figure. However, the BJP experienced its first big setback after Yogi Adityanath's oath-taking when it lost the by-poll in March 2018 from the Gorakhpur and Phulpur Lok Sabha seats vacated by Yogi Adityanath and Maurya, respectively.

As the CM, Yogi Adityanath focussed mainly on law and order in the state and started a crackdown on mafia, targeting people like Atiq Ahmed of Allahabad, Mukhtar Ansari of Ghazipur, Vijay Mishra of Bhadohi, and many more. His government took action against Azam Khan, a prominent SP leader from Rampur who had founded Muhammad Ali Jauhar University. His government's action of seizing properties of protestors and recovering the damages from them, particularly during protests against the Citizenship Amendment Act, 2019, enhanced his popularity among the Hindu hardliners. 'Bulldozer' emerged as a new keyword in the state, as also

[4]"'BJP Leaders Have a Soft Corner for Mulayam'", *Rediff.com*, 16 March 2007, https://tinyurl.com/3u9ca4kk. Accessed on 9 March 2024.

'encounter'—a word that had returned and reminded one of the era of V.P. Singh as the CM. Yogi Adityanath paid special attention to Azam Khan, known for his oratory skills and his hold on voters up to the grassroots level in Rampur. Widely known for his aggressive remarks against inter-faith marriages, conversions and cow-slaughter, when campaigning for by-polls for 11 assembly seats in UP in September 2014, Yogi Adityanath said in Bijnor, '*Aaj Hindustan jaga hai. Ab koi Jodhabai Akbar ke saath nahin jayegi*' (Now the country has awoken, now no Jodhabai will go with any Akbar).[5] Azam responded, '*Itna maloom hai ki pichhli sarkar me band ho gaye the to bahut roye the dahaden maar maar kar. Bahut roye the. Hamein bhi taras aaya tha*' (I know that when he was arrested during the last government's regime, he wept a lot, wept aloud. He wept a lot. I was also sympathetic).[6] Azam Khan was referring to an incident on 12 March 2007, when, in the Lok Sabha, Yogi Adityanath had cried while elaborating on the alleged victimization he faced. He had said, 'I have been the victim of political rivalry and prejudice for some time. I would like to know only this, whether this House will be able to provide protection to the Members before we may also fall prey to some kind of mishap, political conspiracy like Shri Sunil Mahato.'[7] But the coin had flipped, and power had come into the hands of Yogi Adityanath, with Azam Khan sitting on the opposite side. Azam, his wife Tazeen Fatima and their son Abdulla Azam are currently facing

[5]'Ab Koi Jodha Nahi Jayegi Akbar ke Saath', *Jagran* (Hindi), 7 September 2014, https://tinyurl.com/yc8mm22h. Accessed on 8 April 2024.

[6]InKhabar Official, 'Andar Ki Baat: From Now on, No Jodha Will Marry Akbar, Says Yogi Adityanath', *YouTube*, 8 September 2014, http://tinyurl.com/3vee8mtf. Accessed on 3 April 2023; author's translation.

[7]Proceedings of Lok Sabha, 12 March 2007, Lok Sabha Secretariat, New Delhi. Mahto, a Lok Sabha MP of Jharkhand Mukti Morcha from Jamshedpur, was shot dead by Maoists on 4 March 2007 in Jamshedpur.

several criminal charges, and the father–son duo has lost its membership of the assembly due to their conviction. On 18 October 2023, Azam, his wife and son were sentenced to seven-year imprisonment by an MP/MLA court in Rampur for acquiring a fake birth certificate of Abdulla.

As CM, Yogi Adityanath spread the Hindutva agenda by taking a number of decisions. On 16 October 2018, his cabinet decided to rename Allahabad district as Prayagraj, and on 6 November 2018, it renamed Faizabad district as Ayodhya. Thanks to the campaign against cow-slaughter, trading in these animals has been greatly affected, but stray cattle have been seen destroying crops across the state. His government started a scheme for rehabilitation of such animals, but it was not effective. On certain issues like inter-faith marriages, Yogi Adityanath has such strong views that on 17 February 2019, when the then BJP general secretary (Organisation) and RSS pracharak Ramlal's niece got married to her Muslim friend at Hotel Taj in Lucknow, several top leaders, including Governor Ram Naik attended it, but Yogi Adityanath did not.

It was for the second time after 1989 that the same party had a majority government at the Centre and in UP as well. While in 1989–91, the same parties (first it was the Janata Dal, then it was the Janata Dal [S]) were in power in UP as well as at the Centre, in 1998–2002, both the central and UP governments were headed by the BJP, but those were not single-party majority governments. The Congress regimes prior to 1989 had seen clashes of egos among central and state leaders, and the Congress high command had frequently changed CMs, including once under their famous move named the Kamaraj Plan in 1963. None of the Congress CMs in UP had completed a full single tenure. Therefore, when PM Narendra Modi started saying '*Double engine ki sarkar*' (state and central governments are run by the same party) with reference to the performance of the state government, it became a new idiom in political circles for appreciating (also in attracting criticism of) the regime of the same party in the state and at the Centre.

Whenever in power, the BJP governments have often faced criticism from party workers on the grounds that the bureaucracy became dominant, and political workers and elected representatives became ineffective. This started happening in the Yogi Adityanath government as well. There have been several such instances of MLAs of the party criticizing their own government. Nearly 100 BJP MLAs sat on a dharna against their own government in Lucknow on 17 December 2019. However, when MLAs keep requesting for transfer and posting of officials of their choice as well as other favours, it becomes very difficult for any CM to satisfy all MLAs.

Since Independence, almost every CM has faced allegations of promoting and posting people of their own caste to prime positions in the government, and Yogi Adityanath is no exception. He has also been widely criticized for being extremely casteist. However, what is different is that he is not defensive. Just before completing his first five-year tenure, on being asked whether he felt hurt on being labelled a casteist, he said, 'I am not hurt. It is not a crime to be born in a Rajput family. This is one caste in the country in which even God was born, not once but many times. One should take pride in one's caste, and I am proud to be a Rajput.'[8] Yogi Adityanath is fifth person from Rajput (or Thakur) caste on the post.

However, most of the criticism Yogi Adityanath's government faced was from the Brahmins, who were among the largest beneficiaries of the government and the ruling party, including prime postings for officials of this caste. Crackdown

---

[8]Aron, Sunita, 'Yogi Adityanath Interview: "I Do Politics of Development... How Can That Be Divisive"', *Hindustan Times,* 28 January 2022, https://tinyurl.com/ykd5ccrf. Accessed on 7 March 2024.

on alleged criminals like Vijay Mishra of Bhadohi attracted criticism from Brahmins and even from some BJP leaders who agreed with their sentiments. But the BJP had lost nothing politically. When some BJP MLAs started asking questions about how many Brahmins were killed, the former Union MoS in the Congress government, Jitin Prasada, while launching the Brahmin Chetna Parishad on 6 July 2020, stated that '[s] ince the Adityanath government came to power, the crimes and killings against Brahmins have increased manifold. They are being killed, and they aren't being given any justice. At the moment, data tells us that Brahmin killings are disproportionately high, more than the other castes.'[9] This was despite the fact that the then chief secretary R.K. Tiwari, principal secretary home Awanish Kumar Awasthi, and director general of police Hitesh Chandra Awasthy were all Brahmins. Later, Jitin Prasada joined BJP on 9 June 2021 and was sworn in as a prominent minister in Yogi Adityanath's cabinet, and fielded as a BJP candidate for the 2024 Lok Sabha polls from Pilibhit, a seat earlier represented by Varun Gandhi. But some cases of alleged fake encounters are disturbing. A classic example is that of Jhansi's Pushpendra Yadav, who was allegedly killed in a fake encounter on 9 October 2019. An FIR of murder was registered only after the Allahabad High Court passed an order on 12 September 2022. But while waiting for justice, his wife Shivangi Yadav died of suicide on 29 March 2023.

In its first five-year tenure, the Yogi Adityanath government also initiated infrastructure projects like the Ganga Expressway, Bundelkhand Expressway and Uttar Pradesh Defence Industrial Corridor, and completed others that were conceived during

---

[9] @JitinPrasada, *X* (formerly Twitter), 6 July 2020, 2.59 p.m., https://tinyurl.com/4sn866p5. Accessed on 15 March 2024; author's translation.

the previous governments. But anger among the youth towards his government was high because recruitment for government jobs was stuck or delayed, and there were frequent paper leaks in examinations.[10] There was also the allegation of violation of reservation rules in recruitments. Until March 2024, the Yogi Adityanath government has established five state universities in UP.

Many meetings were organized in Lucknow and Delhi in May and June 2021 among the BJP and RSS leaders at different levels. At one point of time, it was certain that Yogi Adityanath was going to be replaced. The central leadership was concerned about the assembly polls, which were only nine months away. Amid his ongoing tussle with Deputy CM Maurya, after intervention from some RSS leaders, he made a surprise visit to Maurya's residence on 22 June 2021 in an attempt to mend fences. Before Yogi Adityanath could be convinced about the change of leadership, the BJP leadership, assessing the situation, realized that if he was removed, the party would only suffer. The dust settled when PM Modi came to Lucknow to address the 56th Conference of Director Generals of Police and Inspector Generals of Police of states/union territories, attended by heads of central armed police forces and central police organizations, on 20–21 November 2021. After meeting the PM at Raj Bhavan, where Modi was staying, Yogi Adityanath tweeted a picture on 21 November in which PM Modi was on a stroll with his hand on Yogi Adityanath's shoulder. He shared a poem with it:

Ham nikal pade hain pran karke
Apna tan-man arpan karke

---

[10]During the assembly polls, I had travelled to many districts, from Lucknow to Gorakhpur, and reported on this anger among the youth in *The Indian Express* in February 2022.

Jid hai ek surya ugana hai
Ambar se uncha jaana hai
Ek bharat naya banana hai

[We have started a journey with a commitment, sacrificing our body and mind, to bring a sunrise; have to go high above the sky and make a new India.]

This put to rest all the recent rumours and made it clear that the party could not afford to replace Yogi Adityanath. He moved ahead, and the 2022 assembly polls were contested with him as the face of the BJP in UP.

Seven-phase assembly polls were announced on 8 January 2022. A high-stakes election campaign was unleashed, and Yogi Adityanath had an upper hand this time as he left his opponents in the party far behind in popularity and acceptability. Unlike in 2017, when the BJP had not projected anyone as the CM, in 2022, Yogi Adityanath was the face of the party for the chair of CM. However, in order to keep Brahmins with the BJP, he hardly mentioned his action against Vikas Dubey in his public meetings.[11]

In his public addresses before the 2022 polls, his speeches made special mention of 'bulldozers'. The central government under PM Modi continued with its scheme of distributing free ration, which was started during Covid-19. Besides this, the benefits of Pradhan Mantri Awas Yojna (rural as well as urban), Pradhan Mantri Kisan Samman Nidhi and other welfare schemes were also reaching the rural masses. Election management by the BJP, supported by the RSS on the ground, was being carried out with full vigour. Along with all his achievements, a song sung by Kanhaiya Mittal, a Chandigrah-

[11]Vikas Dubey was a gangster, whose gang had killed eight policemen on 3 July 2020 when they raided his home. Dubey was killed by the UP police on 10 July 2020 while he was trying to escape from police custody.

based singer, was widely spread during electioneering: '*Jo Ram ko laye hain, ham unko layenge*' (We will vote those people who have brought Ram). It referred to the Ram temple in Ayodhya, which was being built back then, and an idol of Ram Lalla was ceremoniously positioned in the Garbha Griha on 22 January 2024.

Although the SP–BSP alliance had failed during the 2019 Lok Sabha elections, in 2022, the SP was the main Opposition against the BJP. At this time, turncoats had also started switching parties. Yet, against all speculations, calculations, defections and resignations, when results of the 2022 polls were announced, the BJP had won 255 seats.

Yogi Adityanath thus created history by becoming the first-ever CM of the state since Independence to win a consecutive term for his party after completing a full five years in office. The Congress-led governments had won consecutively in the past, but no CM had managed to complete a full term. Two of Yogi Adityanath's predecessors, Akhilesh Yadav (SP, 2012–17) and Mayawati (BSP, 2007–12), had also completed their full tenures as CMs, but they couldn't bring their respective parties back to power again.[12] For the 2022 victory, a big part of the credit was given to Yogi Adityanath, and he emerged much stronger within the BJP, while Keshav Prasad Maurya, who was a strong claimant for the CM's post in 2017, much to his misfortune, lost his own assembly seat, his home turf Sirathu, to Pallavi Patel of the SP.

In Yogi Adityanath's second assembly as the CM, Kanpur's Satish Mahana was elected as the Speaker and Akhilesh Yadav as the LoP. The BJP leadership retained Maurya as the deputy CM, but Dinesh Sharma was replaced by Brajesh Pathak as

---

[12]Yadav, Shyamlal, 'Yogi Creates History for BJP as Congress, BSP Flunk Poll Math', *The Indian Express,* 11 March 2022, https://tinyurl.com/28ts2bwy. Accessed on 7 March 2024.

the second deputy CM. Pathak, who had earlier been with the BSP, joined the BJP in August 2016 and has since consolidated himself as a prominent Brahmin face of the BJP. As the minister of law in the first Yogi Adityanath government, on 12 April 2021, Pathak wrote a letter to principal secretary, Department of Health Education, criticizing the mismanagement in dealing with Covid-19. In the second Yogi Adityanath government, as a deputy CM, Pathak was given charge of the ministries of health and family welfare, medical education, and women and child welfare. Maurya, on the other hand, has become the longest-serving person on the chair of deputy CM, which he has continued to hold since 19 March 2017.

On the electoral turf in UP, there seem to be only two main players left—the BJP and the SP—and the face-off between Yogi Adityanath and Akhilesh goes on. Whenever the former takes the credit for encounters, the latter keeps reminding the public that criminals of the CM's own caste are not being touched.

Yogi Adityanath's focus on crime and his crackdown on the mafia continue in his second stint. The additional director general (law and order) of the UP police, Prashant Kumar, announced that the UP police has neutralized over 178 criminals in as many as 10,713 encounters across the state.[13] But after the killing of Umesh Pal, a key witness in the murder of the BSP MLA Raju Pal in 2005, in Prayagraj on 24 February 2023, the encounters started getting special focus. Accused in the Umesh Pal murder were Atiq Ahmed and members of his family. One of his five sons, 19-year-old Asad, was killed in Jhansi in an encounter with the police on 13 April 2023, in the 183rd encounter killing since Yogi

---

[13]'U.P. Police Eliminated 178 in 10.7k Encounters in 6 Yrs of Yogi Govt: Data', *Hindustan Times*, 16 March 2023, http://tinyurl.com/4kunkt3x. Accessed on 3 April 2023.

Adityanath took oath in March 2017.[14] But a bigger story came two days later. On the night of 15 April in Prayagraj, three youths from three different parts of UP, who had not committed any joint crime prior to that, killed Atiq Ahmed and his brother Ashraf, who were in police custody and were being moved to a hospital for medical examination after interrogation. This was a big blot on the record of the Yogi Adityanath government—of people being killed in police custody. On Atiq's appeal against threat to his life, the Supreme Court had, on 28 March 2023, assured him that the state machinery would take care of him.[15] Yet, Atiq was killed while in the custody of the police. On 28 March 2024, Mukhtar Ansari, too, died at Rani Durgawati Medical College, Banda, while he was in judicial custody in Banda jail. His family alleged that he was slow-poisoned.

In his second stint as the CM, Yogi Adityanath did not give any interview for several months, but after that, he emerged with a massive drive to attract investments from abroad by organizing investors' summits at various levels. He claimed to have attracted investment intent for over ₹32.92 lakh crore.[16] Just before declaration of the Lok Sabha polls 2024, he launched an impressive scheme named Mukhyamantri Yuva Udyami Vikas Abhiyan (MYUVA). Such rosy figures were given by his many predecessors as well, but little arrived on the ground. So, it is

---

[14]Pandey, Bhupendra, 'Count in 6 Yrs of Yogi Govt: Jhansi Killing UP Police Encounter No. 183', *The Indian Express*, 14 April 2023, http://tinyurl.com/334hcs43. Accessed on 19 April 2023.

[15]Justice Ajay Rastogi and Justice Bela M. Trivedi on Writ Petition (Criminal) 107/2023. See 'SC Dismisses Gangster-Turned-Politician Atiq Ahmed's "Threat to Life" Plea', *The Indian Express*, 28 March 2023, http://tinyurl.com/498pdjk7. Accessed on 22 April 2023.

[16]'Global Investors Summit | Got Rs 32.92 Lakh Cr Investment Offers Even before Summit Began: Yogi Adityanath', *The Indian Express*, 11 February 2023, http://tinyurl.com/4m7e3rtw. Accessed on 22 April 2023.

yet to be seen how much of those intended investments have actually fructified.

On 27 February 2023, Yogi Adityanath broke Dr Sampurnananda's record of being the longest serving CM in single tenure, and on 30 March 2024, he broke Mayawati's record of being the longest serving CM of UP. His popularity is on the rise, and his story should not be considered as complete for now.

ACKNOWLEDGEMENTS

This book is a result of the efforts and knowledge of many people. I would like to express my heartfelt thanks to everyone who helped in the making of this book.

I am thankful to my editors Raj Kamal Jha, Unni Rajen Shanker and Ritu Sarin for the support and inspiration I get from them every day. I would like to extend my sincere gratitude to Ram Bahadur Rai and Ashok Mehta, who contributed information crucial for this book. Both read the manuscript word-by-word, and suggested several valuable corrections, additions and deletions.

Many people encouraged me to bring this book to life, including Rajendra Agrawal, Santosh Gangwar, Baleshwar Tyagi, Vindhyawasini Kumar, Jagadish Upasane, Prabaal Maitra, Shankkar Aiyar, Chandramohan Mishra, Shive Kumar Sharma, Santosh Yadav, Amod Kumar, Gaya Prasad Yadav, Anshuman Yadav, Tejvir Singh Rana, Ajmer Singh and Vidya Bhushan Arora. I am very grateful to all of them.

This book needed some lesser-known information, and many people generously offered their assistance for the same. These include, but are not limited to, Ashish Gautam, R.K. Chaturvedi, Arvind Kumar Singh, Sushma Yadav, Balwan Singh Gautam, Shrikant Singh, Jai Prakash Singh, Ram Awadh Yadav, Shashank Singh, Rajnikant Singh, Sheokesh Mishra, Chandra Bhushan Singh, Pradeep Singh, Narendra Pal Verma, Pradeep Yadav, Lalita Yadav, Sanjay Rai, Dinesh Yadav, Jai Shankar Gupta, Bhupendra Kumar, Sudeep Thakur, Ajay Kumar Singh,

Mahendra Parihar, Rajesh Raparia, Shambhunath Shukla, Roop Chaudhary, Omkar Chaudhary, Arvind Mohan, Abhay Pratap, Kumar Harsh and Nalin Chauhan (sadly missing since December 2020). My wholehearted gratitude goes to them.

While writing this book, I had many discussions with young political workers from different parties. I also asked some young students what they would like to know about the people who have ruled the state. I am thankful to all of them for their perspectives and have tried to take their feedback into account in this book.

The secretariats of the UP Assembly, UP Legislative Council, Lok Sabha and Rajya Sabha have put all debates, and most of their other publications, in public domain, which has been a very rich source of information for this book. The proceedings of the UP Assembly were particularly helpful, as was the data from Election Commission of India, which was available in the public domain. I am thankful to all these institutions for making this vast knowledge accessible to me and everyone. I would like to extend my gratitude to the Prime Minister Memorial Museum and Library as well, which I visited quite frequently. I would also like to thank the officials of the Directorate of Information, Government of UP, for providing the pictures of CMs that are included in this book.

I am grateful to Rudra Narayan Sharma at Rupa Publications, who accepted my book proposal very quickly and constantly advised me in giving the manuscript the shape it required. At Rupa, I would also like to extend my thanks to Smita Mathur, Anshuman Yadav, Aditi Mehrotra, Raj Kumari and Birendra Negi for their help and advice. Thank you, Sudhir Pillai, for giving the chapters a once-over before the manuscript was submitted for publication.

At home, over the past five years, I have spent most of my free time away from work writing this book with the help of my family. Without mentioning my better half Renu, son Shikhar and daughter Shreeti (sadly, she left us on 29 November 2023 at just 20 years and two months), the story will not be complete. Their unstinted support made this book possible.

INDEX